베니스
상인의
계산과 기록

1494 베니스 회계

베니스 상인의 계산과 기록
1494 베니스 회계

초판 1쇄 인쇄 2011년 1월 5일
초판 1쇄 발행 2011년 1월 10일

지은이 루카 파치올리
옮긴이 존 B. 가이스빅(영역) · 이원로(번역 및 해설)
펴낸이 김선식
펴낸곳 (주)다산북스
출판등록 2005년 12월 23일 제313-2005-00277호

PD 임영묵
다산북스 이혜원
디자인연구소 최부돈, 황정민, 김태수, 조혜상
마케팅본부 모계영, 신현숙, 김하늘, 박고운, 권두리
광고팀 한보라, 박혜원
온라인마케팅팀 하미연
저작권팀 이정순, 김미영
미주사업팀 우재오
경영지원팀 김성자, 김미현, 유진희, 김유미, 정연주

주소 서울시 마포구 서교동 395-27
전화 02-702-1724(기획편집) 02-703-1725(마케팅) 02-704-1724(경영지원)
팩스 02-703-2219
이메일 dasanbooks@hanmail.net
홈페이지 www.dasanbooks.com

필름 출력 스크린그래픽센타
종이 월드페이퍼(주)
인쇄 (주)현문
제본 (주)광성문화사

ISBN 978-89-6370-462-3 (03320)

· 책값은 표지 뒤쪽에 있습니다.
· 파본은 구입하신 서점에서 교환해드립니다.
· 이 책은 저작권법에 의하여 보호를 받는 저작물이므로 무단 전재와 복제를 금합니다.

베니스
상인의
계산과 기록

1494 베니스 회계

| 루카 파치올리 지음(1494년) |
| 존 B. 가이스빅 영역(1914년) |
| 이원로(李元魯) 번역 및 해설 |

달봉

머리말

국내 최초의 숨마 번역본

이 책은 르네상스 시대의 이탈리아 수학자 루카 파치올리(Luca Pacioli)가 1494년에 저술한 《Summa de Arithmetica, Geometrica, Proportioni et Proportionalita》의 일부분인 "the Treatise De Computis et Scripturis"(상업적 계산과 기록)을 번역한 것입니다. 존 가이스빅(John B. Geijsbeek)의 영역본(1914년)과 히라이 야스타로(平井泰太郎)의 일역본(1918년)이라는 두 개의 번역본을 각각 대조하여 한국어로 다시 번역했습니다.

　① 존 가이스빅의 영역본: Ancient double-entry bookkeeping, 1914년
　　 Lucas Pacioli's treatise(A. D. 1494—the earliest known writer on bookkeeping) reproduced and translated with reproductions, ……
　　 Mainardi, Ympyn, Stevin and Dafforne, by John B. Geijsbeek (Author)
　② 히라이 야스타로의 일역본: 《파치올리 부기서 연구》, 1918년, 고베(神戶) 회계학회

숨마(《Summa de Arithmetica, Geometrica, Proportioni et Proportionalita》를 줄여서 숨마라 일컬음)는 네덜란드인 임핀(Ympyn)이 1543년에 네덜란드어와 프랑스어로, 1544년에 영어로 번역 출판한 이래, 독일·스페인·러시아 등 유럽 각국에서 번역 출판되었고, 1918년에는 일본의 히라이 야스타로가 일본어로도 번역했습니다. 우리나라에도 번역된 것이 있으나 원문 대조 방식이 아니라 다른 나라의 번역본을 참조하여 대강 요약한 수준이고, 또한 정식 책으로 출판된 적도 없으므로 사실상 이 책이 국내 최초의 숨

마 번역본이라 할 수 있습니다.

특히 이 책은 좌측에는 영어 원문을 쓰고, 우측에는 한국어를 쓴 원문 대조 번역인 바, 이는 영역자인 존 가이스빅의 방식(좌측 영역문, 우측 이탈리아어 원문)을 따른 것입니다. 영어 원문을 병기한 이유는 필자의 번역이 원문과 어느 정도 일치하는지를 독자가 직접 판단할 수 있도록 하기 위해서입니다. 원문의 제시가 없는 번역은 정역(正譯)이 아니라 반역(反譯)이나 반역(半譯)이 될 가능성이 큽니다. 요즘은 과거와 달리 영어에 정통한 독자들이 많으므로 혹시 어색한 번역이 있다면 언제든 지적해주시기를 부탁합니다.

숨마는 르네상스 시대 유럽의 진어(眞語)인 라틴어가 아니라 속어 또는 방언(方言)이라 할 수 있는 이탈리아어로 씌었고, 이탈리아어 중에서도 파치올리의 모국어인 토스카나어 50%, 복식부기의 원산지(?)인 베네치아어(베니스어) 50%로 정확히 배분되어 씌었습니다. 따라서 이탈리아인조차도 숨마를 제대로 이해하기는 어렵습니다. 한자로 쓰인 주역의 원문을 현대 중국인이 그대로 이해하지 못하고 영어로 번역한 글을 통해 대충의 의미를 파악하는 것과 마찬가지입니다.

파치올리의 숨마는 본질적으로 여러 의미로 해석될 수 있는 난해한 글입니다. 다음은 숨마의 난해함과 모호성, 불확실성 등에 대하여 스페인의 회계학자가 〈Accounting Historians Journal〉(1994년 6월)에 게재한 글(총 37페이지 분량)입니다. 이 중에서 제1페이지만 번역 소개하고자 합니다.

숨마복식부기의 모호성과 불확실성에 대하여

Comments on some obscure or ambiguous points of the Treatise De Computis et Scripturis by Luca Pacioli, Accounting Historians Journal, The, June 1994 by Hernandez-Esteve, Esteban

When I recently translated Luca Pacioli's treatise De Computis et Scripturis into Spanish, a series of obscurities and difficulties of interpretation were uncovered.

파치올리의 숨마를 최근에 스페인어로 번역하면서 일련의 난해함과 불확실성을 발견하게 되었다.

In this paper, I intend to discuss – though without any pretensions of exhaustiveness – the main obscurities encountered, their difficulty, the interpretation given by a number of scholars who have studied the subject and, finally, my own interpretation and the reasons that led me to consider it as the most correct. This paper is thus an attempt to clarify the questions raised, to offer a basis for judgment to those who are interested in it and, above all, to submit my approach and interpretation to open discussion.

이 글은 숨마를 연구해온 많은 학자들의 해석과 그들이 겪은 어려움, 모호성 등에 대하여 – 완전한 연구는 아니지만 – 논하고자 하는 글이다. 그리고 나 자신의 해석과 나의 해석이 가장 옳다고 여기는 이유를 설명하는 글이기도 하다. 이 글은 제기된 의문에 대한 판단의 근거를 제시하고, 동시에 이 토론을 개시하기 위한 나의 해석과 접근방법을 제시하여 여러 의문을 해결하기 위한 것이기도 하다.

As I point out in my introduction to the translation, Pacioli's prose is surely neither easy nor fluent. Baldi and Annibale Caro, among old authors, and Federigo Melis, among modern ones, have already mentioned this.

이 번역의 서두에서 언급하였듯이 파치올리의 글은 쉽지도 않거니와 유려(流麗)하지도 않다. 이 점에 대해서는 발디(Baldi)를 비롯한 신구 학자들도 이미 지적했다.

The difficulties of this prose are many: it is written in a half Tuscan, half Venetian language; it is still unpolished and lacking clear and precise rules;

the book itself is incunable with the typographical limitations and; above all, it is complicated by abbreviations characteristic of that time. For all these reasons, Luca Pacioli's Treatise contains various types of anomalies, inaccuracies, ambiguities and obscurities that will be convenient to group in different categories for the purpose of this analysis.

숨마에는 난해한 부분이 많다. 반은 토스카나어, 반은 베네치아어로 씌었고 또한 투박하면서 동시에 명쾌함과 정확성이 결여되어 있기 때문이다. 이 책 자체가 인쇄기술이 부족했던 시대의 출판물인 데다, 500여 년 전의 약어와 기호는 이 책을 더욱 어렵게 만들고 있다. 이러저러한 이유로 숨마는 다양한 형태의 변칙성, 부정확성, 모호성, 불확실성 등을 갖고 있지만 오히려 여러 문제점을 다양한 형태로 그룹화하여 분석하는 데는 편리할 것이다.

First, there are purely typographical anomalies and irregularities or mechanical errors. We shall not lose much time on them, although I shall point out the main ones.

첫째로, 숨마에는 인쇄기술상의 변칙성과 오류가 있다. 여기에 분석의 중점을 두지는 않겠지만, 지적은 해야 할 것 같다.

Second, we shall study a small group of obscurities and ambiguities which are basically of a linguistic nature and whose interpretation may cause headaches to translators, though they do not really affect the technical aspect of the work.

둘째로, 회계 자체의 내용에는 영향을 주지 않지만 번역자에게 두통을 안겨주는 것들, 즉 주로 언어적 측면에서의 모호함과 불확실성과 관련된 것들을 모아 연구하고자 한다.

The third group consists of points whose doubtful interpretation does affect in one way or another the accounting, commercial or banking explanations given by the Franciscan monk of Borgo San Sepolcro. This is the largest group of difficulties, obscurities and ambiguities.

셋째 그룹은 파치올리, 즉 보르고 산 세폴크로 출신의 프란체스코 수도회 소속의 수도승이 서술한 것으로서, 회계 및 상업 또는 은행 업무와 관련된 내용이다. 그 번역에 따라 회계에 여러모로 영향을 주는 난해하고 불확실하고 모호한 내용으로 구성되어 있으며, 이들이 이 분석에서 가장 큰 그룹을 형성하고 있다.

Finally, I shall explain some details or passages that make us doubt whether the particular Treatise De Computis et Scripturis is really a single work entirely written on the same occasion and or the same purpose.

마지막으로, 숨마가(산술 및 기하와 관련된 내용 등과) 같은 목적이나 동기로 저술된 일관된 목적을 가진 책인지에 대하여 의문을 갖게 하는 구절에 대하여 설명하고자 한다.

이탈리아인도, 이탈리아어와 언어적으로 가장 가까운 스페인인도, 아니 숨마의 저자인 파치올리 자신도 이해하기 어려운 것이 숨마이므로 그것이 네덜란드어로 번역되었든 프랑스어나 영어, 독일어, 스페인어, 일본어로 번역되었든 정역은 아니라는 뜻입니다. 따라서 이 번역본의 원문인 존 가이스빅의 영역본 또한 정역으로 판단되지는 않습니다. 그러나 번역을 하고 보니, 논리적 일관성 면에서는 아무런 결함이 없는 것으로 보아 거의 정역에 가까운 것으로 사료됩니다. 이 점에 대하여 지금은 이미 고인이 된 존 가이스빅 님께 깊이 감사드립니다.

처음에는 존 가이스빅의 영역본이 있는지조차 몰랐기에, 한국의 보물창고인 국립중앙도서관에서 입수한 히라이의 일역본 해독에 매달리기도 했습니다. 현대 일본어로 쓰인 것이 아니라 고어체, 문어체가 많이 쓰였고, 존 가이스빅의 영역본을 재역한 것이라 매우 난해했지만, 핵심 내용은 파악할 수 있었습니다. 한국인에게 1917년에 출판된《사개송도치부법》이 암호, 즉 코드 그 자체인 것과 마찬가지로, 가이스빅의 영역본이나 히라이의 일역본 역시 그 나라 사람들에게는 코드 그 자체일 것으로 사료됩니다만, 영어 원문을 한국어로 번역하면서 번역의 정확성에 대한 확신이 부족할 때, 히라이의 번역본을 참고하며 확신을 얻었음도 부인할 수 없습니다. 아울러 최대한 정확하게 번역하고자 많은 노력을 기울인 히라이 교수께도 깊이 감사드립니다.

또한 1494년 숨마의 출판 이후, 회계 이론과 장부체계(분개장, 원장, 손익계산서, 대차대조표)의 변화를 관찰하고자 다음 서적들을 참고하였습니다.

- Basil. S. Yamey, 1989, Historic accounting literature series 2, Japan Yushodo (숨마의 유럽 각국어 번역본)

  제1권, 이탈리아, Casanova Alvise, 1558, Specchio lucidissmo

  제2권, 이탈리아, Grisogono Simon, 1609, Il mercante arrichito

  제8권, 영국, Peele James, 1569, Pathewaye to perfectness

  제9권, 영국, Carpenter John, 1632, A most excellent instruction for the exact and perfect keeping merchants books of accounts

  제14권, 프랑스, Ympyn Jan Christoffels, 1543, Nouvelle instruction (네덜란드인 임편의 프랑스어본)

- S. S. Packard 외, 1878, The new Bryant and Stratton common school book-keeping, American book company

- L. Cuthbert Cropper, 1918, Book-keeping and Accounts, London MacDonald and Evans

- B. G. Vickery, 1929, Principles and Practice of book-keeping and accounts, London The Gregg Publishing

- W. W. Bigg 외, 1955, Book-keeping and Accounts, H. F. L.

- Donald. E. Kieso 외, 2003, Fundamentals of intermediate accounting, John Wiley & Sons

- Frank Wood 외, 2005, Business Accounting, Prentice Hall
- Peter J. Eisen, 2006, Accounting, Barron's Educational Series, Inc

그러나 숨마를 비롯하여 앞서 참고한 서적 어느 것에서도 이론은 찾아볼 수 없었습니다. 오직 이럴 땐 이렇게 저럴 땐 저렇게 분개하고, 원장에 전기해야 한다는 내용뿐이었습니다. 즉, 엑셀 사용법처럼 프로그램의 근본 원리는 모른 채 이런 방법으로 입력하면 저런 결과를 얻을 수 있다고 알려주는 수준이었습니다.

현금으로 이자를 지급하면 "차변 지급이자 ○○○ // 대변 현금 ○○○"으로 기록해야 하고, 외상매출이면 "차변 외상매출금 ○○○ // 대변 상품매출 ○○○"으로 기록해야 하는 등 각 경우에 따른 기록방법을 달달 외워야 한다는 내용은 있었지만, 왜 지급이자를 차변에 쓰고, 왜 현금을 대변에 써야 하는지는 설명되지 않았던 것입니다. '왜'가 없는 학문, 학문이 아닌 학문, 그것이 회계학의 현주소라고 할 수 있습니다.

이 '왜'는 일본열도나 베니스가 아니라, 생지지성(生知之聖: 나면서부터 아는 분), 천종지성(天縱之聖: 하늘이 낸 분) 세종대왕의 궁정인 경복궁 그리고 천세 전에 미리 정하신 영원의 수도 서울에서 찾아야 합니다. 행복이 밖이 아닌 안에 있듯이, 회계학의 '왜' 역시 이미 서울에 있었습니다. 이 글은 회계학의 '왜'를 찾는 첫 번째 여정입니다.

2011년 1월
서울에서 이원로

| 차례 |

| 머리말 | 국내 최초의 숨마 번역본 4

| 잊혀진 천재 | 루카 파치올리에 대하여 15

제1편 1494 베니스 회계 번역 및 해설 28

| 제1장 | 훌륭한 상인에게 필요한 것과, 베니스식 장부 기록방법 31
| 제2장 | 이 글의 첫 번째 부분, 재물기(재산 조사표)의 의의와 작성법 35
| 제3장 | 모든 요소를 갖춘 재물기의 사례 37
| 제4장 | 훌륭한 상인에 대한 매우 유용한 충고와 가르침 45
| 제5장 | 이 글의 두 번째 중요 부분인 장부조직과 그 의미, 그리고 상인이 갖추어야 할 세 개의 주요 장부 49
| 제6장 | 일지의 의미와 기록내용 그리고 부기자에 대하여 51
| 제7장 | 여러 도시의 상업장부 인증과 그 이유 55
| 제8장 | 일지의 기록방법과 그 예시 59
| 제9장 | 상인이 매입하는 아홉 가지 방법과, 외상으로 구입해야 할 필요가 있는 상품들 63
| 제10장 | 두 번째 주요 장부인 분개장의 의미와 체계적인 기록방법 67
| 제11장 | 베니스에서 분개장에 사용하는 두 개의 용어, Per(차변)와 A(대변)의 의미 69
| 제12장 | 차변과 대변 방식으로 분개장에 기록하는 방법과 원장에 사용되는 두 개의 용어인 현금과 자본금의 의미 71

| 제13장 | 세 번째 주요 장부인 원장과 그 기록방법, 원장의 알파벳 색인, 그리고 단식 기록방법과 복식 기록방법 79

| 제14장 | 분개장 기록을 원장으로 전기하는 방법과, 한 건의 분개를 두 개의 원장에 전기해야 하는 이유, 그리고 원장으로 전기된 분개 기록에 소인(消印, 전기필 표시)을 하는 방법, 그리고 대차 각 기사의 가장자리에 원장의 페이지 번호를 기록해야 하는 것과 그 이유 81

| 제15장 | 현금과 자본금 분개를 원장의 차변과 대변에 전기하는 방법. 고풍스런 자체로 페이지 상단에 날짜를 쓰는 것과 상황에 따라 원장의 공간을 분할하는 방법 85

| 제16장 | 상품 관련 분개를 원장의 차변과 대변으로 전기하는 방법 93

| 제17장 | 베니스의 관청에서 운영하는 시립 대부은행, 즉 공공기관과 거래하는 방법 99

| 제18장 | 은행 및 기관과 관련된 거래를 일지, 분개장, 원장에 기록하는 방법 103

| 제19장 | 어음 또는 은행이체 지급시 장부 기록방법 111

| 제20장 | 물물교환 거래 및 조합 거래 등을 일지, 분개장, 원장에 기록하는 방법 115

| 제21장 | 조합거래 기록방법 121

| 제22장 | 가계비 및 경상비, 영업비, 임금 등의 기록방법 125

| 제23장 | 지점을 직접운영 또는 위탁운영하는 경우의 거래 기록방법 131

| 제24장 | 은행과의 거래를 분개장 및 원장에 기록하는 방법과 그 의미. 독자가 은행의 고객인 경우와 은행인 경우의 기록방법. 각종 증빙을 복본화해야 하는 이유 135

| 제25장 | 손실과 이익이라는 계정의 의미와 이를 별도의 원장으로 개설하는 이유 143

| 제26장 | 직접출장 또는 위탁출장 관련 거래의 기록방법 145

| 제27장 | 손익계정과 손익이 원장에만 기록되어야 하는 이유 149

| 제28장 | 원장의 공간을 다 사용한 경우 새 원장을 만드는 방법 153

| 제29장 | 원장을 매년 갱신하지 않는 경우 원장의 연도를 바꾸는 방법 157

| 제30장 | 채무자 또는 고용주를 위하여 계정 요약서를 작성하는 방법 **159**

| 제31장 | 실수로 다른 곳에 기록한 것을 교정하는 방법 **163**

| 제32장 | 원장 기록의 검증, 즉 시산표 작성방법과 구 장부의 계정 잔액을
새 장부로 넘기는 방법 **165**

| 제33장 | 결산 도중에 발생하는 거래의 기록방법, 그리고 결산 도중 구 장부에
어떠한 기록도 해서는 안 되는 이유 **171**

| 제34장 | 구 장부 각 계정의 마감과 그 이유. 원장의 차변과 대변 각각의 합계로
결산 및 장부기록을 검증하는 것에 대하여 **173**

| 제35장 | 편지, 증서 및 판결문 등의 보관방법과 문서 수발부 작성에 대하여 **181**

| 제36장 | 장부 기록방법과 그 규칙의 요약 **189**

1494 베니스 회계 요약 **208**

장부 체계 **210**

거래 유형별 분개 예시 **213**

장부의 마감과 결산 **216**

| 번역 후기 | 原文 · 眞文을 보는 것, 그리고 그 原文을 제대로 번역하는 것이
학문의 시작이다 **218**

1494 베니스 회계 원문 **223**

루카 파치올리에 대하여

| 루카 파치올리 개관 |

- **출생지** 이탈리아, 토스카나(초기 로마 시대의 에트루리아), 보르고 산 세폴크로 (Borgo San Sepolcro)
- **출생과 사망** 1445~1515년
- **신분** 평민, 프란체스코 수도사
- **직업** 수학 관련 저술가 겸 수학교수(페루자, 밀라노, 플로렌스, 로마 대학 등)
- **이름**
  - 라틴어 이름: Lucas Paciolus
  - 이탈리아 이름: Luca Pacioli 또는 Luca Paciolo
  - 영어 이름: Lucas Pacioli
- **출신학교** 프란체스코 수도회 소속 학교
- **학습과목** 성경, 문법, 수사학, 대수학, 기하학, 천문학, 음악, 고전문학(Dante, Cicero, Quintalian, Boethius 등의 작품) 등
- **연구 도서관** 특전으로 우르비노(Urbino) 공작의 도서관을 무상출입하며 연구

주요 저서

- 1470년　《대수학》
- 1476년　정방형(대수학과 기하학의 정오방형을 다룸)
- 1480년　《유클리드 기하학》(유클리드 기하학을 이탈리아어로 번역한 것)
- 1481년　《대수학》
- 1494년　《산술, 기하 및 비례 총설》
    - 원제: Summa de Arithmetica, Geometrica, Proportioni et Proportionalita
    - 복식부기 부문: Treatise De Computis et Scripturis
- 1504년　La Scuola Perfetta Dei Mercanti(숨마의 부기편을 다시 인쇄한 것)
- 1505년　Schifanonia(수학적 게임과 체스 문제를 다룸)
- 1508년　De Viribus Quantitatis(숫자의 힘, 기하학 및 수학적 게임을 다룸)
- 1509년　De Divina Proportione(응용수학을 다룸, Leonardo Da Vinch와의 공저)
- 1509년　Campanus' Euclid(유클리드 기하학을 라틴어로 번역한 것)
- 1523년　1494년의 Summa 제2판

숨마의 주요내용

- 산술과 대수학
- 장사와 계산에 있어서 대수와 산술의 응용
- 상업적 계산과 기록(복식부기)
- 화폐와 교환
- 순수기하학과 응용기하학

(참조:《회계사상과 회계기준의 발전》, 정기숙 외, 1995, p. 78~79, 경문사)

루카 파치올리의 업적

파치올리(1445~1515년)는 15세기의 인물로서 당대 최고의 수학자이자 실학자라고 할 수 있습니다. 마틴 루터(1483~1546년)보다 먼저 진어인 라틴어 대신 언문에 해당되는 이탈리아어로 유클리드 기하학 등을 보급하는 데 앞장섰고, 장 칼뱅보다 앞서서 노동의 대가, 그리고 상인의 사업적 성공과 재산축적을 인정하고 장려한 수도사이자 학자였기 때문입니다.

그는 순수 학문인 수학을 현실생활에 적용하는 데 관심이 많았습니다. 수학적 게임에 관한 두 권의 저서와 레오나르도 다빈치와 함께 저술한 《신성 비례》편에서 그러한 관심과 노력을 읽을 수 있습니다. 그리고 그가 창시한 것은 아니지만 그가 소개한 복식부기 역시 수학의 원리를 상업에 적용한 대표적인 사례라고 할 수 있습니다. 파치올리에 대한 당대와 후대의 평가를 요약하여 인용하면 다음과 같습니다.

파치올리의 다양한 업적은 일반적으로 존경과 인정을 받고 있었으나, 개인적으로는 오랫동안 논쟁의 대상이 되었다. 그는 종종 종교적 신비주의자 또는 이단자, 전통주의자 또는 인습 타파주의자, 개방주의자 또는 은둔주의자, 뛰어난 개인주의자 또는 기회주의자, 창의성 있는 학자 또는 표절자 등과 같이 상반된 인격의 소유자로 불리기도 하였다. 그는 1464년의 바오로 2세로부터 시작하여 50년 뒤의 식스투스 6세까지 일곱 분의 교황과 개인적 친분을 맺었으나, 1470년대에 입문한 프란체스코 수도회로부터는 한 번 파문의 위협을 받기도 하였다.

파치올리에 대해서는 여러 가지 논쟁이 있으나 대부분의 전문가는 파치올리가 우수한 저술가, 훌륭한 선생, 신앙심이 깊은 사람, 그리고 수학, 신학, 건축, 군사전략, 스포츠와 게임, 사업계에서 인정받는 뛰어난 학자임을 확신하고 있었다. 그는 일생동안 플로렌스, 밀라노, 페루자, 나폴리 및 로마 등 5개 대학에서 교수하였다. 그는 또 법원과 부유한 가정의 개인교사로도 일하였다.

한편 파치올리는 신앙심은 있었으나, 프란체스코 수도회에 대한 책임감은 민감한 편이 아니었던 것 같다. 그는 이론의 발전과 개발보다는 편집과 번역에 관심이 더 많은 학자였다. 파치올리는 이론도 중요하지만 그것이 실제로 이용되지 않으면 유용하지 않다고 생각하였다. 15세기경 대부분의 책은 라틴어로 저술되어 있었기 때문에 학자들만이 이용할 수밖에 없었다. 그는 각 나라의 자국어(vulgar tongue)로 글을 쓰고 많은 사람에게 지식을 전달하는 데 관심이 있었다. 이러한 목적을 위해 그는 가르치고 글을 쓰는 일에 헌신하였다. 그 결과 수학의 개념과 기술을 사업계에서 운용하는 것과, 각 지방 또는 그 나라의 자국어로 저술하는 데 다대한 공헌을 하였다. 강의에 대한 높은 평판, 저서의 광범한 사용은 그가 명성 있고 성공한 학자였음을 충분히 증명한다.

1874년 보르고 산 세폴크로의 사람들은 파치올리를 기념하는 기념비를 세웠는데, 그 내용을 번역하면 다음과 같다.

"레오나르도 다빈치와 레온 바티스타 알베르티의 친구이고 상담자이면서, 처음으로 대수학을 과학적 구조로 해석하고, 그 중요성을 강조한 루카 파치올리에게.

그는 산술을 기하학에 응용한 위대한 창시자다. 그는 복식부기를 발명하였고, 미래의 사고에 기초가 되는 수학책을 집필하였다. 상업노동자사회(Society of Commercial Workers)의 조사에 의해, 370년 동안 그를 망각한 것을 수치스럽게 생각하면서 산 세폴크로 사람은 이 기념비를 세운다(1878)."

(참조:《회계사상과 회계기준의 발전》, p. 76~77)

파치올리의 숨마는 고전 중의 고전입니다. 숨마에서 파치올리가 제시한 주요 명제는 다음과 같은 의미를 갖습니다.

파치올리는 복식부기의 창시자가 아니라 소개자다!

그는 제1장에서 자신이 복식부기를 창안한 것이 아니라 이미 사용되고 있는 베니스식 부기를 채택하였노라고 밝히고 있습니다. 따라서 그의 고향 사람들이 기념비에 쓴 구절("그는 복식부기를 발명하였고")은 이 위대한 선각자의 저술인 숨마 제1장조차 읽어보지도 않은 결과임을 알 수 있습니다.

제1장 훌륭한 상인에게 필요한 것과, 베니스식 장부 기록방법
이 글은 베니스식 기록방법을 채택한 것이다. 베니스식 부기는 누구나 그 시스템 내에서 기록방법을 찾을 수 있는 가장 우수한 기장방법이다.

복식부기의 창시국은 이탈리아가 아니라 또 다른 위대한 나라입니다.

파치올리는 순이익과 순재산 산출방법을 제시한 최초의 경영·경제학자다!

경제학은 경제주체(가계, 기업, 그리고 국가 등)의 소득과 그 원천 그리고 그 변동을 연구하는 학문입니다. 소득은 총액 개념으로도 사용되고 순액 개념으로도 사용되지만, 결국은 소득에서 합리적 소비를 차감한 잔액인 순소득 또는 순이익을 산출하는 것이 연구의 핵심입니다. 순소득 = 순이익은 어떻게 해석하느냐에 따라 차이가 있을 수 있으나, 순이익을 산출하는 방법 그리고 각 경제주체의 순재산을 산출하는 방법까지 최초로 제시한 학자가 파치올리이고, 이 순이익 산출에 관한 구절은 논어, 맹자, 사기의 화식열전, 플라톤, 아리스토텔레스 그리고 세계 최고의 회계국가였던 조선왕조실록에도 명백하게 나타나 있지 않습니다. 따라서 파치올리는 이에 관해 언급한 최초의 경제학자이자 경영학자라 할 수 있습니다. 순이익이 산출되지 않으면, 경제학이든 경영학이든 성립할 수 없기 때문입니다.

제27장 손익계정과 손익이 원장에만 기록되어야 하는 이유

여러 계정 원장의 뒤에는 지역에 따라 다양하게 명명되는 계정 원장, 즉 손익계정 원장을 설치해야 한다. 각 계정의 잔액은 이 계정으로 이체, 즉 전기되어야 한다. 이에 대하여는 "시산표"편에서 설명하고자 한다. (중략)

손익계정 차변, 날짜, 상품계정의 대변 금액, 즉 손실액을 여기로 전기(轉記)하다. 상품계정의 페이지 번호는 제 몇 페이지다. 만약 상품에서 이익이 난 경우에는 위와 반대로 기록하면 된다. 잔액이 좋은 쪽이든 나쁜 쪽이든 모든 계정에 대하여 상기의 절차를 반복해야 한다. 이렇게 하면 모든 계정의 대차 잔액이 일치하게 된다. 이것이 장부의 정확성을 보여주는 조건이다. 이에 대하여는 "시산표" 편에서 설명하고자 한다. 그리고 이렇게 하면 한눈에 손익 여부와 그 금액을 파악할 수 있다. 그리고 손익계정의 잔액은 자본금계정으로 이체되어야 하는데, 자본금계정은 모든 계정의 종착지라고 할 수 있다.

제34장 구 장부 각 계정의 마감과 그 이유. 원장의 차변과 대변 각각의 합계로 결산 및 장부기록을 검증하는 것에 대하여

이렇게 손익계정으로 이체한 후, 손익계정의 차변 합계와 대변 합계를 산출한 후 이를 비교하면 손익 여부를 쉽게 파악할 수 있다. 손익계정의 차변 금액이 더 크면 손실이 발생한 것이고, 그 반대면 순이익이 발생한 것이다.

이들 계정을 마감하여 순손실인지 순이익인지를 파악한 후에는 이 잔액, 즉 순이익 또는 순손실을 사업개시 시점에 재물 내역을 기록했던 자본금 계정으로 이체하여 손익계정을 마감해야 한다.

파치올리는 최초의 성공학자다!

그는 사업의 성공요소로 ① 현금, ② 신용, ③ 믿음, ④ 부기자 겸 수학자가 될 것, ⑤ 거래의 체계적인 기록 등을 언급했습니다. 오늘날에도 그대로 통하는 내용입니다. 그리고 ④, ⑤번에서 말하는 것처럼 이병철, 정주영 회장 모두 복식부기의 대가였습니다. 특히 이병철

회장은 일본의 와세다 대학 유학시절에 자기보다 수학을 잘하는 사람을 보지 못했다고 합니다. 정주영 회장의 경우에는 초등학교밖에 나오지 않아 수학 실력을 알 수 없지만, 어린 시절에 사서삼경을 암송하였고, 그 어록의 상당수가 주역의 내용과 상통하는 것으로 보아 정주영 회장 역시 또 다른 형태의 수학의 현인이었을 것으로 사료됩니다. 요약하면 이병철 회장과 정주영 회장은 파치올리가 언급한 성공의 조건을 모두 충족시키는 인물입니다.

제1장 훌륭한 상인에게 필요한 것과, 베니스식 장부 기록방법

위대하고도 위대한 우르비노(Urbino) 공의 백성들에게 훌륭한 상인에게 요구되는 모든 법칙을 알려주기 위하여, 나는 이 책에서 이미 다룬 주제 외에 특별한 주제를 추가하여 저술하기로 결정하였다. (중략) 사업에 성공하고자 하는 사람에게 필요한 것이 세 가지 있다. 가장 중요한 것은 현금이다. 현금 없이 되는 사업은 아무것도 없기 때문이다. 자본 없이 신용만으로 거래를 성사시켜 부자가 된 사람도 많다. 기독교적인 믿음에 따르면, 우리는 믿음에 의하여 구원되고 믿음이 없으면 하나님을 기쁘게 할 수 없기 때문이다.

사업에서 두 번째로 중요한 것은 훌륭한 부기자(簿記者, bookkeeper)이자 숙달된 수학자가 되는 것이다. 이렇게 될 수 있도록 하기 위하여 나는 각 거래에 필요한 규칙(후술)을 누구나 자수자득할 수 있게 알려주고자 한다. 따라서 이 첫 장을 이해하지 못하면, 그 다음은 읽어볼 필요가 없다는 것도 알려드리고자 한다.

사업에서 세 번째이자 마지막으로 중요한 것은 모든 거래를 체계적인 방법으로 기록 정리하는 것이다. 누구라도 한눈에 거래 내역을 이해할 수 있도록 차인(나에게 빚진 자)과 대인(내가 빚진 자)으로 정리하여 기록해야 한다. 이것은 상인에게 매우 중요한 일이다. 체계적인 기록과 정리가 없으면 사업을 수행하는 것이 불가능하고 마음의 안식도 없고, 마음은 언제나 혼란스럽기 때문이다.

파치올리는 최초의 사무 관리학자다!

그는 상인에게 모든 것을 기록할 것과, 정리정돈과 질서를 강조하고 있습니다. 각 지점에 보내야 할 편지도 각 지점별로 파우치를 만들어 보관하고 아울러 이의 장기 보전과 보전된 문서를 쉽게 찾는 방법에 대하여도 언급하고 있습니다. 심지어 중요 문서는 단순 보전이 아니라 필사, 복사까지 해둘 것을 요구하고 있습니다.

제1장 훌륭한 상인에게 필요한 것과, 베니스식 장부 기록방법

장부를 체계적으로 기록 유지하고자 하는 사람은 내가 하는 말에 충분히 귀를 기울여야 한다. 진행 절차를 잘 이해하도록 하기 위하여 나는 사업을 이제 처음으로 시작하는 사람을 예로 들어 설명하고자 한다. 그리고 그가 한눈에 그의 사업 상황을 파악하기 위해서 장부를 어떻게 기록 유지해야 하는가를 설명하고자 한다. 모든 것을 제자리에 두지 않는 사람, 즉 사업 상황을 한눈에 파악하지 못하는 사람에게는 언제나 곤란과 혼란만이 남는다. 질서가 없는 곳에는 언제나 혼란이 있기 때문이다.

제4장 훌륭한 상인에 대한 매우 유용한 충고와 가르침

전술한 바와 같이, 상인은 소유하고 있는 모든 것을 세밀하게 기록해야 한다. 유동자산이든 고정자산이든 그것이 만 가지일지라도 하나씩 그 조건과 상태, 빌려준 것인지, 빌린 것인지 여부 등을 기록해야 한다. 상인은 전술한 재물기에 적절한 방식으로 상표, 성명 등을 기록해야 한다. 상인이면 누구나 아는 것처럼, 상인은 발생 가능한 불상사에 대비하여 언제나 모든 것을 분명하게 기록해야 하기 때문이다.

제35장 편지, 증서 및 판결문 등의 보관방법과 문서수발부 작성에 대하여

여기에서는 지출증빙, 어음수취증, 상품을 선물로 제공한 내역 및 기타 비밀문서 등의 각종 서류 보전방법에 대하여 설명한다. 서류는 상인에게 매우 중요한 것이다. 만일 서류를 분실하면 큰 위험이 닥칠 수도 있다.

고객들과 주고받는 사적인 문서에 대하여 설명한다. 월말까지는 작은 책상에 이 문서들을 보관한다. 월말이 되면 묶어서 다른 곳에 옮겨두며, 그 표면에 수신일자 및 발신

일자를 기록한다. 매월 이렇게 하다가 연말에 다시 월 단위 묶음을 크게 묶어서 문서고 등에 보전하되, 표면에 연도를 기록해둔다. 필요하면 이 묶음을 찾으면 된다.

어떤 편지에 대하여 답장을 보낸 후에는 그 답장의 원인이 되는 편지를 적절한 장소에 보관해야 한다. 그리고 이것은 다른 모든 편지에도 적용된다. 그것이 중요한 편지인 경우에는 편지기록부에 기록해야 한다. 그리고 아주 중요한 편지인 경우에는 이 기록부에 글자 그대로 복사해두어야 한다. 그러나 일반적인 편지는 일지에 기록하듯 다음과 같이 핵심 내용만 기록하면 된다. "날짜, 아무개에게 편지를 쓰고, 다음의 것들을 그에게 보냈다. 이 편지는 그가 어느 날짜에 보낸 것에 대한 답장이고, 이 편지는 어느 파우치에 보관되어 있다."

모든 편지는 월 단위 또는 연 단위로 묶어서 문서고 등에 체계적으로 보관해야 한다. 근무시간 중에 편지를 받는 경우, 같은 순서로 임시 보관한다. 그러면 필요시 편지들을 쉽게 찾을 수 있다.

미회수 채권 내역서 등은 좀 더 비밀스러운 곳에 보관할 수도 있다. 비상시를 대비하여 안전한 곳에 보관해야 한다. 그러나 타인에게 현금을 지급할 때는 수취자로 하여금 지불대장에 영수필이라는 의미의 글을 쓰게 해야 한다. 영수증이라는 것은 쉽게 분실되기 때문이다.

각종 중요 문서, 즉 브로커의 각서, 송장, 세관의 상품반출증, 판결문 등은 별도의 장소에 보관해야 하며, 공증서 및 판결문 등도 역시 복사해두어야 한다.

그리고 비망록을 별도로 작성하는 것도 좋다. 비망록은 잊어서는 안 될 것, 잊으면 큰 위험이 되는 것 등을 기록하는 장부다. 매일 저녁 잠들기 바로 전에 해야 할 일은, 이 책을 보고 할 일을 제대로 마쳤는지 확인하는 일이다. 이 장부에는 이웃에게 잠시 빌려준 꽃병, 냄비, 솥 등을 기록해도 된다.

상인은 여기서 제시한 규칙을 준수해야 하며, 지역과 시대의 특성에 따라 가감해도 좋다. 여기서 상업상의 행위규칙에 대한 모든 것을 일일이 다 설명할 수는 없기 때문이다. 상인이 법률가보다 더 많은 능력을 필요로 한다는 속담이 있다. 지금까지 내가 설명한 것을 제대로 이해한다면, 여태까지 배운 것으로 당신의 사업을 성공적으로 수행할 수 있을 것으로 확신한다.

파치올리는 최초의 자본주의자다!

그는 우르비노 공의 백성을 훌륭한 상인으로 만들기 위하여 이 글을 썼고, 아울러 노력의 대가로 금품을 받는 것이 정당하다는 것과 체계적이고 합법적인 노력으로 성공하고 성장하는 것을 상인의 목표로 보았습니다. 이러한 견해는 부의 축적을 정당화하고 경제적 활동을 보장함으로써 자본주의 탄생의 중요한 기틀을 마련한 장 칼뱅보다 수십 년 앞서서 전개한 것이므로 그를 최초의 자본주의자라고 보아도 틀리지 않을 듯합니다.

제1장 훌륭한 상인에게 필요한 것과, 베니스식 장부 기록방법

위대하고도 위대한 우르비노 공의 백성들에게 훌륭한 상인에게 요구되는 모든 법칙을 알려주기 위하여, 나는 이 책에서 이미 다룬 주제 외에 특별한 주제를 추가하여 저술하기로 결정하였다.

제2장 이 글의 첫 번째 부분, 재물기(재산 조사표)의 의의와 작성법

모든 상인의 목표는 합법적으로 충분한 이익을 획득하여 자신의 사업을 성장시키는 데 있다.

제24장 은행과의 거래를 분개장 및 원장에 기록하는 방법과 그 의미. 독자가 은행의 고객인 경우와 은행인 경우의 기록방법. 각종 증빙을 복본화(複本化)해야 하는 이유

여기서 당신의 역할은 두 채권자 사이의 중개인 또는 대리인, 증인 등에 해당된다. 잉크비, 종이값, 집세, 수고비, 시간비 등 때문에 당신은 수수료를 받는데, 이것은 합법적인 것이다. 이러한 이체거래를 통하여 현금의 직접운송에 따른 위험 및 여행의 위험 등이 제거되기 때문이기도 하다.

숨마에서 파치올리가 사업의 성공을 위하여 가장 강조한 것은 다음의 세 가지로 요약됩니다.
① 상인은 자기 사업의 전부를 정확히 알아야 한다.
② 아는 것도 한눈에(at a glance) 알아야 한다.

③ 모든 것을 한눈에 알려면 베니스 부기, 즉 복식부기를 알고 실천해야 한다. 즉, 모든 거래를 베니스 방식으로 체계적으로 기록 및 정리해야 한다.

제23장 지점을 직접운영 또는 위탁운영하는 경우의 거래 기록방법

계정 원장이라는 것은 상인이 항상 염두에 두어야 할 사건을 정리 기록하는 것에 불과하다. 상인이 이 시스템을 채용하면 자신이 하는 사업 전부를 알게 될 것이고, 자신의 사업이 잘 운영되는지 아닌지를 정확하게 알게 될 것이다. "사업을 하는 자가 자기 사업 전부에 대하여 알지 못한다면 그의 돈은 날아가버릴 것이다. 즉, 실패할 것이다."라는 속담이 있으니 명심하기 바란다.

제34장 구 장부 각 계정의 마감과 그 이유. 원장의 차변과 대변 각각의 합계로 결산 및 장부 기록을 검증하는 것에 대하여

사업을 하는 자가 장부 기록방법을 모르는 것은 눈을 감고 헤매는 격이고, 결국은 거대한 손실로 귀착되기 때문이다. 그러므로 상인은 내가 이 훌륭한 책에서 충분히 설명한 방법에 따라 유능한 부기자가 되도록 모든 노력을 기울여야 한다.

제1장 훌륭한 상인에게 필요한 것과, 베니스식 장부 기록방법

그리고 그가 한눈에 그의 사업 상황을 파악할 수 있기 위해서 장부를 어떻게 기록 유지해야 하는가를 설명하고자 한다. 모든 것을 제자리에 두지 않으면, 즉 사업 상황을 한눈에 파악하지 못하는 사람에게는, 언제나 곤란과 혼란만이 남는다. 질서가 없는 곳에는 언제나 혼란이 있기 때문이다.

"사업 상황 전부를 정확히 한눈에 파악하는 것, 그것이 성공의 핵심 조건이고, 그렇지 않으면 실패할 것이다."라는 파치올리의 말은 진리 중의 진리입니다. 또한 이 말은 상업적 사업뿐 아니라 인간이 이루고자 하는 모든 사업에 적용된다고 할 수 있습니다. 숨마 복식부기 편은 내용은 그리 긴 편이 아니지만 성공을 위한 진리가 모두 들어 있는 글이라고

할 수 있습니다.

특히, 복식부기는 단순한 기록이 아니라 사업 상황을 한눈에 정확히 파악할 수 있게 해주는 불멸의 시스템입니다. 파치올리가 언급한 성공의 조건을 모두 갖춘 인물로는 대표적으로 빌 게이츠가 있습니다. 그의 표현을 빌리면, 생각의 속도로 모든 사업 상황을 한눈에 정확히 파악할 수 있는 유일한 시스템이 복식부기입니다. 그래서 파치올리는 상인이라면 유능한 부기자가 되도록 모든 노력을 기울여야 한다고 강조하고 있습니다.

파치올리가 또 위대한 것은 고전의 번역에 앞장섰다는 점입니다. 그는 수학의 고전인 《유클리드 기하학》을 1480년에는 필사본으로, 1509년에는 인쇄본으로, 한번은 이탈리아어로, 또 한번은 라틴어로 번역 보급한 바 있습니다. 아마도 이 번역 때문에 표절자라는 비난을 받았을지도 모릅니다. 그러나 비록 그리스보다는 대략 2,000년이나 늦게 이탈리아에서 수학이 시작되었지만, 기왕이면 제대로 가르치고 배워야 한다는 마음에서 그리스어로 된 원문을 두 개의 언어로 번역 출판한 것으로 사료됩니다. 그리스어로 씌었고, 그 후 아랍어로 먼저 번역된 《유클리드 기하학》이 이탈리아와 라틴어라는 서유럽어로 번역된 최초의 사례인 듯합니다. 이 번역은 학문의 시작이 정확한 번역에 있음을 직접 보여준 대표적인 사례입니다. 필자 역시 선현의 글을 번역하는 것을 글의 시작으로 삼고자 합니다.

그러나 고전의 번역은 선현의 말씀을 번역자의 가감 없이 그대로 전하는 술이부작(述而不作)에 있지, 술이조작(述而造作)이나 술이날조(述而捏造)에 있지 않습니다. 필자는 이 번역이 술이부작의 원칙을 지키고자 노력하였음을 알리기 위해 영어 원문과 대조하는 방식으로 편집하였습니다.

복식부기에 의한 결산, 즉 재산과 채무, 그리고 손실과 이익의 확정이 없이는 현대 경제사회가 존재할 수 없습니다. 숨마 복식부기 편은 중세 이탈리아에서 시작된 상업혁명을 완결함과 동시에 근대와 현대를 여는 책이며 사업과 경제의 진리를 밝히는 위대한 책입니다. 파치올리, 이 위대한 분에게 깊이 감사드립니다.

끝으로 파치올리는 숨마의 후반부인 제34장에서 다음과 같이 말하였습니다.

And remember to pray God for me so that to his praise and glory I may always go on doing good.

　　잊지 말고 나를 위해 하나님께 기도하여 주기 바란다. 그분에 대한 찬양과 영광을 위하여 내가 언제나 하나님의 뜻에 맞는 선한 일을 하며 살 수 있도록.

Section Nine
Treatise XI

Particulars of reckonings and their recording

상인의 계산과 기록

제1편
1494 베니스 회계 번역 및 해설

CHAPTER 1

THINGS THAT ARE NECESSARY TO THE GOOD MERCHANT AND THE METHOD OF KEEPING A LEDGER WITH ITS JOURNAL, IN VENICE AND ELSEWHERE

In order that the subjects of His Illustrious Highness, the most honorable and magnanimous Duke of Urbino (D. U. D. S –*Docis Urbini Domini Serenissimi*), may have all the rules that a good merchant needs, I decided to compile, in addition to the subjects already treated in this work, a special treatise which is much needed. I have compiled it for this purpose only, *i. e.*, that they (the subjects) may whenever necessary find in it everything with regard to accounts and their keeping. And thereby I wish to give them enough rules to enable them to keep all their accounts and books in an orderly way. For, as we know, there are three things needed by any one who wishes to carry on business carefully. The most important of these is cash or any equivalent, according to that saying, *Unum aliquid necessarium est substantia*. Without this, business can hardly be carried on.

It has happened that many without capital of their own but whose credit was good, carried on big transactions and by means of their credit, which they faithfully kept, became very wealthy. We became acquainted with many of these throughout Italy. In the great republics nothing was considered superior to the word of the good merchant, and oaths were taken on the word of a good merchant. On this confidence rested the faith they had in the trustworthiness of an upright merchant. And this is not strange, because, according to the Christian religion, we are saved by faith, and without it it is impossible to please God.

The second thing necessary in business is to be a good bookkeeper and ready mathematician. To become such we have given above (in the foregoing sections of

제1장
훌륭한 상인에게 필요한 것과, 베니스식 장부 기록방법

　위대하고도 위대한 우르비노 공의 백성들에게, 훌륭한 상인에게 요구되는 모든 법칙을 알려주기 위하여, 나(루카 파치올리)는 이 책에서 이미 다룬 주제 외에 특별한 주제를 추가하여 저술하기로 결정하였다. 필요시 언제나 이 책에서 기록과 계산에 관한 모든 것을 찾을 수 있게 할 목적으로 이 글을 쓴다. 그래서 나는 그들이 체계적인 방법으로 기록과 계산을 하기에 충분한 법칙을 알려주고자 한다. 우리 모두 잘 알다시피, 사업에 성공하고자 하는 사람에게 필요한 것이 세 가지 있다. 가장 중요한 것은 현금이다. 현금 없이 되는 사업은 아무것도 없기 때문이다.

　자본 없이 믿음과 신용만으로 거래를 성사시켜 부자가 된 사람도 많다. 이런 사람들을 우리는 이탈리아 전역에서 어렵지 않게 볼 수 있다. 이 위대한 공화국에서 상인의 말보다 더 높이 평가되는 것은 없다. 그리고 이 공화국에서는 하나님에 대한 맹세도 '훌륭한 상인의 이름'으로 행하여 진다. 훌륭한 상인의 진실함에 대하여 그들이 갖는 믿음은 이러한 자신감에 기인한다. 그리고 이러한 상황은 이상한 일이 아니다. 기독교적인 믿음에 따르면, 우리는 믿음에 의하여 구원되고, 믿음이 없으면 하나님을 기쁘게 할 수 없기 때문이다.

　사업에서 두 번째로 중요한 것은 훌륭한 부기자(簿記者, bookkeeper)이자 숙달된 수학자가 되는 것이다. 이렇게 되기 위하여 나는 각 거래에 필요한 규칙(후술)을 누구나 자수자득할 수 있게 알려주고자 한다. 따라서 이 첫 장을 잘 이해하지 못하면 그 다음은 읽어볼 필요가 없다는 것도 알리고자 한다.

the book) the rules and canons necessary to each transaction, so that any diligent reader can understand it all by himself. If one has not understood this first part well, it will be useless for him to read the following.

The third and last thing is to arrange all the transactions in such a systematic way that one may understand each one of them at a glance, *i. e.*, by the debit (*debito*—owed to) and credit (*credito*—owed by) method. This is very essential to merchants, because, without making the entries systematically it would be impossible to conduct their business, for they would have no rest and their minds would always be troubled. For this purpose I have written this treatise, in which, step by step, the method is given of making all sorts of entries. Although one cannot write out every essential detail for all cases, nevertheless a careful mind will be able, from what is given, to make the application to any particular case.

This treatise will adopt the system used in Venice, which is certainly to be recommended above all the others, for by means of this, one can find his way in any other. We shall divide this treatise in two principal parts. The one we shall call the Inventory, and the other, Disposition (arrangement). We shall talk first of the one and then of the other, according to the order contained in the accompanying Table of Contents, from which the reader may take what he needs in his special case.

He who wants to know how to keep a ledger and its journal in due order must pay strict attention to what I shall say. To understand the procedure well, we will take the case of one who is just starting in business, and tell how he must proceed in keeping his accounts and books so that at a glance he may find each thing in its place. For, if he does not put each thing in its own place, he will find himself in great trouble and confusion as to all his affairs, according to the familiar saying, *Ubi non est ordo, ibi est confusio* (Where there is no order, there is confusion). In order to give a perfect model to every merchant, we will divide the whole system, as we have said, in two principal parts, and we will arrange these so clearly that one can get good results from them. First, we will describe what the inventory is and how to make it.

사업에서 세 번째이자 마지막으로 중요한 것은 모든 거래를 체계적인 방법으로 기록 정리하는 것이다. 누구라도 한눈에 거래 내역을 이해할 수 있도록 차인(借人, 나에게 빚진 자)과 대인(貸人, 내가 빚진 자) 방식으로 정리 기록하는 것이 필요하다. 이것은 상인에게 매우 중요하다. 체계적인 기록과 정리가 이루어지지 않으면 사업을 수행하는 것이 불가능하고, 마음의 안식도 얻을 수 없어, 마음이 언제나 혼란스럽기 때문이다. 내가 이 글을 쓰는 이유도 그 때문인데, 모든 기록방법은 단계적으로 하나하나씩 설명될 것이다. 비록 모든 사례를 들어서 설명하지는 못하지만, 수의정독하면 이 글만 읽어도 설명되지 않은 거래 유형까지 터득하여 스스로 기록할 수 있을 것이다.

이 글은 베니스식 기록방법을 채택한 것이다. 베니스식 부기는 누구나 기록방법을 그 시스템 내에서 찾을 수 있는 가장 우수한 기장 방법이다. 나는 이 글을 두 개의 주요 부분으로 나누고자 한다. 하나는 기초재산의 기록방법이고, 또 하나는 체계적인 정리 기록방법이다. 우선 첫 번째 것부터 순서대로 설명하고자 한다. 목차를 참조하면, 누구나 각자의 상황에 맞는 해결책을 찾을 수 있을 것이다.

장부를 체계적으로 기록 유지하고자 하는 사람은 내가 하는 말에 충분히 귀를 기울여야 한다. 진행절차를 잘 이해하도록 하기 위하여 나는 사업을 이제 처음으로 시작하는 사람을 예로 들어 설명하고자 한다. 그리고 그가 한눈에 그의 사업 상황을 파악할 수 있기 위해서 장부를 어떻게 기록 유지해야 하는가를 설명하고자 한다. 모든 것을 제자리에 두지 않는 사람, 즉 사업 상황을 한눈에 파악하지 못하는 사람에게는 언제나 곤란과 혼란만이 남는다. 질서가 없는 곳에는 언제나 혼란이 있기 때문이다. 모든 상인에게 적용 가능한 완벽한 모델을 만들기 위하여 나는 이 글을 전술한 바와 같이 두 개의 주요 부문으로 나눌 것이고, 누구나 이 글로부터 좋은 결과를 얻을 수 있도록 명료하게 설명할 것이다. 첫째로 나는 기초재산이 어떤 의미이고, 어떻게 작성해야 하는가를 설명하고자 한다.

CHAPTER 2

FIRST PART OF THIS TREATISE, WHICH IS CALLED INVENTORY— WHAT INVENTORY IS, AND HOW TO MAKE IT

First, we must assume that every action is determined by the end in view, and in order to pursue this end properly, we must use every effort. The purpose of every merchant is to make a lawful and reasonable profit so as to keep up his business. Therefore, the merchants should begin their business with the name of God at the beginning of every book and have His holy

> *Note—The words in parentheses are the author's. as also the punctuation and paragraphing, as the original is extremely deficient in these. The words in italics are copied exact from the original.*

name in their minds. To begin with, the merchant must make his inventory (*inventario*) in this way: He must always put down on a sheet of paper or in a separate book whatever he has in this world, personal property or real estate, beginning with the things that are most valuable and most likely to be lost, such as cash, jewels, silver, etc., for the real estate, such as houses, lands, lakes, meadows, ponds, etc., cannot be lost as personal property. Then all the other things must be put down one after another. In the said inventory give always first the day, the year, the place and your name. This whole inventory must be completed in one day, otherwise there will be trouble in the future in the management of the business.

As an example for you, I will give you, now, an idea as to how the inventory is to be made, so that you may use it as a guide in any particular case.

제2장
이 글의 첫 번째 부분, 재물기*(재산 조사표)의 의의와 작성법

우선, 우리는 모든 행동이 목표를 기반으로 결정된다는 것을 알아야 한다. 즉, 목표가 행동을 결정한다는 것을 명심해야 한다. 이러한 목적을 적절히 수행하기 위하여 우리는 모든 노력을 기울여야 한다. 모든 상인의 목표는 합법적으로 충분한 이익을 획득하여 그의 사업을 성장시키는 데 있다. 그러므로 상인은 그의 모든 장부의 첫 머리에 하나님의 이름을 기록하여 하나님의

<small>주의 — 괄호는 번역자(존 가이스빅)가 쓴 것이다. 파치올리 원문은 구두점, 단락구분 표시 등이 매우 부족하다. 그리고 이탤릭체의 글씨는 파치올리 원문에서 복사한 것이다.</small>

이름을 기억하면서 사업을 시작해야 한다. 먼저, 상인은 재물기*(재산 조사표)를 이런식으로 작성해야 한다. 상인은 항상 문서 또는 장부에 자신의 동산, 부동산을 기록해야 한다. 기록은 현금, 보석 등의 잃기 쉬운 자산부터, 건물, 토지 등의 부동산의 순서로 기록해야 한다. 이 재물기는 적어도 하루 이내에 작성되어야 한다. 그렇지 않으면 괜한 혼란이 초래되기 때문이다.

이제 나는 재물기를 작성하기 위한 예시를 들고자 하며, 이 예시를 보고 각자의 재물기를 작성할 수 있게 될 것이다.

---

* 재물기: 재산 및 채무 조사표

CHAPTER 3

EXAMPLE OF AN INVENTORY WITH ALL ITS FORMAL REQUIREMENTS

In the name of God, November 8th, 1493, Venice.

The following is the inventory of myself, N. N., of Venice, Street of the Holy Apostles.

I have written down systematically, or had written by Mr. So-and-So, this inventory of all my property, personal and real, what is owed to me (*debiti*), and what is owed by me (*crediti*), of which I on this said day find myself possessed in this world.

First Item: First I find myself possessed in cash, in gold and coin of so many ducats, of which so many are Venetian, and so many gold Hungarian ; of so many large florins made up of Papal, Siennese and Florentine, etc. The rest consists of many different kinds of silver and copper coins, *i. e.*, *troni*, *marcelli*, papal and royal *carlini* and Florentine *grossi*, and Milanese *testoni*, etc.

Second Item: I also possess, in set and unset jewels, so-and-so many pieces, among which are many *balassi* set in gold, rings weighing so-and-so-many ounces, carats, grains, etc., per piece or in bulk, etc., which you can express in any manner you wish. There are so-and-so-many sapphires set on clamps for women ; they weigh so much. And there are so-and-so-many rubies, unset, weighing so much. The rest consists of unpolished pointed diamonds, etc. Here you may give such descriptions and weight as you desire.

Third Item: I have clothes of many kinds ; so many of such kind ; and so many

제3장
모든 요소를 갖춘 재물기의 사례

하나님의 이름으로, 1493년 11월 8일 베니스.

다음은 내가 보유하는 재산 및 채무에 관한 목록인 재물기이다. 그리고 나의 이름은 N. N.이고, 나의 주소는 베니스 공화국, 성스러운 사도들의 거리이다.

나는 재물기를 체계적으로 기록했고 또는 타인으로 하여금 기록하도록 하였다. 재물기는 오늘 현재로 나에게 귀속되는 모든 채권과 재산, 그리고 채무로 구성되어 있다.

제1번 항목: 첫째로, 나는 베네치아 화폐와 금, 동전 등을 소유하고 있다. 그리고 헝가리 금화도 소유하고 있다. 그리고 교황령, 시에네, 플로렌스(피렌체) 등지의 은화를 소유하고 있다. 그리고 다양한 지역의 은화와 동전을 소유하고 있다.

제2번 항목: 나는 또한 가공, 미가공 보석들을 소유하고 있다. 금, 반지 등은 개 또는 무게 단위로 거래되는데, 이 단위는 작성자가 원하는 단위로 기록하면 된다. 그리고 사파이어, 루비, 다이아몬드 등도 보유하고 있고 무게는 얼마이다. 여기에 이런 식으로 무게와 해설을 기록하면 될 것이다.

제3번 항목: 나는 여러 종류의 옷감을 소유하고 있다. 이러한 것은 그 상태와 색상, 스타일 등을 기록하면 된다.

of such-and-such kind, etc., describing their condition, colors, linings, styles, etc.

Fourth Item: I have several kinds of silverware, as cups, basins, rammi, cosileri, piromi, etc. Here describe all the different kinds one by one, etc., and weigh each kind diligently. Keep an account of pieces and weights, and of the alloy, whether the Venetian or the one used at Ragusa, etc. Also mention the stamp or mark that they might have.

Fifth Item: I have so much *massaria dei lini*—that is, bed sheets, table cloths, shirts, handkerchiefs, etc., so many of each. Of the bed sheets, so many are made three-piece sheets, and so many are three and one-half, etc., mentioning whether the linen is Padua linen or some other kind, new or used ; length so many *braccia*, etc., so many shirts, etc.; table cloths of so many threads ; so many big handkerchiefs and so many small, mentioning whether new or used, giving the different kind in your own way.

Sixth Item: I have so many feather beds and their respective pillows, mentioning whether the feathers are new or used, whether the pillow-cases are new or used, etc., which altogether or one by one weigh so much, marked with my mark or with some other mark, as the custom is.

Seventh Item: I have at home or in the store so much goods of different kinds : First, so many cases of ginger *michino*, weighing so many pounds, marked with such-and-such mark, and so on, describing each kind of said goods with all their marks that you might possibly give and with all the possible accuracy as to weight, number, measurement, etc.

Eighth Item: I have so many cases of ginger *bellidi*, etc., and so many sacks of pepper, long pepper or round pepper, depending on what it is; so many packages of cinnamon, etc., that weigh so much; so many packages of cloves, etc., that weigh so much, with *fusti polvere* and *cappelletti* or without, etc., and so many pieces of *verzini* weighing so much, and so much sandalwood, red or white, weighing so much, and so on, entering one item after another.

Ninth Item: I have so many skins of coverings, that is, so many white kids and so many *albertoni* or *marchiani*, etc., so many of such-and-such kind, etc., so many fox skins, so many tanned and so many raw, so many chamois skins tanned, and so many raw.

제4번 항목: 나는 컵, 대야 등 여러 종류의 은 제품을 소유하고 있다. 여기에 종류별로 하나씩 무게 등을 기록해야 한다. 그리고 그 개수와 무게, 합금 여부, 주로 이용되는 나라, 그리고 마크 등을 기록하면 된다.

제5번 항목: 나는 침대 시트 및 테이블보, 셔츠, 손수건 등을 소유하고 있다. 침대 시트는 3조각 짜리이며, 리넨은 파두아 리넨인지 아니면 다른 지역의 리넨인지, 그리고 새것인지 헌것인지, 길이는 얼마인지도 기록해야 한다. 그리고 셔츠, 테이블보, 손수건 등도 그 크기, 새것인지 헌것인지 등을 각자의 방법으로 기록하면 된다.

제6번 항목: 나는 새의 깃으로 만들어진 침대와 베개 등을 소유하고 있다. 이 역시 새것인지 헌것인지를 기록해야 한다. 그리고 베개 상자 역시 새것인지 헌것인지 등을 기록해야 한다. 그리고 각각에 대하여 부피, 마크 등을 기록해야 한다. 그것이 상관습이다.

제7번 항목: 나는 집 또는 가게에 잡제품을 소유하고 있다. 첫째로, 생강 michino 상자 수, 무게, 표시된 마크 등을 기록해야 한다. 그리고 보유하고 있는 상품 각각에 대한 무게, 개수 등을 가능한 한 정확하게 기록해야 한다.

제8번 항목: 나는 생강 몇 상자를 보유하고 있고, 후추 몇 자루를 보유하고 있다. 후추는 긴 모양 또는 둥근 모양이다. 그리고 계피 몇 팩을 보유하고 있고 그 무게는 얼마이다. 정향 및 백단향이 몇 팩이고 그 무게는 얼마이다 등을 차례로 기록해야 한다.

제9번 항목: 나는 여러 종류의 가죽제품을 소유하고 있다. 이 역시 그 종류와 가공, 미가공 여부 등을 기록해야 한다.

제10번 항목: 나는 여러 종류의 고급 가죽제품을 소유하고 있다. 진실이 당신을 언제나 올바른 길로 인도할 수 있도록 매번 세심하고 정확하게 기록해야 한다. 즉, 개수로 기록해야 할 것과, 무게로 기록해야 할 것, 양으로 기록해야 할 것 등을 구분해야 한다. 이 세

Tenth Item: I have so many fine skins, *fore armenti, dossi varii, zebelini*, etc., so many of such-and-such kind, and so many of such-and-such kind—defining diligently and truthfully each time so that truth will always guide you, etc., distinguishing the things that ought to be entered by pieces from those that ought to be entered by weight, and those that ought to be entered by measurement, because in these three ways business is conducted everywhere; certain things are reckoned by the bushel, others by the hundreds, others by the pound, others by the ounce, others by number, others by a *conto* (by single numbers) as leather goods or skins, others by the piece, as precious stones and fine pearls, etc.; so you will make a notation of each thing. These examples will serve as a guide for all the rest, etc.

Eleventh Item: I have in real estate: first, a house with so many stories, so many rooms, court yard, wells, garden, etc., situated in St. Apostle Street over the Canal, etc., adjoining such-and-such parties, etc., giving the names of the boundary line properties, making reference to the oldest and most reliable deeds, if there are any; and so, if you have more houses in different localities, you will enter them in a similar way.

Twelfth Item: I have so many pieces of land under cultivation (fields or *staiore* or *panora*) etc., entering them by the name according to the usage of the country where you are, saying where they are situated, etc., as, for instance, a field of so many *tavole*, or *canne*, or *pertiche*, or *bevolche*, etc., situated in such-and-such town in the Province of Padua or somewhere else, adjoining the land of so-and-so, giving all the boundary lines and referring to deeds or the description from the recorder's office, for which land you pay taxes in such-and-such municipality, which are worked by so-and-so with a yearly income of so much, and so on; you will enter all your possessions, etc., cattle, etc.

Thirteenth Item: I have in deposit with the Camera de l'Impresti (a bank), or with another bank in Venice, so many ducats; or with the parish of Canareggio, etc., or part in one parish and part in another, giving the names under which they have been deposited, mentioning the book of the bank, the number of the page where your account is, and the name of the clerk who keeps said book, so that you can easily find your account when you go to get money, because in such offices they must keep very many accounts on account of the big crowd that sometimes goes

가지 방식으로 어디서나 장사가 이루어지기 때문이다. 즉, 물품의 종류에 따라 어떤 것은 부셀 단위로, 100개 단위로, 파운드 단위로, 온스 단위로 계산이 되고, 가죽 제품 등은 단일 숫자 단위로, 보석 및 진주 등은 개수 단위로 계산이 되므로 당신은 각 물품에 대하여 이러한 표시를 해야 한다. 여기까지의 기록 예시를 보고 나머지 물품도 이 예시와 같이 기록하면 될 것이다.

제11번 항목: 나는 부동산을 소유하고 있다. 즉, 부동산을 소유하는 경우 먼저, 집의 경우, 층수, 방의 수, 정원, 우물 보유 여부, 그리고 성 사도 거리 등의 주소와 인접건물 등을 기록하면 된다. 그리고 다른 지역에 또 집을 소유하고 있는 경우에는 상기와 같이 기록하면 될 것이다.

제12번 항목: 나는 몇 필지의 땅(fields or staiore, panora)을 소유하고 있다. 이 경우 거주하고 있는 시군의 관청이 정한 규정에 따라 그 농경지의 명칭을 정하여 재물기에 기록해야 한다. 예를 들면, tavole, canne, pertiche, bevolche 등의 땅은 Padua 주 또는 다른 주의 어느 도시에 위치하는지, 그리고 누구의 땅에 인접하여 있는지, 토지의 경계는 어떠한지, 사무실에서의 접근방법은 어떠한지 등을 기록해야 한다. 그리고 토지세는 어느 도시에 납부하는지, 타인에게 경작시키는 경우 그 임대로 인한 연소득이 얼마인가 등을 기록해야 한다. 이러한 방식으로 모든 재산을 기록해야 한다. 또한 소를 키운다면 그 소 역시 이런 방식으로 기록해야 한다.

제13번 항목: 나는 Camera de I'Impresti 은행 또는 베니스의 다른 은행과 거래를 하고 있다. 즉, 은행 예치금을 갖고 있다. 은행에 현금을 예치한 경우, 은행에서 돈을 인출하고자 할 때 당신의 통장을 쉽게 찾을 수 있도록 은행 명칭, 예금조건, 금액, 통장의 페이지 수, 은행의 담당자 명칭 등을 기록해야 한다. 은행은 언제나 많은 사람들과 거래를 하므로 그 관리하는 통장이 많아 실수할 우려가 있다. 따라서 만기가 언제인지 이자는 얼마인지를 쉽게 알 수 있도록 모든 날짜가 정확하게 기록되어 있는지를 확인해야 한다.

there, and you must also see that dates are put down precisely so that you know when everything falls due and what the per cent. is.

Fourteenth Item: I have so many debtors (*debitori*) : one is so-and-so, who owes me (*me dee dare*—shall give me) so many ducats, and so on, giving the names of each one, putting down all annotations as to the names, their family names, and how much they owe you (*te debbono dore*—shall have to give you) and why ; also whether there are any written papers or notarial instruments. In total I have so many ducats to collect, you will say, of good money, if the money is due from good people, otherwise you will say of bad money.

Fifteenth Item: I am debtor in total to the extent of so many ducats, etc. I owe so many to so-and-so. Here mention your creditors (*creditori*) one by one, writing down whether there are any documents or writings or instruments; if possible, mention the persons present when the debt was incurred, the reason, the time and the place, for any case that might arise in court or out of court.

제14번 항목: 나에게는 다수의 채무자가 있다. 나에게 빚진 사람, 즉 나에게 돈을 주어야 할 사람이 누구이고, 그 금액이 얼마인지 각각의 이름과 금액을 기록해야 한다. 즉, 그들의 성과 이름, 빚진 금액, 이유 등을 자세히 설명하는 방식으로 기록해야 한다. 또한 채무 성립과 관련된 문서 또는 공증문서의 존재 여부 등을 각 인명별로 하나씩 기록해야 한다. 도합하여 나는 얼마를 회수해야 하는지를 기록하되, 회수 가능한 채권은 회수 가능분으로, 악성채무자에 대한 것은 악성채무로 분류하여 기록해야 한다.

제15번 항목: 나는 도합하여 얼마의 채무가 있다. 나는 누구누구에게 빚지고 있다. 여기에 채권자 명칭을 하나하나씩 기록하고, 동시에 관련문서의 존재 여부도 기록해야 한다. 가능하다면 법정 내외의 소송 또는 시비에 대비하여 차입 당시의 입회자, 이유, 때와 장소 등도 기록해두어야 한다.

CHAPTER 4

VERY USEFUL ADMONITION AND GOOD ADVICE TO THE GOOD MERCHANT

And so, as we have said, you shall enter diligently every thing that you have, whether personal property or real estate, one by one, even if there were ten thousand items, putting down the condition and nature, whether deposited or loaned, etc. You will have to mention each thing in proper order in the said Inventory with all marks, names, surnames—as far as possible—for things are never too clear to a merchant on account of the different things that may happen in business, as anybody in business knows. Right is the proverb which says: More bridges are necessary to make a good merchant than a lawyer can make. Who is the person that can count all the things that can happen to a merchant—on the sea, on land, in times of peace and abundance and times of war and famine, in times of health or pestilence? In these crises he must know what to do, in the marketplaces and in the fairs which are held now in one place and now in another. For this reason it is right to say that the merchant is like a rooster, which of all the animals (*animale*) is the most alert and in winter and summer keeps his night vigils and never rests. And they say of the nightingale that it sings throughout the whole night; however, this may be in the summer during the hot weather, but not during the winter, as experience shows. Also it is said that the head of the merchant has a hundred eyes, and still they are not sufficient for all he has to say or to do. These things are told by people who have had experience in them, such as the Venetians, Florentines, Genoans, Neapolitans, Milanese, people of Ancona, Brescia, Bragama, Aquila, Sienna, Lucca, Perugia, Urbino, Forosempronio, Cagli, Ugubio, Castello,

제4장

훌륭한 상인에 대한 매우 유용한 충고와 가르침

전술한 바와 같이, 상인은 소유하고 있는 모든 것을 세밀하게 기록해야 한다. 유동자산이든 고정자산이든 그것이 천 가지, 만 가지일지라도 하나씩 그 조건과 상태, 빌려준 것인지, 빌린 것인지의 여부 등을 기록해야 한다. 상인은 전술한 재물기에 적절한 방식으로 상표, 성명 등을 기록해야 한다. 상인이면 누구나 아는 것처럼, 상인은 발생 가능한 불상사에 대비하여 언제나 모든 것을 분명하게 기록해야 하기 때문이다. 그런 면에서 "변호사보다 상인에게 더 많은 퇴로(a bridge of gold, 타개책)가 필요하다."라는 속담은 명언인 것으로 보인다. 상인은 땅에서 바다에서, 평시 또는 전시, 풍년 또는 흉년, 평년 또는 유행병의 시기 등에 상인에게 발생할 수 있는 모든 상황을 예측하고 대비해야 한다. 이러한 위기시에 상설시장 또는 여기저기서 열리는 임시시장에서 상인이 해야 할 바를 알아야 한다. 이러한 이유로 상인은 수탉과 비슷하다고 할 수 있다. 수탉은 겨울이든 여름이든 언제나 기민하고, 항상 경계하며 쉬지 않기 때문이다. 흔히 나이팅게일이란 새는 밤새워 노래한다고 한다. 그러나 이것은 날씨가 좋은 여름에만 그렇고, 겨울에는 그렇지 않다. 이것은 직접 들어보면 알 수 있을 것이다. 그리고 보통 상인은 눈을 100개나 갖고 있으면서도, 그가 해야 할 말과 업무가 많아 그 100개나 되는 눈도 부족하다고 말한다. 이러한 얘기는 베니스, 플로렌스, 제노바, 나폴리, 밀라노, 인코나, 브레시아, 브라가마, 아킬라, 시에나, 루카, 페루자, 우르비노, 포로셈프로니오, 칼리, 우구비오, 카스텔로, 브로고, 풀리뇨, 피사, 볼로냐, 페라라, 만투아, 베로나, 빈센차, 파두아, 트라니, 레체, 비톤토 등 이탈리아 전역의 상인을 겪어본 사람들이 하는 얘기다. 이 도시들은 상업을 최우선으로 하는 제1급 도시이

Brogo, Fuligno, Pisa, Bologna, Ferrara, Mantua, Verona, Vincenza, Padua, Trani, Lecce, Bitonto, which are among the first cities of Italy and have the first place in commerce—especially the cities of Venice and Florence, which adopt rules that respond to any need. And well say the municipal laws: *Vigilantibus et non dormientibus jura subveniunt*—which means, The law helps those that are awake, not those that sleep. So in the divine functions of the Holy Church they sing that God promised the crown to the watchful ones, and this was the instruction that Virgil gave to Dante as to his son, in Canto 24 of the Inferno, where he exhorts him to the work by which one can reach the hill of virtue: Now, my son, it behooves that you quit your laziness, said my master, for he who lies on feathers or under covers will never amount to anything. Whoever spends his life in this way, he said, will leave on this earth the same trace as the smoke in the air or foam on the water, etc.; and another Italian poet admonishes us in the same way, saying: Work should not seem to you strange, for Mars never granted a victory to those that spent their time resting. And it is also very good to quote that sage who said to the lazy man to take the ant as an example; and the Apostle Paul says that no one will be worthy of the crown except he who shall fight valiantly for it.

I wanted to bring in these reminders for your own good, so that the daily care about your business would not seem heavy to you, especially the writing down everything and putting down every day everything that happens to you, as we shall unfold in the next chapters. But above all, remember God and your neighbor; never forget to attend to religious meditation every morning, for through this you will never lose your way, and by being charitable, you will not lose your riches, as the poet says: *Nec caritas, nec Missa minuit iter*, etc. And to this our Savior exhorts us in the book of St. Mattew, when he says: *Primum quaerite regulum dei, et haec omnia adiicietur vobis*, which means: Seek you, Christians, first the kingdom of God and then the other temporal and spiritual things you will easily obtain, because your Heavenly Father knows very well your needs, etc.

And this I hope will be sufficient as an instruction for you to make the Inventory, etc., and to do other things well.

고, 특히 베니스와 플로렌스는 상인에게 필요한 것을 즉시 지원하는 법규를 갖고 있을 정도다. 그리고 "법은 깨어 있는 자는 도와주지만, 잠들어 있는 자는 돕지 않는다."라는 말이 있다. 신성한 교회에서도 "하나님은 경계하는 자에게 영광을 약속하셨다."라고 한다. 이것은 베르길리우스가 단테에게 《신곡》 지옥편 제24장에서 준 가르침이다. 거기서 그는 아들에게 간곡히 타이른다. 덕의 경지에 이를 수 있는 일을 하라고 아들아, 이제 그 게으름을 버려야 한다. 이부자리에 누워만 있는 자는 성공에 이를 수 없기 때문이다. 누구라도 이런 식으로 인생을 허비하면 공중의 연기, 물가의 거품과 같은 허망한 흔적만을 남기게 되기 때문이다. 또 다른 이탈리아 시인도 같은 방식으로 우리를 훈계한다. 일이라는 것이 너에게는 이상하게 보일 수도 있겠으나, 우리의 마르스(Mars) 신께서는 시간을 허비하는 자에게 승리를 허락하지 않는다. 그리고 게으른 사람을 훈계한 현인이 개미를 예로 든 것은 매우 타당한 것으로 보인다. 그리고 사도 바울도 "용감하게 투쟁하는 사람만이 영광을 차지할 수 있다."라고 말씀하신 바가 있다.

내가 매일 사업에 신경 써야 한다는 것이 여러분들에게 큰 정신적 부담으로 되지 않도록 하기 위하여 이 글을 쓰는 것이다. 특별히 매일 당신에게 발생하는 것을 기록해야 한다는 것을 너무 무겁게 느끼지 않도록 하는 마음에서다. 이제 다음 장을 펼치고자 한다. 그러나 무엇보다 먼저 하나님과 이웃을 기억해야 한다는 것을 잊지 말기 바란다. 매일 아침 종교적 명상에 참여하라. 이렇게 하면 당신의 길 그리고 자비심을 잃지 않을 것이고, 또한 당신의 재산도 잃지 않을 것이다. 시인은 말한다. 그리고 마태복음에서 우리의 구원자께서는 우리에게 말씀하신다. 너희 기독교인들아, 먼저 하나님의 나라를 찾아라. 그러면 다른 것들을 쉽게 얻을 것이다. 하나님 아버지께서는 네가 무엇을 필요로 하는지 잘 알고 계시기 때문이다.

그리고 여러분들이 재물기를 작성하기 위한 지침과 경영지침은 이 정도면 충분할 것이다.

CHAPTER 5
SECOND PRINCIPAL PART OF THIS TREATISE NAMED DISPOSITION (ARRANGEMENT) —WHAT IS UNDERSTOOD BY IT— WHAT IT CONSISTS OF IN BUSINESS, AND THE THREE PRINCIPAL BOOKS OF THE MERCHANT

Comes now the second principal part of this treatise, which is called disposition, and of this I have to talk more at length than of the first part, in order to make it very clear. I will divide it in two parts. We shall call the one, *Corpo overo monte de sutto el trafico*; the other, *Corpor overo monte de botega* (Commerce in general, and Your store in particular).

First, we shall speak of commerce in general and its requirements. Immediately after the Inventory, you need three books to make the work proper and easy. One is called Memorandum (*Memoriale*), the second Journal (*Giornale*), and the third Ledger (*Quaderno*). Many, on account of their small business, use only the last two, that is, the journal and the ledger.

We shall speak about the first—that is, of the memorandum book, and thereafter of the other two, about their makeup, and how they should be kept. First of all, we will give the definition of the memorandum book.

제5장
이 글의 두 번째 중요 부분인 장부조직과 그 의미, 그리고 상인이 갖추어야 할 세 개의 주요 장부

이제 이 글의 두 번째 부분이고, 장부조직이라고 불리는 부분에 왔다. 이것에 대하여 나는 그 의미를 명확히 하기 위하여 첫 번째 부분보다는 좀더 길게 설명하고자 한다. 나는 이것을 두 부분으로 나누고자 한다. 첫 번째는 상업총론이고, 두 번째는 상업각론이다.

첫째로 나는 상업총론과 그 요건에 대하여 설명하고자 한다. 재물기를 작성한 직후에 당신은 업무를 효율적으로 처리하기 위하여 세 개의 장부를 준비해야 한다. 첫 번째는 영업일지(약칭: 일지, 이탈리아어 Memoriale)이고, 두 번째는 분개장(이탈리아어 Giornale, 영어 Journal)이고, 세 번째는 원장(이탈리아어 Quaderno, 영어 Ledger)이다. 작은 가게의 경우에는 보통 분개장과 원장만을 사용하는 경우도 많다.

이제 나는 첫 번째 장부인 (영업)일지부터 설명하고, 다음에 나머지 두 장부를 만드는 방법과 작성방법에 대하여 설명하고자 한다. 우선 일지의 의미에 대하여 설명하겠다.

| 해설 | 영어 arrange, dispose 등에 대응되는 이탈리아어는 organizzare, disporre이므로 arrangement를 조직화, 즉 장부조직(장부의 구성)으로 번역하였다. 실제로 본 장의 내용은 영업일지, 분개장, 원장으로 이어지는 장부 체계 및 조직화에 관한 것이다.

CHAPTER 6

OF THE FIRST BOOK, WHICH IS CALLED MEMORANDUM BOOK (*MEMORIALE*), OR SCRAP BOOK (*SQUARTA LOGLIO*), OR BLOTTER (*VACHETTA*). WHAT IS UNDERSTOOD BY IT AND HOW ENTRIES SHOULD BE MADE IN IT AND BY WHOM

The memorandum book, or, according to others, scrap book or blotter, is a book in which the merchant shall put down all his transactions, small or big, as they take place, day by day, hour by hour. In this book he will put down in detail everything that he sells or buys, and every other transaction without leaving out a jot; who, what, when, where, mentioning everything to make it fully as clear as I have already said in talking about the Inventory, so that there is no necessity of saying it over again in detail. Many are accustomed to enter their inventory in this book, but it is not wise to let people see and know what you possess. It is not wise to enter all your personal property and real property in this book. This book is kept on account of volume of business, and in it entries should be made in the absence of the owner by his servants, or his women if there are any, for a big merchant never keeps his assistants idle; they are now here, now there, and at times both he and they are out, some at the market place and some attending a fair, leaving perhaps at home only the servants or the women who, perhaps, can barely write. These latter, in order not to send customers away, must sell, collect or buy, according to the orders left by the boss or owner, and they, as well as they can, must enter every transaction in this memorandum book, naming simply the money and weights which they know; they should note the various kinds of money that they may collect or take in or that they may give in exchange. As far as this book is concerned, it is not as important to transfer to standards the various kinds of coin handled as it is with the journal and ledger, as we will see hereafter.

제6장
일지의 의미와 기록내용 그리고 부기자에 대하여

일지는 스크랩북(scrap book) 또는 블로터(blotter, 사건 기록부)라고도 하며, 발생하는 모든 거래를 크든 작든 상인이 기록하는 장부다. 이 장부에 상인은 조금도 빠짐없이 사고파는 것을 비롯한 모든 거래를 자세하게 기록해야 한다. 이미 재물기에서 설명한 바와 같이 모든 일을 명료하게 처리하기 위하여 누가, 무엇을, 언제, 어디서 했는지를 기록해야 한다. 이에 대해 더 이상 잔소리할 필요가 없을 것이다. 많은 사람이 재물 내역을 이 장부에 기록하고 있으나, 자신의 재산 상태를 이 장부에 기록하여 남들이 보게 하는 것은 현명한 일이 아니다. 즉, 일지에 개인적으로 소유하는 동산, 부동산 등을 기록하는 것은 현명한 일이 아니다. 이 장부는 거래량이 많기 때문에 기록하는 것이다. 주인이 부재시에는 그의 점원 또는 부인 또는 딸 등이 기록하면 된다. 대상인일수록 점원들을 놀리지 않기 때문이고, 이들은 시장과 거래처 여기저기를 돌아다녀야 한다. 간신히 읽고 쓸 줄 아는 소수의 사람들만 가게에 남겨둔 채, 이들 기록 담당자들은 고객을 내쫓지 않도록 주인의 지시에 따라 팔거나, 거두거나, 사거나 해야 한다. 그리고 그들은 가능한 한 모든 거래를 일지에 기록해야 한다. 그들이 아는 대로 무게와 화폐 명칭을 기록할 뿐만 아니라, 그들이 주고받는 다양한 화폐의 종류를 기록해두어야 한다. 일지에서 다양한 화폐를 하나로 표준화하여 기록하는 것은 중요하지 않다. 그 이유는 나중에 알게 될 것이다.

부기자는 분개장에 기록하기 전에 먼저 일지에 거래를 기록해야 한다. 주인이 돌아오면 일지를 검사한 후, 더 좋은 기록방법 또는 위치를 지시할 것이다. 그러므로 이 일지는 사업을 크게 하는 상인에게 더욱 필요하다. 그러나 거래가 발생하자마자 모든 거래를 질

The bookkeeper will put everything in order before he transcribes a transaction in the journal. In this way, when the owner comes back he will see all the transactions, and he may put them in a better order if he thinks necessary. Therefore, this book is very necessary to those who have a big business. It would be too much trouble to put down in a beautiful and orderly way every transaction immediately after it take place, in books which are authentic and kept neat with care. You must make a mark on the cover of this book, as well as on all the others, so that you can distinguish them when, in the process of the business, the book is filled or has served for a certain period of time and you take another book. You must take another book when the first one has been used entirely, yet many are accustomed in different localities to balance annually these books although they are not full; and they do likewise with the other books not yet mentioned, as you will see hereafter.

On the second book you should put another mark different from the first, so that at any time you can trace your transaction easily. For this purpose we use the date. Among true Christians there is the good custom to mark their first books with that glorious sign from which every enemy of the spiritual flees and before which all the infernal spirits justly tremble—that is, the holy cross, by which in our tender years we begin to learn to read. The books that follow, you may mark in alphabetical order, calling A the second, and B the third, etc. So that we call the first books with the Cross, or Memorandum with Cross, and the second Memorandum A, Journal A, Ledger A. The pages of each of these books ought to be marked for several reasons known to the merchant, although many say that this is not necessary for the Journal and Memorandum books. The transactions are entered day by day, one under the other, in such way that it may be easy to trace them. This would be all right if all the transactions of one day would not take more than one page; but, as we have seen, for many of the bigger merchants, not one, but several pages have to be used in one day. If some one would wish to do something crooked, he could tear out one of the pages and this fraud could not be discovered, as far as the dates are concerned, for the days would follow properly one after the other, and yet the fraud may have been committed. Therefore, for this and other reasons, it is always good to number and mark each single page in all the books of the merchants; the books kept in the house or kept in the store.

서정연하게 보기 좋게 기록하는 것은 부담이 클 수도 있으므로, 일지는 신뢰성 있고, 간결하게 기록한다. 그리고 일지의 표지에는 식별 기호를 표시해야 한다. 장부를 다 사용했는지 또는 어느 기간의 장부인지 등을 식별할 수 있어야 하기 때문이다. 그리고 장부가 모두 사용되면 새 장부로 바꾸어야 한다. 그러나 다른 지역에서는 아직 다 사용하지 않았어도 해가 바뀌면 마감하고 새 장부로 바꾸는 관행도 있다. 다른 장부의 경우에도 마찬가지인데, 이에 대해서는 곧 알게 될 것이다.

두 번째 일지는 첫 번째 일지와 다른 기호를 표시해야 한다. 아무 때나 거래기록을 쉽게 추적할 수 있도록 하기 위해서다. 이러한 목적으로 우리는 날짜를 사용한다. 진정한 기독교인은 그들의 첫 책을 영광스러운 십자가 기호로 시작한다. 십자가 기호는 모든 마귀를 떨게 하고 또 도망가게 하기 때문이다. 그리고 십자가 기호는 우리가 어린 시절 글을 배우기 시작할 때 맨 처음 배운 것이기도 하다. 따라서 다음의 일지들에 알파벳 순서로 번호를 붙이면, A일지는 두 번째 일지, B일지는 세 번째 일지가 된다. 물론 첫 번째 일지는 십자가 일지 또는 십자가 기호 일지로 칭하고, 두 번째 일지는 일지 A, 분개장 A, 원장 A 등으로 칭한다. 많은 사람들이 일지와 분개장에는 페이지 번호가 필요 없다고 말하지만, 일지에는 여러 이유로 반드시 페이지 번호가 표시되어야 한다. 거래는 그 거래를 추적하기 쉽도록 하기 위하여 매일 순서대로 기록한다. 하루에 발생한 거래를 한 페이지에 기록할 수 있는 경우에는 페이지 번호 무용론이 옳을 것이다. 그러나 보다시피, 큰 상인의 경우에는 하루의 거래가 한 페이지가 아니라 다수의 페이지에 기록될 수도 있다. 누군가가 장부조작을 위하여 그중 한 페이지를 떼어내면 그 조작은 발각되지 않는다. 이렇게 해도 날짜순으로 기록되므로 언제든 장부 조작이 발생할 수 있다. 이러한 이유로 상인이 기록하는 모든 장부는 그것이 가정용이든 상업용이든 모든 장부에는 매 장마다 페이지 번호가 반드시 표시되어야 한다.

| 해설 | 중세유럽의 알파벳은 26자가 아니라 27자였다. 당시의 교회, 학교 등에서는 글자를 가르칠 때, A가 아니라 십자가(Cross) 기호부터 가르쳤다고 한다. 따라서 모든 기호의 시작은 A가 아니라 십자가 기호였으므로, 장부의 순서는 첫째로 십자가 장부, 두 번째로 A장부, 세 번째로 B장부 이런 식으로 진행되는 것이다.

CHAPTER 7

OF THE MANNER IN WHICH IN MANY PLACES MERCANTILE BOOKS ARE AUTHENTICATED, WHY AND BY WHOM

All these books, according to the good customs of several countries where I have been, should be taken and shown to a certain mercantile officer such as the Consuls in the City of Perosa employ, and to him you should state that those are the books in which you intend to write down, or somebody else write down for you, all your transactions in an orderly way; and also state in what kind of money the transactions therein should be entered—that is, whether in *lire di Picioli*, or in *lire di Grossi*, or in *ducats* and *lire*, etc., or in *florins* and *denari*, or in ounces, *tari*, *grani*, *denari*, etc. The good merchant should put down these things always on the first page of his book, and if afterwards the handwriting should be done by somebody else than the one stated at the beginning of the book, this should be recorded at the office of the said officer. The clerk should mention all this in the records of the said officer—that is, on such and such a day you presented such and such books, marked with such and such mark, which books are named, one so-and-so, the other so-and-so, etc.; of which books one has so many pages, another so many, etc., which books you said would be kept by you or by so-and-so; but that it may be that in said Memorandum Book or Scrap Book or Blotter, some person of your family might enter said transaction, as explained before. In this case, the said clerk shall write down on the first page of your books, in his own handwriting, the name of the said officer, and will attest to the truth of everything and shall attach the seal of that office to make the books authentic for any case in court when they might be produced.

제7장
여러 도시의 상업장부 인증과 그 이유

　내가 다녀본 여러 국가의 관행에 따르면, 이 모든 장부는 페로사 시의 Consul 등과 같은 상업 감독관청의 관리에게 제출되어야 한다. 그리고 감독관에게 상인은 이 모든 장부가 자기 또는 대리인에 의하여 체계적인 방법으로 모든 거래가 기록된 것임을 증언해야 한다. 동시에 어떤 종류의 화폐로 기록하였는가도 증언해야 한다. 훌륭한 상인이라면 이런 것들을 장부의 첫 페이지에 기록해야 한다. 그리고 후에 장부의 첫 부분에 언급된 사람이 아닌 다른 사람에 의하여 기록되는 경우, 이러한 사실은 감독관리의 사무실에 보고되어야 한다. 관공서의 서기는 감독관의 기록에 이 모든 것을 언급해야 한다. 즉, 어느 날짜에 상인이 장부를 제출하였고, 그 장부에는 어떤 기호가 표시되어 있었으며, 각 장부의 이름은 무엇이고, 페이지 수는 얼마인가 등을 언급해야 한다. 그러나 일지에 상인의 식구 중 누군가가 거래를 기록하는 경우도 있는데, 이 경우 서기는 친필로 상인이 제출한 장부의 첫 페이지에 감독관의 이름을 기록해야 한다. 그리고 법률적 분쟁에 대비하여 감독관의 도장을 찍어 그 장부가 인증된 것임을 확인해주어야 한다.

　이런 관행은 지극히 추천할 만한 것이다. 이러한 관행이 실천되는 도시 또한 그러하다. 많은 상인들이 장부를 두 벌로 작성하여, 하나는 구매자에게 또 하나는 판매자에게 보여주는데 이것은 그리 좋지 않은 관행이다. 왜냐하면 이런 방식으로 거짓말을 하기 때문이다. 감독관에게 장부를 제출함으로써 상인은 쉽게 거짓 또는 조작을 할 수 있다. 이 장부들은 조심스럽게 기록되고 인증을 받은 후 작성자의 집 또는 가게에 하나님의 이름으로 보관되어야 한다. 그래야 상인은 그의 사업을 시작할 준비가 완료된 것이다. 그러나 먼

This custom ought to be commended exceedingly; also the places where the custom is followed. Many keep their books in duplicate. They show one to the buyer and one to the seller, and this is very bad, because in this way they commit perjury. By presenting books to the said officer, one cannot easily lie or defraud. These books, after they have been carefully marked and authenticated, shall be kept in the name of God in your own place, and you are then ready to start your business. But first you shall enter in an orderly way in your Journal all the different items of the Inventory in the way that I will tell you later. But first you must understand how entries should be made in this Memorandum Book.

저 상인은 후술하는 방법으로 재물 내역을 분개장에 전기*해야 하므로 상인은 일지 작성법부터 배워야 한다.

---

* 전기(転記): 분개장에서 원장으로 또는 일지에서 분개장으로 옮겨 적는 것

CHAPTER 8

HOW ENTRIES SHOULD BE MADE IN THE SAID MEMORANDUM BOOK, AND EXAMPLES OF THE SAME

We have said already, if you will remember, that any one in your family can make entries in the said Memorandum Book, or Scrap Book or Blotter. Therefore, it cannot be fully stated how the entries should be made, because some members of your family will understand and some will not. But the common custom is this: Let us say, for instance, that you bought several pieces of cloth—for instance, 20 white *bresciani*, at 12 ducats apiece. It will be enough simply to make the entry in this way: On this day we have or I have bought from Mr. Filippo d'Rufoni of Brescia, 20 pieces of white *bresciani*. These goods are at Mr. Stefano Tagliapietra's place; one piece is so long, according to the agreement, and paid for at so many ducats, etc., marked with such and such number, etc. You mention whether the cloth is *a trelici*, or *a la piana*, wide or narrow, fine or medium, whether the Bergamo kind, or Vincenza, or Verona, or Padua, or Florence, or Mantua. Also you have to state here whether the transaction was made through a broker and whether it was made in cash entirely or part only in cash and part on time, stating the time, or whether it was part in cash and part in trade. In this case you must specify the things that were given in exchange, number, weight, measurement, and the price of the bushel or of the piece, or of the pound, etc., or whether the transaction was all by payment on time, stating the time when the payment should be made, whether on *Galia de Barutto*, or on *Galia de Fiandra*, or on the return day of a ship, or on the date of some fair, or other festivity, as for instance, on the next harvest day or on next Easter, or on next Christmas, or on Resurrection day or Carnival day, etc., according to what

제8장
일지의 기록방법과 그 예시

　가족 중 누구라도 일지를 기록할 수 있다는 것에 대하여는 이미 말한 바가 있으므로 일지 기록방법에 대해서는 상세히 설명할 필요가 없을 것이다. 가족 중 일부는 문맹이기 때문이다. 그러나 공통된 기록방법은 다음과 같다. 예를 들어, 개당 12더컷(ducat)에 20개의 흰색 브레시아니 천을 구입한 경우, 간단하게 다음과 같이 기록하면 충분할 것이다. 이 날 나는 필리포 씨로부터 흰색 브레시아니 20개를 구입했다. 물건은 스테파노 씨의 창고에 보관되어 있다. 개당 길이, 금액, 표시된 숫자는 이러이러하다 등을 기록한다. 또한 그 천이 넓은지 좁은지, 상급인지 중급인지, 베르가모, 빈센차 또는 베로나 종류인지 등도 기록해야 한다. 또한 그 거래가 거간을 통하여 이루어졌는지, 전액 현금인지, 현금외상 혼합인지, 현금과 물물교환 혼합거래인지, 그리고 그 거래일자 등도 언급해야 한다. 이 경우 기록자는 교환으로 받은 것의 세부 내역, 즉 개수, 무게, 단위당 가격, 외상 여부, 만기 지급일자 등을 자세히 기록해야 한다. 만기 지급일자가 Baruto or Fiandra 일인지, 선박 귀항일인지, 장날인지, 축제일인지, 추수감사절인지 아니면 다음 부활절인지, 다음 크리스마스인지, 사육제 날인지 등을 기록해야 한다.

was understood in the transaction. Finally, I must say that in this memorandum book nothing should be omitted. If it were possible, it should be noted what many others had said during the transaction because, as we have said about the Inventory, the merchant never can be too plain.

마지막으로 언급하면 이 일지에서 생략될 수 있는 것은 아무것도 없다는 것이다. 가능한 한 거래 교섭시 다른 사람들이 한 말을 많이 기록해야 한다. 재물기편에서 말했듯이, 상인은 언제나 용의주도해야 하기 때문이다.

CHAPTER 9

OF NINE WAYS IN WHICH THE MERCHANT USUALLY BUYS, AND THE GOODS WHICH IT IS MORE OR LESS NECESSARY TO BUY ON TIME

Since we are talking about buying, you must know that usually you can make your purchase in nine ways—that is: either in cash or on time; or by exchanging something, which is usually called a trade; or partly in cash and partly on time; or partly in cash and partly by trading and partly on time; or by draft (*assegnatione de ditta*); or partly by draft and partly on time, or partly by draft and partly by trading. In these nine ways it is customary to make purchases. If you would make your purchases in some other way you must state in your memorandum book with precision the way that you have made the purchase, or have somebody else do it for you, and you will do well.

You buy on time usually when you buy *guati* or oats, wines, salt, remnants from a butcher shop, and fats. In these cases, the seller promises to the buyer to give all the *guati* that he will have in that season. The butcher will sell you and promises to give you all the hearts, skins, fat, etc., that he will have during that year. This kind for so much a pound, that kind for so much a pound, etc., and similarly for the fat of beef, of mutton, etc.; the black skins of mutton at so much apiece; and the white mutton skins, etc., and so with the oats, or *guati*; you must specify the price for each bushel or other measure and the kind of oats as is the custom at Chiusi de Perugia. In buying *guati* you must see whether they are of our city San Sepolcro, or Mercatello, or Sant' Angelo, or Citta de Costello, or Forli, etc.

In this memorandum book, whether kept by you or by others, you must mention every single point. You state the things in a simple way as they happened,

제9장
상인이 매입하는 아홉 가지 방법과, 외상으로 구입해야 할 필요가 있는 상품들

상인이 매입하는 방법에는 다음과 같이 아홉 가지가 있음을 알아야 한다. ① 현금매입, ② 외상매입, ③ 물물교환, ④ 현금외상 혼합매입, ⑤ 현금외상 물물교환 혼합매입, ⑥ 어음매입, ⑦ 어음외상 혼합매입, ⑧ 어음 물물교환 혼합매입 등이다. 이 아홉 가지(실제로는 여덟 가지) 방법이 가장 흔한 매입방법이다. 상인이 상기 이외의 방법으로 매입을 하게 되는 경우에는 그 매입방법을 영업일지에 정확히 기록해야 한다. 또는, 대리인을 시켜서 자세히 기록해야 한다. 그래야 일을 잘하는 것이다.

상인이 귀리, 포도주, 소금, 축산 부산물, 지방 등을 살 때는 보통 외상으로 산다. 이 경우 판매자는 구매자에게 그해에 그가 수확하는 모든 귀리를 주기로 약속한다. 또 푸줏간 주인은 구매자인 상인에게 그해에 그가 갖게 되는 심장, 가죽, 지방 등을 주기로 약속한다.

이것은 파운드당 얼마, 저것은 파운드당 얼마 등과 같이 단위당 가격을 페루자 식으로 기록해야 한다. 쇠고기 및 양고기 지방에 대하여도 같다. 검은 양 가죽, 하얀 양 가죽 등은 개당 얼마인지, 또한 귀리의 경우에도 단위당 얼마인지 등을 기록해야 한다. 즉, 귀리의 종류에 따라 단위당 가격을 정확하게 기록해야 하는 바, 그것이 페루자의 관행이다. 그리고 귀리를 살 때에는 그것이 우리의 도시인 San Sepolcro 또는 mercatelo 또는 Sant'Angelo 또는 Citta de Costello 또는 Forli 산인지 확인해보아야 한다.

이 일지에는 상인이 기록하든 다른 사람이 기록하든 모든 사항을 기록해야 한다. 일어난 상황을 간결하게 기록하면, 숙달된 부기자가 며칠 후 또는 매일 이 일지 기록을 분개장으로 전기할 수 있기 때문이다. 분개장 전기시 일지에 기록된 긴 내역을 모두 기록할 필

and then the skillful bookkeeper, after four or five days, or eight days, may enter all these transactions from the said memorandum book into the Journal, day by day; with this difference, though, that it is not necessary for him to put down in the Journal all the long lines of words that were used in the memorandum book, because it is sufficient to put them down in an abridged way, and besides, references should always be made from one book to the other. Those that are used to keeping these three books in the way we have said never must enter one thing in Journal if they have not first entered it in the memorandum book. This will be enough as to the arrangement of the said memorandum book, whether it is kept by you or others. Remember that there are as many ways to buy as to sell; therefore, I need not explain the ways of selling, because you knowing of the ways of buying can understand the selling.

요는 없다. 기록을 생략해도 되는 이유는 기록 후 일지와 분개장을 대조하면 되기 때문이다. 내가 설명하는 방식의 일지 기록에 익숙한 사람들은 애초에 일지에 기록되지 않은 사항은 단 한 개라도 분개장에 전기하지 않는다. 이 정도면 일지 기록방법을 충분히 설명한 것으로 판단된다. 사고파는 방법에는 여러 가지가 있으므로 나는 판매방법까지 설명하고 싶지는 않다. 매입방법을 이해하면 판매방법은 스스로 터득할 수 있기 때문이다.

CHAPTER 10

THE SECOND IMPORTANT MERCANTILE BOOK WHICH IS CALLED JOURNAL; WHAT IT IS, AND HOW IT SHOULD BE KEPT IN AN ORDERLY WAY

The second common mercantile book is called the Journal (*Giornale*) which, as we have said, must have the same mark that is on the memorandum book and the pages marked as we have said in talking of the memorandum book.

Always at the beginning of each page you must put down the date, and then, one after another, enter all the different items of your inventory.

In this Journal, which is your private book, you may fully state all that you own in personal or real property, always making reference to the inventory papers which you or others may have written and which are kept in some box, or chest, or *filza*, or *mazzo*, or pouch, as is customary and as is usually done with letters and other instruments of writing.

The different items entered in the said Journal ought to be entered there in a neater and more systematic way, not too many or too few words, as I will show in the few following examples. But first of all you must know that there are two words or expressions (*termini*) necessary in the keeping of a Journal, used according to the custom of the great City of Venice, and of these I will now speak.

제10장
두 번째 주요 장부인 분개장의 의미와 체계적인 기록방법

　두 번째로 중요한 상업장부는 분개장이다. 분개장에는 일지와 같은 기호가 표시되어야 하고, 또한 반드시 페이지가 기록되어야 한다.

　언제나 분개장 각 페이지의 첫머리에는 날짜를 기록한 후, 재물기의 각 항목을 순서대로 전기해야 한다.

　상인의 사적 장부인 분개장에 상인은 모든 재산을 항목별로 기록하되, 항상 이미 기록된 재물기를 참조하여야 한다. 분개장 등의 문서는 상자 또는 주머니 등에 보관하는 것이 관행이다.

　분개장에 전기할 때에는 간결하고 체계적으로 기록해야 한다. 말이 너무 많아도 안 되고 너무 적어도 안 된다. 이에 대하여는 후술할 것이다. 먼저 상인은 위대한 도시 베니스에서 분개장 기록에 사용하는 두 개의 용어부터 알아야 한다.

CHAPTER 11

THE TWO EXPRESSIONS USED IN THE JOURNAL, ESPECIALLY IN VENICE, THE ONE CALLED "PER," AND THE OTHER "A," AND WHAT IS UNDERSTOOD BY THEM

As we have said, there are two expressions (*termini*) used in the said Journal; the one is called "per," and the other is called "a," each of which has a meaning of its own. "Per" indicates the debtor (*debitore*) one or more as the case may be, and "a," creditor (*creditore*), one or more as the case may be. Never is any item entered in the Journal which also is to be entered in the Ledger, without preceding it by one of the two expressions. At the beginning of each entry, we always provide "per," because, first, the debtor must be given, and immediately after the creditor, the one separated from the other by two little slanting parallels (*virgolette*), thus, //, as the example below will show.

제11장
베니스에서 분개장에 사용하는 두 개의 용어, Per(차변)와 A(대변)의 의미

전술한 바와 같이 분개장에는 두 개의 용어가 사용된다. 하나는 Per라 불리고, 또 하나는 A라 불리며, 그 각각의 의미는 다르다. Per는 1인 또는 다수의 채무자를 의미하고, A는 1인 또는 다수의 채권자를 의미한다. 이 두 개의 용어 중 어느 하나를 앞세우지 않고는 분개장 기사를 원장으로 전기할 수 없다. 분개장 기사의 서두에 언제나 Per부터 기록해야 하는데, 이는 채무자를 먼저 쓰고 나중에 채권자를 쓰는 것이기 때문이다. 채무자와 채권자 사이, 즉 per와 A 사이에는 이중사선(//)을 그어 양자를 구분해야 한다.

| 해설 | 여기서 채무자, 채권자는 자기 또는 회사의 채무자, 회사의 채권자라는 뜻이다. 즉 회계 기록을 실시하는 회사가 채권, 채무의 주체이다.

CHAPTER 12

HOW THE ENTRY SHOULD BE MADE INTO THE JOURNAL BY MEANS OF THE DEBIT AND THE CREDIT, WITH MANY EXAMPLES. THE TWO OTHER EXPRESSIONS USED IN THE LEDGER, THE ONE CALLED "CASH," AND THE OTHER "CAPITAL," AND WHAT SHOULD BE UNDERSTOOD BY THEM

With the name of God you shall begin to enter into your Journal the first item of your Inventory, that is, the quantity of cash that you possess, and in order to know how to enter this Inventory into the Ledger and Journal, you must make use of the two other expressions (*termini*); the one called "cash" (*cassa*) and the other "capital"(*cavedale*). By cash is understood your property or pocketbook (*borscia*: from *bursa*, or bag); by capital is understood the entire amount of what you now possess.

This capital must always be placed as creditor (*creditore*) in all the principal mercantile Ledgers and Journals and the cash always debtor. Never at any time in the management of your business may cash be creditor, but only debtor unless it balances. For if, in balancing your book, you find that cash is in the credit, it would denote a mistake in the book, as I will remind you hereafter at its proper place. Now this entry ought to be made in the Journal, and ought to be arranged in this way:

EXAMPLE OF MAKING AN ENTRY IN THE JOURNAL
FIRST. November 8, MCCCCLXXXXIII in Venice.

Debit 1.   Per cash // A—Capital of myself so and so, etc. In cash I have at present, in gold and coin, silver and copper of different coinage as it appears in the first sheet of the Inventory in cash, etc., in total so many
Credit 2.   gold ducats and so many silver ducats. All this is our Venetian money; that is counting 24 *grossi* per ducat and 32 *picioli* per *grosso* in gold is

제12장

차변과 대변 방식으로 분개장에 기록하는 방법과 원장에 사용되는 두개의 용어인 현금과 자본금의 의미

하나님의 이름으로 재물기를 분개장으로 전기하기 시작해야 한다. 현금보유액과, 재물기를 분개장과 원장으로 전기하려면, 현금과 자본금이라는 두 개의 용어를 사용할 줄 알아야 한다. 현금은 재산 또는 주머니라는 의미이고, 자본금은 보유재산 총액을 의미한다.

| 해설 | 자본금은 재산 총액이 아니라 순재산 총액이다.

자본금은 분개장과 원장에서 항상 채권자로서 위치하고, 현금은 항상 채무자로 위치한다. 현금은 그 어느 경우에도 (회사의) 채권자가 될 수 없고, 잔액이 있는 경우에는 채무자로 존재한다. 마감할 때 현금이 대변에 있으면 이는 기록이 잘못되었음을 의미한다. 이에 대하여는 다시 언급할 기회가 있을 것이다. 이제 분개를 예시하면 아래와 같다. 재물기 기재 사항은 분개장에 전기(분개)되어야 하는 바, 그 방법은 아래와 같다.

| 해설 | 자본금이 항상 채권자로 위치한다는 것은 음수 잔액이 존재할 수 없다는 것을 의미한다. 또한 현금이 항상 채무자로 위치한다는 것은 현금 잔액 역시 음수 잔액이 존재할 수 없다는 것을 의미한다.

〈분개의 예시〉

제1번 항목, 1493년 11월 8일, 베니스

Debit 1.   Per 현금 // A 나의 자본금, 나는 현재 재물기 첫 장에 기록된 바와 같이 금화, 은화, 동화 등을 보유하고 있다. 모두 합하면 금으로 몇 더컷이

worth: L____(*Lire*), S____(*Soldi*), G____(*Grossi*), P____(*Picioli*)

For the second item you shall say this way:

SECOND. Per mounted and unmounted precious stones of several kinds //. A capital ditto for so many mounted *belassi*, etc., weighing, etc., and so many sapphires, etc., and rubies and diamonds, etc., as the said Inventory shows to which, according to current prices I give these values: *Belassi* worth, etc.; and so you shall state a price for each kind in total that are worth so many ducats. Their value is

L____, S____, G____, P____

After you have once named the day, the debtor and the creditor, you may say for brevity—if you don't make any other entry in between: On the day ditto, per ditto, // a ditto.

THIRD. Per silver //. A ditto—by which capital is understood—for several kinds of silver which at present I possess—that is, wash basins so many, so many coppers, so many cups, so many *pironi*, and so many *cosilier*, etc., weighing in total so much. Their value is: L____, S____, G____, P____

You shall give all the details in entering these items for everything as you have them in the Inventory, giving to each thing a customary price. Make the prices rather higher than lower; for instance, if it seems to you that they are worth 20, you put down 24, so that you can make a larger profit; and so you will enter everything, putting down for each thing its weight, number, value, etc.

Credit 2.   고, 은으로는 몇 더컷이다. 모두 베니스 화폐이며, 더컷당 20grossi이고, 금으로는 grosso당 32picioli의 가치가 있다. L___(Lire), S___(Soldi), G___(Grossi), P___(Picioli).

| **분개 해설** | 차변 현금 ○○○ // 대변 나의 자본금 ○○○

Debit 1, Credit 2에서 숫자 1, 2는 원장의 페이지 번호이다. 그리고 원문의 Line of the debit.은 특별한 의미가 없다.

재물기의 두 번째 항목은 다음과 같이 기록한다.

제2번 항목, Per 가공 및 미가공 보석류 // A 나의 자본금, 미가공 벨라시, 사파이어, 루비, 다이아몬드 등 재물기에서 설명한 바와 같이 재물은 현재가로 기록해야 한다. 그리고 상인은 각 품목별 단가와 총액을 기록해야 한다. 그 총액은 얼마이다.

L____, S____, G____, P____

| **분개 해설** | 차변 보석재산 ○○○ // 대변 나의 자본금 ○○○

날짜, (회사의) 채무자, (회사의) 채권자를 기록한 후에는 그 사이에 다른 기록을 하지 않고, 아래와 같이 간략하게 기록해도 된다.

일자 상동, Per 상동 // A 상동(나의 자본금)

제3번 항목, Per 은제품 // A 상동(상동은 출자자를 의미한다), 나는 예닐곱 가지의 은 제품을 보유하고 있다. 즉, 몇 개의 세숫대야 및 구리 제품, 컵, pironi, cosilier 등을 갖고 있다. 이들의 총 무게는 얼마이며, 총액은 얼마이다.   L____, S____, G____, P____

| **분개 해설** | 차변 은제품 ○○○ // 대변 나의 자본금 ○○○

재물기에 기재된 모든 항목을 분개장에 전기하되, 품목별 가격은 수취 가능가격(Customary price)으로 매겨야 한다. 낮게 매기기보다는 높게 매겨야 한다는 뜻이다. 즉, 자신이 20의 가치가 있다고 판단하는 경우, 이를 24로 기록해야 하는데, 이렇게 하면 큰 이익을 얻을 수 있기 때문이다. 가격을 고가로 기록한 후, 무게 등의 비망사항을 기록

FOURTH. Per woolen clothes //. A ditto, for so many clothes of such and such color, etc., of such and such style, etc., lined, etc., new or used, etc., for myself or for my wife or for my children, I give the total value, according to the current price, so many ducats. And for cloaks, so many of such and such color, etc., and so on, for all the other clothes: L____, S____, G____, P____

FIFTH. Per linen //. A ditto, for so many bed sheets, etc., and put down their number and value as the Inventory shows: L____, S____, G____, P____

SIXTH. Per feather beds //. A ditto, etc., for so many feathers—and here put down all that the Inventory shows, number and value: L____, S____, G____, P____

SEVENTH. Per ginger //. A ditto, for so many packages, etc., giving all the details that are contained in the Inventory, number, value, according to common prices, etc., so many ducats: L____, S____, G____, P____

하면 된다.

| **해설** | 재산의 과대 계상은 루카 파치올리 최고의 오류다. 재산을 과대 계상하는 것 자체가 불합리한 것이고, 또 과대 계상을 하더라도 차익을 얻을 수 없기 때문이다. 즉, 기초 재산을 낮게 기록하든 높게 기록하든 대변과 차변을 일치시켜서 기록해야 하므로 자본 총액, 즉 출자 총액이 증감할 뿐 순이익은 증가할 수 없기 때문이다.

제4번 항목, Per 모직물 // A 상동, 색상과 스타일은 이러저러하며, 나 또는 아내 또는 아이들의 것이다. 시가로 총 얼마에 해당된다. 그리고 이러저러한 색상의 외투와 기타 의류를 갖고 있다.   L____, S____, G____, P____

| **분개 해설** | 차변 모직물 ○○○ // 대변 나의 자본금 ○○○

제5번 항목, Per 리넨 // A 상동, 재물기에 기록된 대로 개수와 가액을 기록한다.
           L____, S____, G____, P____

| **분개 해설** | 차변 리넨 ○○○ // 대변 나의 자본금 ○○○

제6번 항목, Per 깃털침구류 // A 상동, 재물기에 기록된 대로 개수와 가액을 기록한다.   L____, S____, G____, P____

| **분개 해설** | 차변 깃털침구류 ○○○ // 대변 나의 자본금 ○○○

제7번 항목, Per 생강 // A 상동, 보통 가격으로 재물기에 기록된 그대로 기록한다.
           L____, S____, G____, P____

| **분개 해설** | 차변 생강 ○○○ // 대변 나의 자본금 ○○○

In this way you can continue to enter all the other items, making a separate entry for each different lot, and as we have said before, giving the current prices, number, marks, weights, as the Inventory shows. Indicate only one kind of money, to which you reduce the estimated values. In the column for the amounts, only one kind of money should appear, as it would not be proper to have appear in this column different kinds of money.

You shall close each entry in the Journal by drawing a line from the end of the last word of your descriptive narrative (explanation) up to the column of the figures. You shall do the same in the memorandum book, and as you transfer an entry into the Jouranal from the memorandum book, you shall draw a single diagonal line (*una sola riga a traverso*) through it in this way /; this will show that this item has been entered (*posta*) in the Journal.

If you should not draw this line through the entry, you shall check off (*lanciarai*) the first letter of the beginning of the entry, or the last letter, as we have done at the beginning of this; or otherwise you shall use some other sign by which you will understand that the said item has been transferred into the Journal. Although you may use many various and divers expressions or marks, nevertheless you must try to use the common ones which are used by the other merchants, so that it will not look as if you would deviate from the usual mercantile custom.

이런 방식으로 재물기에 기재된 모든 항목을 분개장에 전기해야 한다. 가격은 시가로 하고, 나머지 사항인 개수, 무게, 상표 등을 순서대로 기록하면 된다. 단, 평가액이 축소될지라도 동일한 화폐 단위로 금액을 기록해야 한다. 즉, 금액란에는 한 가지 화폐만 출현해야 한다. 금액란에 여러 가지 화폐가 출현하는 것은 적절하지 않기 때문이다.

　그리고 설명문의 끝부터 숫자란까지 선을 그어서 분개장 기록, 즉 분개를 마무리해야 한다. 일지도 같은 방식으로 마무리해야 한다. 그리고 일지의 기록을 분개장으로 전기할 때에는 사선(/)을 그어 그 기사가 분개장으로 전기되었음을 표시해야 한다.

　사선을 긋지 않는 대신에 기사의 첫 글자 또는 마지막 글자에 체크 표시를 해도 된다. 이 글이 시작될 때 말했던 것처럼 전기필, 즉 전기완료 기호로 다른 기호를 쓸 수도 있으나, 가급적 여러 상인들이 사용하는 공통의 기호를 사용하는 것이 좋다. 그래야 통상적인 상업관습에서 이탈하지 않은 것으로 보일 수 있기 때문이다.

CHAPTER 13

THIRD AND LAST PRINCIPAL MERCANTILE BOOK CALLED THE LEDGER. HOW IT IS TO BE KEPT. ITS ALPHABET (INDEX), AND HOW THIS CAN BE KEPT SINGLE AND DOUBLE

After you have made all your entries in the Journal in an orderly way, you must transfer them to the third book, called Ledger (*Quaderno Grande, i. e.*, big book). This Ledger contains usually twice as many pages as the Journal. In it there must be an alphabet or repertory or *"trovarello"* (finding key) according to some; the Florentines call it *"Stratto."* In this index you shall write down all the debtors and creditors in the order of their initial letter, together with the number of their respective pages. You shall put the names that begin with A in the A page, etc.

This Ledger, as we have said before, must bear the same sign or mark that is on the Journal and memorandum book; its pages should be numbered; and at the top at the right margin as well as at the left margin, you shall put down the date. On the first page you shall enter cash as debtor. As in the Journal, so in the Ledger, cash should be entered on the first page. It is customary to reserve the whole of the first page to cash, and not to enter anything else either under the debit (*in dare*) or the credit (*in havere*). This because the cash entries are more numerous than all others on account of almost continuously paying out and receiving money; therefore, it needs much space. This Ledger must be ruled, and should have as many lines as there are kinds of money that you want to enter. If you enter *lire*, *soldi*, *denari* and *picioli*, you shall draw four lines, and in front of *lire* you shall draw another line in order to put in the number of the pages of the Ledger debit and credit entries. Before these lines you shall draw two more lines wherein to mark the dates as you go on, as you have seen in the other books, so that you may find each item quickly. This book shall also bear the sign of the cross as the others.

제13장
세 번째 주요 장부인 원장과 그 기록방법, 원장의 알파벳 색인, 그리고 단식 기록방법과 복식 기록방법

재물기 기사를 분개장으로 전기한 후에는 다시 그것을 원장(big book, 큰 책)으로 전기해야 한다. 원장은 분개장의 두 배 분량의 장수를 갖는다. 원장에는 반드시 색인(trovarello)이 필요하다. 플로렌스에서는 색인을 스트라토(stratto)라고도 한다. 색인 또는 목차란에는 채무자와 채권자의 이름을 알파벳 순서로 쓰고, 그 인명별 페이지 번호도 함께 기록해야 한다. 즉, A페이지에는 A로 시작하는 인명을 기록하라는 의미이다.

| **해설** | 루카 파치올리의 원본 부기는 현행 부기와 달리 인명부기였으므로, 원장도 인명별로 작성하므로 상기와 같이 원장을 인명별로 색인하게 되는 것이다.

원장 역시 일지 및 분개장과 같은 부호와 기호를 사용하며, 페이지 번호 또한 반드시 표시되어야 한다. 그리고 원장의 우상단 및 좌상단에는 반드시 날짜를 기입해야 한다. 그리고 원장의 첫 페이지에는 현금을 채무자로 기록해야 한다. 분개장과 같이 원장에서도 현금은 첫 페이지에 기록되어야 한다. 첫 페이지 전부를 현금 기록용으로 유보해두는 것이 관행이다. 거래 중에서 현금거래가 제일 많기 때문에 현금원장은 많은 공간을 필요로 한다. 원장에는 상인이 기록하고자 하는 화폐 단위의 수만큼 선을 그을 수 있다. 상인이 리르, 솔디, 데나리, 피치올리 단위로 기록하는 경우 네 개의 선을 그어야 하고, 리르 앞에는 원장의 페이지 번호를 기입하기 위하여 선을 하나 더 그어야 한다.

이 선들의 앞에 날짜를 기록하기 위하여 두 개의 선을 더 그어야 하는데, 그 이유는 기사를 쉽게 찾기 위함이다. 또한 이 장부에는 다른 장부처럼 십자가 기호(†)가 포함되어야 한다.

CHAPTER 14

HOW THE ENTRIES SHOULD BE TRANSFERRED FROM THE JOURNAL INTO THE LEDGER AND WHY, FOR EACH ENTRY OF THE JOURANL, YOU HAVE TO MAKE TWO IN THE LEDGER; HOW ENTRIES IN THE JOURNAL SHOULD BE CANCELED. THE TWO NUMBERS OF THE PAGES OF THE LEDGER WHICH ARE PLACED IN THE MARGIN OF EACH ENTRY AND WHY

For each one of all the entries that you have made in the Journal you will have to make two in the Ledger. That is, one in the debit (*in dare*) and one in the credit (*in havere*). In the Journal the debtor is indicated by per, the creditor by a, as we have said. In the Ledger you must have an entry for each of them. The debitor entry must be at the left, the creditor one at the right; and in the debitor entry you must indicate the number of the page of the respective creditor. In this way all the entries of the Ledger are chained together and you must never make a credit entry without making the same entry with its respective amount in the debit. Upon this depends the obtaining of a trial balance (*bilancio*) of the Ledger.

There can not be a closing (*saldo*) because there must be as much in credit as there is in debit. In other words, you shall add together all the debit entries, even if there are ten thousand, on a separate sheet, and then add together in the same way all the credit entries; the totals of the one should be the same as the totals of the other; otherwise it would show that some mistake has been made in the Ledger. We will speak at length about this when we talk about the way of making the trial balance (*bilancio*). And since for one entry of the Journal you make two in the Ledger, you shall draw two diagonal lines as you make the transfer –that is, if you first transfer the debit entry, you shall first draw a diagonal line (*riga a traverso*) at the beginning of the entry in the Journal which shows that the entry has been posted (*posta*) to the debit into the Ledger. If you transfer the credit entry, either at this time or later, as it often happens that the bookkeeper can make two or three entries on

제14장

분개장 기록을 원장으로 전기하는 방법과, 한 건의 분개를 두 개의 원장에 전기해야 하는 이유, 그리고 원장으로 전기된 분개 기록에 소인(消印, 전기필 표시)을 하는 방법, 그리고 대차 각 기사의 가장자리에 원장의 페이지 번호를 기록해야 하는 것과 그 이유

원장에서는 한 건의 분개에 대해 두 번 전기해야 한다. 차변과 대변으로 나누어 전기해야 하기 때문이다. 분개에서 채무자는 Per, 채권자는 A로 표시되고, 원장에는 이 둘을 모두 기록해야 한다. 채무자는 원장의 좌측에, 채권자는 원장의 우측에 기록해야 한다. 채무자 기록시 반드시 그 짝이 되는 채권자가 기록된 원장의 페이지 번호를 기록해야 한다. 이렇게 하면, 원장의 모든 기록이 쇠사슬처럼 연결된다. 그리고 차변 기록 없이 대변을 기록해서는 안 된다. 즉, 반드시 차변과 대변을 동시에 기록해야 한다. 이러한 기록에 의하여 시산표(균형표, 일치표)가 작성되기 때문이다.

차변과 대변 합계가 다른 상태에서 마감해서는 안 된다. 달리 말하면, 분개 건수가 1만 건이라 하더라도 모든 차변과 대변 금액을 합산해야 하고, 차변과 대변 각각의 합계 금액은 언제나 같아야 한다. 만약 다르다면 원장 기록에 오류가 있다고 판단해야 한다. 이에 대하여는 시산표 작성시 길게 설명할 것이다. 그리고 분개장 기록을 원장에 전기할 때에는 전기필 표시로 사선(/)을 그어야 한다. 분개 기록 중 차변 기사를 전기한 경우에는 분개 행 서두에 사선을 긋고, 대변 기사를 전기한 때에는 분개 행의 끄트머리에 사선을 그어야 한다. 이 두 개의 사선은 다음 표에서 볼 수 있으며, 첫 번째 사선은 차변 선, 두 번째 사선은 대변 선이라고 한다. 그리고 분개 기록 직전에 두 개의 숫자를 기록해야 한다. 위의 숫자는 차변에 기록된 계정 원장의 페이지 번호이고, 아래 숫자는 대변에 기록된 계정 원장의 페이지 번호다. 이 두 숫자는 상기 예시한 1, 2와 같으며, 숫자 사이에 사선은 없다. 어떤 사람들은 숫자 사이에 1/2과 같이 사선을 긋기도 하는데 이것은 중요한 문제가 아니

the same page in order to prevent his coming back to write on that same page—in which case he should draw a line at the right side where the entry terminates. This will show that the entry has been transferred to the credit of the Ledger. These two lines, you may see in the preceding diagram, drawn in the margin by the first cash entry; the one is called debit line, and the other credit line. At the side, in the marginal part, you shall write down two numbers before the beginning of the entry, the one under the other. The upper indicates at what page of the Ledger the debit entry is, and the lower indicates the page of the Ledger where the credit is, as you will see at the cash entry in the above example, like this, $\frac{1}{2}$, without a line between them. Some are accustomed to draw a line in between, like this, $\frac{1}{2}$. This does not matter, but it looks nicer without the line between, so that the figures will not appear to the reader as if they were fractions. The upper figure, 1, means cash was entered in the first page of the Ledger, and capital was entered in the second page of the said Ledger; the cash on the debit, and the capital on the credit side. You should know that the closer to the debtor you can place the creditor, the nicer it will look. It is just the same, however, no matter where it is; but it may look bad on account of the date which at times must be put between entries, and it makes it difficult then to find the dates. We can not tell you everything fully, but you with your natural ingenuity must guide yourself. Therefore you always try to put the said creditor immediately after its debtor on the same line or on the line immediately following without entering anything else in between, for whenever there is a debit item there must exist at the same time a credit item. For this reason, get the one as near as possible to the other.

다. 그러나 사선이 있으면 원장의 페이지 번호가 아니라 분수기호로 보이므로 사선이 없는 것이 더 좋다. 그리고 상기의 숫자 1은 원장의 첫 페이지에 전기되었다는 의미이고, 아래의 숫자 2는 원장의 두 번째 페이지에 전기되었다는 의미이다. 즉, 현금은 원장의 1페이지의 차변에, 나의 자본금은 2페이지의 대변에 기록되었다는 의미이다. 그리고 채권자를 채무자에 가깝게 기록할수록 더 좋게 보인다는 것을 알아야 한다. 물론 그것이 어디에 기록되든 의미는 같지만, 분개 사이에 날짜가 기록되는 경우에는 그 날짜 때문에 혼란스럽게 보일 우려가 있기 때문이다. 이런 경우에는 날짜를 알아보기 어려워진다는 문제가 있다. 여기서 모든 것을 다 설명해줄 수는 없으므로, 슬기로운 독자라면 나머지 사항은 유추하여 쉽게 이해할 수 있을 것이다. 다시 말하면, 언제나 채무자 기록 바로 다음에 채권자를 기록해야 하며, 분개 행을 달리 하는 경우에는 그 행 사이에 아무것도 기록하지 말고 바로 채권자를 기록해야 한다. 이는 차변이 있으면 반드시 대변이 있어야 하기 때문이다. 이러한 이유로 채무자와 채권자의 기록 위치는 가까울수록 좋은 것이다.

| 해설 | 본 장 그리고 본 서에서 채권자, 채무자라는 단어는 회사에 채권을 가진 사람, 회사에 채무를 진 사람의 명칭, 즉 인명을 의미한다. 부기는 송도부기처럼 인명 간의 입출을 기록하는 것이므로 그 주고받은 인명을 기록할 수밖에 없는 것이다. 이 인명이 계정이다. 차입금, 전기료 등의 과목이 계정이 아니다. 과목은 2차 계정에 불과하고, 1차 계정은 인명이다. 현행 부기의 원본인 숨마부기는 순수한 인명부기이다. 과목은 계정으로 언급되지도 않았다.

인명 간 입출을 대차로 나누어 기록하고, 이를 각 인명원장의 대차변에 전기하여, 각 인명별로 잔액을 산출한다, 이 인명별 잔액 중 손익에 관계된 것을 손익계정 대변 또는 차변에 전기하여 순이익을 산출함으로써 결산이 완료되는 부기가 숨마부기이다.

숨마부기에서는 원칙적으로 현행 부기방식의 시산표, 대차대조표는 언급되지 않았다. 숨마의 시산표는 모든 원장의 대변과 차변 기록을 전기하여 대차 각각의 합계를 산출하여 그 일치 여부를 확인하는 것이었지, 각 인명별 잔액을 전기하여 인명별 채권채무를 일람하는 표가 아니었다.

CHAPTER 15

THE WAY IN WHICH THE CASH AND CAPITAL ENTRIES SHOULD BE POSTED IN THE LEDGER IN THE DEBIT AND THE CREDIT. THE DATE WHICH AT THE TOP OF THE PAGE IS WRITTEN DOWN ACCORDING TO THE ANCIENT USE. CHANGING OF THE SAME. HOW TO DIVIDE THE SPACE ON THE PAGES FOR SMALL AND LARGE ACCOUNTS AS THE BUSINESS REQUIRES

After having told you these things for your instruction, we write now the first entry of the cash in the debit column, and then the first entry of the capital in the credit column, in the Ledger. But, as we have said, you shall write down in the Ledger the year in the old way by using the alphabet, thus: MCCCCLXXXXIII, etc. It is not customary to put the day at the top in the Ledger as in the Journal, because one account in the Ledger may have several dates, and therefore you can not keep the dates in order by putting them at the top; but you shall put the days in the body of the entry, as you will understand hereafter.

We put the day to one side, in the space of which I have spoken, just before the entry. If an item refers to a transaction which happened in a different year than that written at the top of the page, which happens when one does not balance and transfer his books at the end of each year, then this year shall be put on the side, in the margin near the entry of the item to which it refers. This only happens in the Ledger, and can not happen in the other books. In making this entry for the year, use the antique letters, which are neater, although it does not matter very much.

Thus you shall put it this way:

JESUS_____MCCCCLXXXXIII.

Cash is debtor (*dee dare*—shall give) on November 8, "per" capital. On this day I have in moneys of different kinds, gold and other coins; page 2:

L.X^m, S____, G____, P____

Here you do not need to be very lengthy if you have already given the

제15장

현금과 자본금 분개를 원장의 차변과 대변에 전기하는 방법. 고풍스런 자체로 페이지 상단에 날짜를 쓰는 것과 상황에 따라 원장의 공간을 분할하는 방법

    앞에서 이미 설명한 바와 같이 첫 번째 현금 기사는 원장의 차변에, 첫 번째 자본금 출자 기사는 원장의 대변에 기록해야 한다. 그러나 연도는 옛날식으로 MCCCCLXXXXIII (1493)과 같이 알파벳을 사용하여 기록해야 한다. 그리고 날짜를 원장의 상단에 기록하는 것은 옳지 않다. 원장의 한 페이지에는 다수의 날짜가 기록될 수 있기 때문이다. 따라서 날짜는 기사란의 중간에 써야 하는데, 이에 대하여는 곧 이해하게 될 것이다.

    날짜는 기사 바로 앞의 공간에 써야 한다. 원장의 상단에 쓰여진 연도와 다른 연도의 거래를 참조하고자 하는 경우도 있으므로, 이런 경우에는 연도를 그 참조하고자 하는 기사 근처의 여백에 기록해야 한다. 다른 연도의 기록을 참조하게 되는 것은 매년 장부를 마감하지 않는 경우에 발생한다. 이런 상황, 즉 다른 연도의 거래를 참조하는 경우는 원장에서만 발생하고, 다른 장부에서는 발생하지 않는다. 따라서 아주 중요한 내용은 아니지만, 연도를 기록할 때에는 식별이 용이하도록 고풍스런 자체로 쓰는 것이 더 좋다.

    즉, 이렇게 기록해야 한다.

JESUS _____ 1493년

    현금이 채무자(나에게 주어야 할 사람)이며, 날짜는 11월 8일, 상대계정은 자본금, 이날 현재 나는 여러 종류의 화폐, 금, 은, 동 등을 보유하고 있다. 상대계정 페이지는 2이다.

L.X^m, S____, G____, P____

    상기의 기록은 길게 할 필요가 없다. 이미 분개장에서 자세히 기록하였기 때문이다. 가급적 간결하게 기록하라.

description in the Journal. Try to be very brief.

At the beginning of the page we say more, but in the entries following it is enogh to say: on ditto, "per" such and such; page, etc.,   L____, S____, G____, P____

After you have made entry in this way, you shall cancel in the Journal as I have explained to you. Then in the credit side you shall write down this way:

JESUS_____MCCCCLXXXXIII.

Capital of myself, so and so, is creditor (*dee havere*—shall have) on November 8, "per" cash. On this day I have in cash, in gold and other kinds of money; page 1:

This entry is also sufficient; express yourself briefly for the reason above said. If there are other items to be entered in the same account, it will be enough to say, on ditto, "per" such and such, etc., as has just been shown. At the end of this treatise, I will give you an example, and thus you will go on expressing yourself briefly especially in those things which are private—that is, of which you do not have to give an account to any one. But as to other things for which you have to give an account to other people, it will be better for you to be more explicit, although for explanations we always rely on the Journal. Then you will cancel, by drawing a line, the credit entry in the Journal as I have said above in Chapter 12. In the margin, just opposite the entry, you shall write down the two numbers of the pages where the debit and credit entries are. That is, you should put the number of the debit page above, and the number of the credit page below, as we have done above in the cash entry. Then you shall at once enter in the alphabet or repertory (index) this debtor and this creditor, each one under its own letter as I have told you before. That is, cash at the letter C, by saying in this way: Cash, page 1. And capital also at the letter C, saying: Capital belonging to me, page 2. And so on, you shall enter (in this repertory) all the creditors under their respective letters, so that you may find them easily in the Ledger mentioned.

Take notice, that if by any chance you should lose this Ledger through robbery, or fire, or shipwreck, etc., if you have either of the other two books, that is, the memorandum book or Journal, you can, by means of this book always make up another Ledger with the same entries, day by day, and enter them on the same pages on which they were in the last book; especially so, if you have the Journal in which, when you transferred the different entries into the Ledger, you wrote down

그리고 다음 번에 상기의 내용이 반복될 때에는 상동, 상대계정 페이지 등과 기록하면 된다. 이런 식으로 기록한 후, 전술한 바와 같이 분개장에 소인(전기필 표시)을 해야 한다. 그러고 나서는 대변에 아래와 같이 기록해야 한다.

JESUS _____ 1493년

나의 자본금, 즉 내가 (회사의) 채권자며, 날짜는 11월 8일, 상대계정은 현금, 이날 현재 나는 화폐와, 금, 은, 동 등을 갖고 있다. 상대방은 현금이고, 현금원장의 페이지는 1이다.

이 건에 대한 분개는 이것으로 충분할 것이다. 그리고 가급적 거래의 사유를 간결하게 기록하라. 만약 같은 계정 원장에 기록될 항목이 더 있는 경우에는 전술한 바와 같이 상동, per 아무개 등과 같이 기록하면 될 것이다. 이 글의 끝에서 예시를 하겠지만, 사적인 계정 원장, 즉 아무에게도 공개할 필요가 없는 계정 원장의 경우에는 보다 더 간결하게 기록해야 할 것이다. 그러나 다른 사람에게 공개해야 하는 계정 원장의 경우에는 분개장에 그 사유를 솔직하고도 분명하게 기록하는 것이 좋다. 그러고 나서는 제12장에서 언급한 바와 같이 선을 그어 대변을 소인(전기필 표시하기)해야 한다. 가장자리, 즉 바로 맞은편에 대변과 차변 계정 원장의 페이지 번호를 기록해야 한다. 즉, 현금 분개에서처럼 차변 계정 원장의 페이지 번호를 쓴 다음 그 바로 밑에 대변 계정 원장의 페이지 번호를 기록해야 한다. 그리고 즉시 알파벳 순서로 된 목차를 작성해야 한다. 즉, cash는 문자 C 부문에 "Cash, Page 1"로 기록하고, Capital 역시 문자 C 부문에 "Capital 출자자 이름, page 2"로 기록한다. 그 후에 채권자를 그 이름순으로 목차에 기록하는데, 그 이유는 계정 원장을 쉽게 찾기 위해서다.

| 해설 | 채권자 이름 순으로 목차를 작성한다는 것은 인명이 계정이고, 과목은 계정이 아니라는 뜻이다.

도난, 화재, 난파 등의 이유로 원장을 분실한 경우에는 일지나 분개장 중에서 어느 하나만 있어도 원장을 원래 상태로 복구할 수 있다. 특히 분개장만을 갖고 있는 경우에는 분개장 기사를 원장으로 전기할 때, 원장의 페이지 번호를 아래 위로 기록해야 하고, 이렇게 하여 원장을 완전하게 복사할 수 있는 것이다. 이것은 기사 중 첫 번째 항목의 전기에 관한 것이다.

at the margin the two numbers of the debit entry page, and the credit entry page, the one above the other, which two numbers indicated the pages of the ledger where the two entries had been entered. In this way you can duplicate your Ledger. This is enough said for the posting of one entry.

For the second entries, which pertains to precious stones, you shall enter in the Ledger as follows:

FIRST, without my telling it to you over again, you shall write down at the top of the page the date, if there has been no date written before because of another account, for at times on the same page two or three accounts are made. Sometimes you won't give much space to one special account because you know that you will not have to use that account over again. Therefore you will give to this account a smaller space than the space you give to other accounts which you had to use more, as we have said above in Chapter 13, when talking about cash and capital, to which we give the whole page, as we have to use these two accounts very often because of the many transactions. This is done in order to lessen transfers.

Now then, after you have found the proper place (in the ledger), you shall write down on the left—because the debtor must always be at the left: Precious stones of many kinds debit (*dicnno dare*—shall give), on November 8, per capital, for so many pieces, etc., weighing so much, so many are counted *balassi*, etc., and so many sapphires, etc., and so many rubies, etc., and so many unpolished diamonds in bulk (or divide the different kinds), for a value of so many ducats; page 2: L40; S0; G0; P0.

You shall cancel this item in the Journal on the debit side by drawing a line as I have told you in Chapter 12. And then you will go to capital, and you shall enter this entry with fewer words, for the reasons above expressed in this chapter, writing it down on the credit side under the first entry that you have already made, and you shall express yourself this way:

On the day, or ditto, for precious stones of several kinds, as it appears at page 3:
L40; S0; G0; P0.

After which you shall draw another line on the credit side of the Journal, as I have shown in Chapter 12; you shall put down in the margin the two numbers of the pages of the Ledger in which you have made these entries, one above the other, as

보석과 관련된 두 번째 항목의 전기는 다음과 같이 한다.

먼저, 다른 계정 때문에 적어놓지 않은 경우 두말할 것도 없이 페이지 상단에 날짜를 기입해야 한다. 가끔 같은 페이지에 2~3개의 계정 원장이 사용될 수도 있기 때문이다. 그리고 특정 계정, 즉 특정 인명과의 거래가 적을 것으로 예상되는 경우에는 그 계정 원장의 공간을 적게 할당하는 경우가 있는데, 이러한 경우에는 이 계정에 대하여는 거래가 많을 것으로 예상되는 인명의 계정 원장에 비하여 더 적은 공간을 할당해야 한다. 그러나 제13장에서 설명한 바와 같이 현금과 자본금계정은 빈번히 사용되는 계정이므로 페이지 전체를 그 계정용으로 할당해두어야 한다. 이것은 전기 업무를 줄이기 위한 것이기도 하다.

이제 적당한 위치를 발견하였으면 그 왼쪽에 기록해야 한다. 채무자는 반드시 왼쪽에 위치해야 하기 때문이다. 여러 종류의 보석은 채무자이고, 11월 8일, 상대계정은 자본금, 각 보석별 무게, 개수 그리고 금액, 페이지 2 : L40; S0; G0; P0.

이미 제12장에서 설명한 바와 같이 선을 그어, 분개장의 차변을 소인해야 한다. 그러고 나서 자본금계정 원장으로 이동하여 간결하게 상기의 내용을 기록해야 하며, 이미 전기된 대변 기록 밑 부분에 아래와 같이 기록해야 한다.

11월 8일, 상동(나는 가게의 채권자이다), 상대계정은 여러 종류의 보석, 페이지 3, 금액 : L40; S0; G0; P0.

그리고 제12장에서 예시한 바와 같이, 분개장의 대변 항목에 선을 그어 소인해야 한다. 즉, 분개 기록 여백에 두 계정 원장의 페이지 번호를 기록해야 한다. 이것은 차변 기사(보석류)는 3페이지에, 대변 기사(자본금)는 2페이지에 전기되었음을 의미한다.

I have told you. We shall say, for instance, that you have entered the debit entry at page 3; the capital entry will still appear at page 2, as long as that page is not filled.

This example will guide you in other cases.

After you have made the entries in the Ledger and marked it in the Journal, you shall put it at once in the index as I have told you above in this chapter—that is, under the letter G or Z, according as to how *Gioie* (stone) is pronounced. In Venice the custom is to pronounce it with Z; in Tuscany, with G. Guide yourself according to your own understanding.

이 예시는 다른 거래의 원장 전기에도 적용된다.

상기와 같이 보석 원장에 전기하고, 분개장에 소인한 후에는 즉시 색인을 작성해야 한다. 이 경우에는 보석을 뜻하는 이탈리아어인 Gioie(jewel)를 어떻게 발음하느냐에 따라 보석 원장의 색인문자는 G 또는 Z가 될 것이다. 베니스에서 G는 Z로 발음되고, 토스카나에서는 G로 발음되기 때문이다. 따라서 이 경우에는 각자의 취향에 따라 G 또는 Z로 쓰면 될 것이다.

CHAPTER 16

HOW THE ENTRIES RELATIVE TO THE MERCHANDISE OF WHICH ONE IS POSSESSED ACCORDING TO HIS INVENTORY, OR OTHERWISWE, SHOULD BE MADE IN THE LEDGER BOTH IN THE DEBIT AND THE CREDIT

You will be able to transfer easily by yourself from the Inventory to the Journal the four items of your personal goods—that is, silver, linen, feather beds, clothes, etc., exactly as you write them in the Inventory, as we explained in Chapter 6. This Inventory was not contained in the memorandum book, for the reasons therein expressed.

And as to how to make these entries in the Journal and the Ledger, and as to how to record them in the Index, I will leave to your ability, on which I count very much.

We shall proceed to enter in the Journal, as well as in the Ledger, the seventh item (of the Inventory), which pertains to Ginger. This must be a sufficient instruction for you by which to make any other entry relative to your merchandise. You should always have in mind their number, weights, measurements and values according to the different ways in which it is customary to make purchases or sales among merchants in the Rialto, or elsewhere. It is not possible to give here full examples for all these operations, but from those few that we give here you will be able to understand how to go ahead in any other case. For if we wanted to give you an example of all the ways in which merchants do business in Tirani, Lecce, Bari and Bitonto—that is, to give you the names of their weights, measurements, etc., and also to tell you about the ways that they use them in Marca and in our Tuscany, this would make our treatise very long, which, on the contrary, I intend to make short.

제16장

상품 관련 분개를
원장의 차변과 대변으로 전기하는 방법

이제 독자는 쉽게 재물기에 기록된 은, 리넨, 깃털 침대, 의류 등의 네 가지 유동재산 항목을 제6장에서 설명한 방식에 따라 분개장으로 전기할 수 있을 것이다. 그러나 이 재물기는 아직 일지에 기록되지는 않은 것이고 그 이유는 후술한다.

그리고 분개장과 원장에 분개 및 전기하는 것과 색인작성법 등에 대하여는 독자의 능력에 맡기고자 한다.

이제는 새물기의 일곱 번째 항목, 즉 생강류를 분개장과 원장에 기록하는 것에 대하여 알아보고자 한다. 이 설명이면 다른 재산항목을 기록하는 것에 대한 충분한 설명이 될 것이다. 이탈리아 전역의 상거래에서 사용되는 다양한 방식의 숫자, 무게 및 금액 등에 대하여 기록자는 항상 염두에 두어야 한다. 여기에서 모든 예제를 드는 것은 어려우나, 제시하는 몇 가지 사례만 익히면 다른 경우에 적용하여 활용하는 데 큰 문제가 없을 것이다. 이탈리아 각지에서 사용하는 단위 등에 대하여 모두 언급하면 이 글이 너무 길어질 것 같아 짧게 하고자 한다.

일곱 번째 항목을 분개장으로 기록하는 것은 다음과 같이 실시한다.: Per 생강(벌크 또는 패키지 단위) 나머지 설명사항은 임의로 기록해도 된다. // A 상동 – 바로 앞의 기록에서, 즉 두 번째 항목을 기록할 때 자본금을 언급하였으므로 상동은 자본금을 의미한다 – 보유하고 있는 생강의 패키지 수, 무게, 양 등을 기록한다. 현재 가격으로 평가하면, 총액은 얼마이다.

L____, S____, G____, P____

As to this seventh item to be entered in the Journal, we shall proceed thus: Per Ginger in bulk or package—you shall express yourself as you like— // a ditto—by which capital is understood, because you have already mentioned it in the entry immediately preceding, when you entered your second item from the inventory, that is, precious stones—as we said in Chapter 12—I possess on this day so many packages weighing so much, or I possess so many pounds, if in bulk, according to the current prices, of a value by the hundred or by the pound, of so many ducats; in total I give them the value of so many ducats.   L____, S____, G____, P____

After you have entered it in the Journal in this way, you shall cancel it in the memorandum book or inventory, as we have said in Chapter 12, and you shall do the same for the other items. Of this entry, as we have said, as well as of any entry made in the Journal, you shall make two different entries in the Ledger; that is, one in the debit and the other in the credit.—See Chapter 14. In making the entry in the Ledger in the debit, you shall proceed in this way: First you shall put the year, in case there is none, at the top of the page, without there putting down the day, for, as we have said in Chapter 15, it is not customary to put down the day at the beginning of the page of the Ledger because on that same page several entries may be made under the debit and credit which, while belonging to the same year, refer to transactions made in different months and days. Even if on that page of the Ledger there was only one cash entry or other entry, the day put at the top of the page could not be very well kept because, under the said entry, it would be necessary to write down transactions which happened in different months and days. For this reason the ancient people never put the day at the top of the pages in mercantile ledgers, as they saw that there was no justification for it, etc.

You shall make this entry in the debit (in the Ledger) in the following manner: Ginger in bulk, or so many packages, debit (*dee dare*—shall give) on November 8 per capital, for so many pieces, weighing so many pounds, which I on this day have in my store, or at home in my house, and which according to current prices are worth so many ducats and in total so many *ducats, grossi, picioli*, etc.; Page 2:   L____, S____, G____, P____

Then you shall cancel this entry on the debit side of the Journal—that is, at the left, as I have told you often, and then you shall enter it on the credit side under

| **분개 해설** | 차변 생강 ○○○ // 대변 출자자 명칭(자본금) ○○○

상기와 같이 분개장에 전기한 후, 제12장에서 설명한 바와 같이 일지 또는 재물기를 소인해야 한다. 그리고 다른 항목에 대하여도 같은 절차를 반복해야 한다. 이 기사뿐만 아니라 분개장에 기록되는 모든 기사를, 원장으로 두 번 전기해야 한다. 즉, 차변과 대변 양방으로 전기해야 한다. 원장 차변으로의 전기는 다음과 같이 실시한다. 먼저 그 페이지 상단에 연도를 기입해야 한다. 그러나 날짜는 기록하지 않는다. 같은 페이지에 날짜가 다른 기사가 전기될 수 있기 때문이다. 이러한 이유로 옛 사람들은 상업장부의 최상단에 날짜를 기록하지 않았다.

다음과 같은 방식으로 원장의 차변에 기록해야 한다. : 생강(벌크용), 차변(그는 나에게 주어야 한다), 11월 8일, 상대계정은 자본금, 개수, 무게 그리고 이는 이날 현재로 자신의 가게, 집 등에서 현재 보유하고 있는 것이고, 이에 대한 시가가 얼마라고 기록한다.
페이지 2:   L____, S____, G____, P____

이렇게 전기한 후에는 분개장 기사 왼쪽의 차변 기사를 소인해야 한다. 그리고 나서 자본금 원장의 대변에 전기해야 한다. 이는 제15장의 보석 관련 기록방법에서 설명한 바와 같다.

| **해설** | Dee Dare(데 다레)와 Dee Havere(데 하베레)는 송도부기의 봉차(捧次), 급차(給次)를 번역한 것이다. Dee Dare = must give, Dee Havere = must have인바 이는 회계 상대방 입장에서의 표현이고, 봉차, 급차는 회계자 입장에서의 표현이므로 양자는 같은 말이다. 즉, 차변(借邊)과 대변(貸邊)은 상대방 입장에서 본 것이고, 봉차와 급차는 자기 입장에서 본 것이므로 양자는 같은 말이다.

- Dee Dare = Must give
  ⇒ He must give me the money.
    = I must receive the money from him.
    = 봉차(捧次) : 내가 (채무자에게) 받아야 한다.

- Dee Havere = Must have
  ⇒ He must receive the money from me.
    = I must give him the money.
    = 급차(給次) : 내가 (채권자에게) 주어야 한다.

Capital, as I have shown you in entering the precious stones item in Chapter 15, that is:

On ditto per Ginger in bulk or packages, etc.; Page 3:

$$L\_\_\_\_, S\_\_\_\_, G\_\_\_\_, P\_\_\_\_$$

After you have entered it in this way, you shall cancel the entry on the credit side of the Journal—that is, at the right—as I have shown you before, and you shall also write down at the margin the numbers of the respective pages of the Ledger one above the other—that is, three above and two below, as you have made the debit entry at Page 3 and the credit entry at Page 2, and you shall thereafter enter it in the alphabet or repertory under its respective letter, which may be Z or G, for the reasons given in the preceding chapter.

상동, Per 생강(벌크용), 기타 등등 ; 페이지 3 :　　　L___ , S___ , G___ , P___

이런 식으로 원장에 전기한 후, 분개장의 대변 기사를 소인해야 한다. 이번에는 분개장 기사의 오른쪽에 소인해야 한다. 다음에는 분개장 왼쪽 여백에 전기된 원장의 페이지 번호를 기록해야 하는데, 이 예제상으로는 차변은 페이지 3, 대변은 페이지 2가 될 것이다. 그리고 색인을 작성해야 한다. 생강은 Ginger 또는 Zinger로 쓸 수 있으므로, 생강 원장은 색인(목차)의 G 또는 Z 부분에 위치하게 될 것이다.

CHAPTER 17

HOW TO KEEP ACCOUNTS WITH PUBLIC OFFICES, AND WHY. THE CAMERA DE L'IMPRESTI (MUNICIPAL LOAN BANK) IN VENICE, WHICH IS MANAGED BY *SESTIERI* (DISTRICTS),

I shall not give you any more rules for the other items—that is, leather goods for coverings, tanned or raw, etc., for each of which you shall make entries in the Journal and Ledger, carefully writing down everything and checking off, etc., without forgetting anything, because the merchant must have a much better understanding of things than a butcher.

If you have accounts with the Camera de L'Impresti, or with other banks, as in Florence, or with the Monte de La Dote, in Genoa, as well as similar offices or bureaux with which you have business, see that you keep these accounts very clearly and obtain good written evidence as to debits and credits in the handwriting of the clerks in those institutions. This advice you will carefully follow, for reasons to be explained in chapter on documents and letters. Because in these offices they often change their clerks, and as each one of these clerks likes to keep the books in his own way, he is always blaming the previous clerks, saying that they did not keep the books in good order, and they are always trying to make you believe that their way is better than all the others, so that at times they mix up the accounts in the books of these offices in such way that they do not correspond with anything. Woe to you if you have anything to do with these people. Therefore, be very careful when dealing with them, and be observant at home and keep your head in the store. Maybe they mean well, nevertheless they may show ignorance. In this way you shall keep accounts with the *Gabellari* and *Datiarii* (revenue officers) as to the things that you might sell or buy, things that you grow, things that you plant,

제17장
베니스의 관청에서 운영하는 시립 대부은행, 즉 공공기관과 거래하는 방법

이제 재물기의 나머지 항목을 일기장 및 원장으로 전기하는 세부적인 설명은 하지 않으려 한다. 어느 하나도 빠짐없이 신중하게 각 장부로 전기하기 바란다. 이 글을 읽는 상인 여러분은 푸줏간 주인보다는 더 이해력이 좋을 테니 각자 알아서 잘하리라 믿는다.

그리고 은행 또는 상업 감독관청 등과 거래할 때에는 그 기록을 세밀하게 해야 하고, 동시에 당해 기관의 서기로부터 채권 또는 채무에 관하여 그가 친필로 쓴 문서를 확보해 두어야 한다. 이 충고는 문서관리편에서 언급한 바와 같이 반드시 이행해야 한다. 이러한 기관에서는 자주 담당 서기를 교체하는데, 이 서기들은 자기 나름의 방법으로 기록하는 경향이 있다. 그는 언제나 전임 서기가 장부를 제대로 정리하지 않았다고 비난한다. 그는 자신의 방법이 그 어느 누구의 방법보다 우월하다고 주장하는 경향이 있다. 가끔 그 서기들은 그 어느 장부에도 근거가 없는 방식으로 관련 장부를 엉터리로 작성한다. 만약 상인이 이러한 서기를 담당으로 만난다면 그것은 큰 불행이다. 그러므로 이런 서기들은 조심해서 다루어야 하고, 집이든 가게든 어디서든 항상 경계를 해야 한다. 그들은 일을 잘하는 것처럼 보이지만, 결국은 무지를 드러낼 것이기 때문이다.

상인은 그가 심고 가꾸고 팔고 사는 모든 것에 대하여 상기와 같이 감독관청에 내역을 제출해야 한다. 그리고 감독관청에 대한 거래 수수료는 2~4%이다. 상인은 거래담당 브로커의 장부를 그의 장부에 명시해야 하고, 또한 그 브로커가 하는 특별한 표시도 언급해야 한다. 브로커의 장부는 베니스인들이 Chiamans라고 부르는 장부로서, 모든 거래 내역이 기록되는 장부이다. 브로커마다 사무실에 장부가 있고, 그는 시민 또는 외국인과 행

etc., as it is the custom in Venice where people are used to keeping an account through the office of the *Messetaria* (market master or exchange), some at 2%, some at 1%, some at 4%. You should mention the book of the broker through whom the transaction was made, and also mention the special mark that the broker has in this book—that is, the book in which he makes a record of the market transaction at said office which they call "*Chiamans*" in Venice. For each broker has a book in the said office, or a place in some book in the said office, in which he has to make a record of all the transactions which he has with the citizens of the town or with outsiders. If the broker should not do that he would be fined and dismissed.

And justly the glorious republic of Venice punishes them and their clerks who should misbehave. I know of many who in the past years have been heavily punished, and right they are in having one officer whose only duty is to oversee all these officers and their books whether they are well kept or not, etc.

한 모든 거래를 이 장부에 기록해야 한다. 만일 브로커가 이를 이행하지 않으면 벌금을 물고 동시에 해임된다.

당연히 영광스런 베니스 공화국에서는 이런 불법행위를 하는 서기들을 징계한다. 나는 중벌을 받은 브로커를 꽤 많이 알고 있다. 그리고 공화국 정부는 브로커들이 제대로 기록하는지 아닌지만을 감독하는 관리관을 두고 있다.

CHAPTER 18

HOW YOU SHOULD KEEP YOUR ACCOUNTS WITH THE OFFICE OF THE *MESSETARIA* IN VENICE. HOW TO MAKE ENTRIES PERTAINING THERETO IN THE MEMORANDUM BOOK, JOURNAL AND LEDGER, AND ABOUT LOANS

When you want to do business with the said offices, you shall always charge to the Camera de L'Impresti (municipal loan bank) so many per cent. on all your funds or capital, naming the district where one resides. Likewise, for the amount of the daily sales for many are the sales made for you or for others, as those people know who are familiar with the Rialto. Be careful to put down the name of the party that buys and his place of business, etc. When you withdraw said funds, you shall always credit the said bank, day by day and district by district.

In doing business with the office of the *Messetaria* (exchange), you shall keep the account in this way: When you buy any merchandise through brokers, you shall credit the said office of the *Messetari* with the 2% or 3% or 4% of the whole amount, and shall charge it to that specific merchandise, for you are thus paying for it, etc. Therefore the buyer, when he makes his payments to the seller, should always retain that percentage, no matter whether the payments are made in cash or otherwise, as the said office does not concern itself about anything except the rate (%) to which it is entitled. The brokers make a report of the transaction, how and what for and with whom made, in order to have things clear in case any question should arise, which may happen.

A common proverb says: Who does nothing, makes no mistakes; who makes no mistakes learns nothing, etc.

If any question should arise and the parties wish to settle it, they would go and examine the records of the transaction made by the broker, to which records,

제18장

은행 및 기관과 관련된 거래를 일지, 분개장, 원장에 기록하는 방법

은행 및 거래소 등의 기관과 거래를 하고자 할 때는, 항상 은행(the Camera de L' Impresti: 시립은행)에 자금의 일부 또는 전부를 공탁해야 하며, 주소도 기록해야 한다. 거래소 사정에 정통한 사람들이라면 잘 아는 일이지만, 본인 명의의 매출이든 타인 명의의 매출이든 일일 매출액 중 일정 금액을 공탁해야 한다. 그리고 반드시 구매자의 이름과 주소를 기록해두어야 한다. 공탁한 자금을 인출할 때에는 그 은행을 대기해야 한다.

| 분개 해설 |
① 공탁할 때: 차변 은행 명칭 ○○○ // 대변 현금 ○○○
② 인출할 때: 차변 현금 ○○○ // 대변 은행 명칭 ○○○

거래소 또는 교환소와 거래시의 기록방법은 다음과 같다. 브로커를 통하여 구매를 하는 경우에는 교환소를 대기(貸記, 대변 기입)하되, 금액은 총액의 2~4%로 해야 한다. 그리고 구입한 상품을 차기(借記, 차변 기입)해야 한다. 따라서 구매자가 판매자에게 그 대금을 지급할 때, 구매자는 그 수수료 비율 해당금액을 유보해야 한다. 지급방법이 현금이든 다른 것이든 상관없다. 거래소는 비율 외에는 관심이 없기 때문이다. 브로커는 분쟁에 대비하여 거래 상대방, 거래방법 및 거래사유 등을 기록한다.

이런 속담이 있다. 아무것도 시도하지 않는 자는 실수를 하지 않는다. 그러나 실수를 하지 않는 자는 아무것도 배우지 못한다.

분쟁이 발생하면 법에 따라 브로커가 작성한 기록을 검토한다. 기관이 작성한 문서는

according to the public decrees, as full faith is given as to a public notarial document, and according to these records very often the office of the Consuls of the merchants issues its judgment.

I say, then, when you buy anything, you must always know what is due to the *Messetaria*, and you withhold half of this from what you pay to the seller; that is, if the particular thing that you buy is subject to a 4% payment to that office, as per public decrees of the Republic, you withhold 2% of what you give to the seller. You give him that much less in order that he receives what is due him. You then will become a debtor for the whole amount which is due the said office, and you shall credit the said office with it in your Ledger when you keep an account with that office and charge it to the goods that you have bought, as we have said, because that office does not interest itself in the party who sells out, but in the party who buys. In accordance with this, the buyer will be allowed to take out of the official warehouses merchandise in proportion to the brokerage paid and according to their books kept at the shipping counter, whether it came by land or sea. Therefore, the merchants should keep a careful account with the said office so that they know how much merchandise they can take out. They are not allowed to take out more than they have bought unless they have paid the extra brokerage.

Of these purchases, I will give you here an example and how the transaction with the said office must be recorded in the Journal and in the Ledger. First, you shall express yourself in the memorandum book in the following manner:

I (or we), on this day above mentioned, have bought of Mr. Zuan Antonio, of Messina, so many boxes of Palermo sugar, and so many loaves of the net weight—that is, without the boxes, wrappers, ropes and straw—so many pounds at so many ducats per hundred; I deduct for what is due to the *Messetaria* at the rate of so much per cent., so many *ducats*, *grossi*, *picioli*, etc. The broker was Mr. Zuan de Gaiardi; net value, so many *ducats*, *grossi*, *picioli*, paid in cash.

The same should be entered in the Journal in the following manner:

Per Palermo sugar // A cash. Cash paid to Mr. Zuan Antonio of Messina for so many boxes and so many loaves, of the net weight—that is, without the boxes, wrappers, ropes and straw—so many pounds; at so many ducats per hundred, it amounts to so many ducats; I deduct what is due to the *Messetaria* at so much per

전적인 신뢰를 받게 되며, 상업감독관청은 그 기록에 따라 판결을 한다.

상품을 구입하면 반드시 거래소에 줄 돈, 즉 거래소에 대한 채무를 확정해야 한다. 그리고 그 금액의 반을 유보해두어야 한다. 구입하는 상품이 4% 수수료 조건이면 2%를 유보해두어야 하므로, 판매자에게 줄 돈은 훨씬 줄어든다. 구매자는 거래소에 지급할 총액에 대한 채무자가 된다. 이 거래를 기록할 때 거래소를 대기하고 상품을 차기해야 한다. 이것은 거래소가 판매자에게는 관심이 없고, 구매자에게만 관심을 갖기 때문이다. 지급된 브로커 수수료에 비례하여 그리고 장부 기록에 근거하여 구매자가 상품을 인출하는 것이 허용된다. 따라서 상인은 거래소와의 기록에 충분한 주의를 기울여야 한다. 그래야 상품을 얼마나 인출할 수 있는지 알 수 있기 때문이다. 또한 추가적인 브로커 수수료를 지급하지 않으면 구매금액 이상으로 상품을 인출할 수 없기 때문이다.

이제 이런 구매거래를 분개장과 원장에 어떻게 기록해야 하는가에 관하여 예제를 들어 설명하고자 한다. 먼저 일지에 다음과 같이 기록해야 한다. :

나는 상기한 일자에 주안 안토니오 씨로부터 팔레르모 설탕을 구입했다. 무게와 덩어리 수는 얼마이고, 박스 없는 설탕, 포장재, 로프, 스트로 등. 나는 몇 퍼센트의 비율로 거래소에 줄 돈을 공제했다. 브로커는 주안 데 가이아르디 씨이고, 현금으로 얼마를 지급했다.

같은 내역이 분개장에 다음과 같이 전기되어야 한다.

Per 팔레르모 설탕 // A cash, 메시나의 주안 안토니오에게 거래소에 줄 돈을 공제한 잔액을 현금으로 지급했다. 브로커는 주안 데 가이아르디 씨다.

L____, S____, G____, P____

| 분개 해설 | 차변 팔레르모 설탕 ○○○ // 대변 현금 ○○○

원장에는 다음과 같이 기록한다.

팔레르모 설탕 차변(그가 나에게 줄 돈 또는 내가 그에게 받을 돈) 메시나의 주안 안토니오에게 지급한 현금. 금액은 ____이고, 페이지 1:   L____, S____, G____, P____

그리고 다음에는 같은 금액으로 현금을 대기해야 한다. 그리고 거래소를 대기하되, 금액은 구매자가 구매금액에서 유보한 금액의 두 배로 기록해야 한다. 그 이유는 수수료

cent., so many ducats, etc.; net residue, so many ducats, etc. The broker was Mr. Zuan de Gaiardi.

L____, S____, G____, P____

In the Ledger you shall make the entries as follows:

Palermo sugar debit (*dee dare* or shall give) cash. Cash paid to Mr. Zuan Antonio of Messina for so many boxes and so many loaves, weighing, net, so many pounds, at so many ducats per hundred, which amounts to—Page 1:

L____, S____, G____, P____

And you shall credit cash with the same amount, and shall always credit the *Messetaria* with twice the amount which you withhold from the price paid to the seller—that is, for the commission due by the seller and by you.

Immediately after, you shall make another entry crediting the said office with the said sugar and charging the said merchandise. This will do for a purchase by cash. Now we shall consider one made partly in cash and partly on time.

First, in the memorandum book you shall say as follows: By cash and on time on such and such day, I have bought on the said date of Mr. Zuan Antonio of Messina so many loaves of Palermo sugar, weighing net so many pounds, at so many ducats per hundred, making a total of so many ducats. This is in part payment; for the rest I shall have time to pay until the whole month of August next, etc. The broker was Mr. Zuan de Gaiardi.   D____, G____, P____

You must understand that you do not need to have a written paper containing the terms of the transaction, for the broker shall record that in the said Office. This record is enough for you, but as a precaution, sometimes people require a contract.

You will make the entry in the Journal as follows: First you shall credit Mr. So-and-So, for the total amount, and then charge him for the money that he has received.

JESUS_____ 1493

On such and such a day of such and such month, etc., per Palermo sugar // A Mr. Zuan Antonio, of Messina, for so many loaves, weighing net so many pounds at so many ducats per hundred, making a total of so many ducats; deducting for his share of the brokerage at so much per cent., so many ducats, leaving a net balance of so many ducats, of which now I have to pay so many, and as to the rest I have

는 구매자와 판매자 양방이 부담하기 때문이다.

그리고 나서 바로 거래소를 대변으로, 상품을 차변으로 하는 분개를 실시해야 한다. 이 사례는 현금거래에 적용된다.

| 분개 해설 | 차변 팔레르모 설탕 ○○○ // 대변 거래소 ○○○

| 해설 | ① 수수료 공제 후 현금지급 분개: 차변 팔레르모 설탕 ○○○ // 대변 현금 ○○○
② 거래소에 대한 수수료 채무계상 분개: 팔레르모 설탕 ○○○ // 대변 거래소 ○○○

다음에는 현금외상 혼합거래에 대하여 설명하고자 한다.

먼저 일지에 다음과 같이 기록한다. 현금외상 혼합으로 모일에 나는 메시나의 주안 안토니오 씨로부터 팔레르모 설탕을 구입했다. 미지급액은 8월 말에 완불할 것이다. 브로커는 주안 가이아르디 씨다.　　　　　　　　D____, G____, P____

브로커를 통하여 거래하는 경우에는 거래와 관련된 문서가 필요하지 않다. 브로커가 기록할 것이기 때문이다. 이 정도면 충분하나, 만약의 사태를 대비하여 계약서 작성을 요구하는 사람도 있다.

분개장에는 다음과 같이 기록한다. 먼저 아무개 씨를 총액으로 대기하고, 그가 대금을 일부 받았으므로 그를 차기해야 한다.

　　　　　　　　JESUS _____ 1493년

몇 월 몇 일, Per 팔레르모 설탕 // A 메시나의 주안 안토니오 씨, 지불 총액은 얼마이고, 나머지 미지급액은 8월 말에 지급하기로 하다. 브로커는 주안 데 가이아르디 씨다. 금액　　　　　　　　　　　　　　　　L____, S____, G____, P____

| 분개 해설 | 차변 팔레르모 설탕 ○○○ // 대변 주안 안토니오 ○○○ (매입총액)

다음에는 거래소 수수료를 기록해야 한다. 거래소를 대기, 상품을 차기한다.

Per 팔레르모 설탕 // A 메시나의 사무실(거래소), 수수료율은 몇 %이고, 내 부담과 판매자의 부담은 얼마이며, 총액은 얼마이다.　　　L____, S____, G____, P____

| 분개 해설 | 차변 팔레르모 설탕 ○○○ // 대변 거래소 ○○○ (거래소 수수료 계상)

time until the end of next August. The broker was Mr. Zuan de Gaiardi; value

L____, S____, G____, P____

Immediately after, credit the office of the *Messetaria* with the commission due to it: Per ditto // A Office of the *Messetaria*. For the amount above mentioned—that is, so many ducats at the rate of so much per cent. for my share and for the share of the debtor (seller), in all amounting to so many *ducats, grossi, picioli*: value:

L____, S____, G____, P____

For the cash payment, you shall charge him and credit cash in the following manner:

Per Mr. Zuan Antonio, of Messina // A cash. By cash paid him for part payment of said sugar according to the terms of the transaction, so many ducats, as it appears from his receipt written in his own handwriting. Value: L____, S____, G____, P____

In the Ledger you shall write down as follows:

Palermo sugar debit (*dee dare*—shall give) on such and such a day of November, per Zuan Antonio of Messina, for so many loaves, weighing net so many pounds, etc., at so many ducats per hundred, making a total, net of the brokerage; Page 4:

L____, S____, G____, P____

These items shall be entered in the credit column as follows:

Mr. Zuan Antonio of Messina, credit (*dee havere*—shall have), per Palermo sugar so many loaves, weighing net so many pounds, at so many ducats per hundred, amounting, net of the brokerage, so many ducats, of which I must now pay so many ducats, and for the rest I have time until the end of next August. Broker, Mr. Zuan de Gaiardi; Page 4; value: L____, S____, G____, P____

For the cash payment you shall put in the debit column:

Mr. Zuan, debit (*dee dare*—shall give), on such and such a day, etc., per cash to him paid for part payment on sugar—I received from him according to our agreement—so many ducats, as it is shown by his own handwriting in his book; page 1:

The account of the *Messetaria* in the Ledger shall be as follows:

Office of the *Messetaria*, credit (*dee havere*—shall have), on such and such day, per Palermo sugar bought from Mr. Zuan Antonio, of Messina, for the amount of so many ducats, at so many ducats per hundred. Broker, Mr. Zuan de Gaiardi; Page, etc.:   L____, S____, G____, P____

현금 지급분에 대하여는 그를 차기하고, 현금을 대기해야 한다.

Per 메시나의 주안 안토니오 씨 // A 현금, 계약에 따라 현금을 일부 지급했고, 그 수령액은 그가 직접 쓴 문서에 표시되어 있다.

| **분개 해설** | 차변 주안 안토니오 ○○○ // 대변 현금 ○○○ (외상 총액 중 현금 지급분)

원장에는 다음과 같이 전기한다.

팔레르모 설탕 차변, 11월 몇 일, 상대 계정 메시나의 주안 안토니오, 금액; 페이지 4:

$$L\_\_\_\_, S\_\_\_\_, G\_\_\_\_, P\_\_\_\_$$

대변은 다음과 같이 기록한다.

메시나의 주안 안토니오 씨 대변, 차변은 팔레르모 설탕, 미지급액은 8월 말에 지급하기로 하다. 브로커는 주안 데 가이아르디 씨다. 페이지 4; 금액

$$L\_\_\_\_, S\_\_\_\_, G\_\_\_\_, P\_\_\_\_$$

현금 지급분에 대하여는 인명 원장, 즉 주안 계정에 차기한다.

주안 씨, 차변, 몇 월 몇 일, 대변은 현금이며, 총 구입액 중 일부를 현금으로 지급하다. 나는 계약에 따라 그로부터 얼마를 받았다. 이 내용이 주안 씨의 장부에 그의 진필로 기록되었다.

거래소 수수료는 다음과 같이 원장에 전기한다.

거래소 대변, 몇 월 몇 일, 차변은 팔레르모 설탕이며, 이는 메시나의 주안 안토니오 씨로부터 구입관련 수수료다. 브로커는 주안 데 가이아르디 씨다.

$$L\_\_\_\_, S\_\_\_\_, G\_\_\_\_, P\_\_\_\_$$

CHAPTER 19

HOW WE SHOULD MAKE THE ENTRIES IN OUR PRINCIPAL BOOKS OF THE PAYMENTS THAT WE HAVE TO MAKE EITHER BY DRAFT OR THROUGH THE BANK

And as to the purchases, this should be sufficient to guide you, whether the payment of the purchase should be made all in cash or part in cash and part on time; or part in cash or part by bill of exchange or draft (*ditta*); or all through the bank; or part in cash and part through the bank; or part through the bank and part on time; or part through the bank and part by bill of exchange; or part through the bank, part in cash, part by bill of exchange and part by merchandise, etc.

For in all these ways it is customary to make purchases, and in each case you shall make entries, first in the Day Book, then in the Journal, then in the Ledger, taking as a guide the foregoing example.

But when you make a payment part through the bank and part by bill of exchange, deliver first the bill of exchange and then settle through the bank, which is safer. Many observe this precaution on good grounds, whenever they have to make payments part in cash to settle this balance through the bank, etc. If you make payments part through the bank, part by trading something or part by a bill of exchange and part in cash, you shall charge the seller for all these things and you shall credit each of the said things, each thing in its own place.

Now that you know how to go ahead whenever you make purchases, you will also know what you have to do when you sell. In this case, you shall charge the different buyers and shall credit the different goods that you sell and shall charge cash if you get money for the same, and you shall charge bills of exchange if you get a bill of exchange in payment, and credit the latter when the bank pays the

제19장
어음 또는 은행이체 지급시 장부 기록방법

구매에 관해서는 이것으로 충분할 것이다. 구매방법에는 ① 전액 현금, ② 일부 현금, 일부 외상, ③ 일부 현금, 일부 어음, 일부 환어음, ④ 전액 은행이체, ⑤ 일부 현금, 일부 은행이체, ⑥ 일부 은행이체, 일부 외상, ⑦ 일부 은행이체, 일부 어음, ⑧ 일부 은행, 일부 현금, 일부 어음, 일부 물물교환 등의 방법이 있다.

구매는 상기의 방법으로 이루어지며, 어느 경우에나 기록을 해야 한다. 먼저 일지에 그리고 분개장에, 다음에는 원장에 기록해야 한다. 기록방법은 후술하는 예를 참고하라.

그러나 은행을 통한 지급과 어음을 통한 지급을 혼합해야 하는 경우에는, 먼저 어음으로 지급하는 것이 더 안전하다. 이것에 대하여는 많은 사람들이 상당한 장점이 있다고 한다. 만약 일부 은행이체, 일부 물물교환, 일부 어음, 일부 현금으로 지급하고자 하는 경우에는, 판매자를 차기하고 앞에서 언급한 것들을 대기해야 한다. 즉, 모든 것을 제자리에 기록해야 한다.

이제 당신은 어떤 유형의 구매거래라도 처리할 수 있게 되었다. 다음에는 당신이 판매자가 되었을 때의 처리방법을 알아야 한다. 이 경우에는 (외상) 구매자(이름)를 차기하고, 당신이 판매하는 상품을 대기하면 된다. 돈을 받으면 현금을 차기하고, 어음을 받게 되면 어음을 차기하면 된다. 그리고 은행이 그 어음을 지급하는 경우에는 그 어음을 대기하면 된다. 판매에 대하여 요약하면, 구매자로부터 외상대금을 받는 경우에는 구매자를 대기하면 된다는 것이다.

이 정도면 이 주제에 관하여는 충분히 설명한 것으로 보인다.

exchange.

Therefore, referring again to the purchase, you shall credit the purchaser with all that he gives you in payment, etc.

This will be enough for your instruction on this subject.

| **분개 해설** 1 | 외상판매

① 외상판매: 차변 외상구매자 명칭 ○○○ // 대변 상품 명칭 ○○○
② 외상대금의 현금회수: 차변 현금 ○○○ // 대변 외상구매자 명칭 ○○○
③ 외상대금의 어음회수: 차변 받을어음 ○○○ // 대변 외상구매자 명칭 ○○○
④ 어음대금의 현금수취: 차변 현금 ○○○ // 대변 받을어음 ○○○
⑤ 외상대금의 이체수취: 차변 은행 명칭 ○○○ // 대변 외상구매자 명칭 ○○○

| **분개 해설** 2 | 외상매입

① 외상매입: 차변 상품 명칭 ○○○ // 대변 외상매입처 명칭 ○○○
② 외상대금의 현금지급: 차변 외상매입처 명칭 ○○○ // 대변 현금 ○○○
③ 외상대금의 어음지급: 차변 외상매입처 명칭 ○○○ // 대변 지급어음 ○○○
④ 외상대금의 상품지급: 차변 외상매입처 명칭 ○○○ // 대변 상품 명칭 ○○○
⑤ 외상대금의 이체지급: 차변 외상매입처 명칭 ○○○ // 대변 은행 명칭 ○○○

CHAPTER 20

ENTRIES FOR THE WELL-KNOWN AND PECULIAR MERCANTILE CUSTOMS OF TRADING AND PARTNERSHIP, ETC. HOW THEY SHOULD BE ENTERED IN THE MERCANTILE BOOKS. FIRST: SIMPLE TRADINGS, THEN COMPLEX TRADINGS AND EXAMPLES OF ENTRIES FOR THEM IN THE MEMORANDUM BOOK, JOURNAL AND LEDGER

Now we shall speak of how certain well-known and peculiar entries should be made which are of the highest importance in commerce, and which usually are kept separate from the others so that they can show their respective profits and losses (*pro e danno*). They cover tradings, partnerships, suggested business trips, trips on your own ventures, commissions from others, drafts (*ditta*) or bills of exchange (*bancha descritta*), actual trades, store accounts, etc. I will tell you briefly about these accounts, how you should make the entries in your books so that you don't get mixed up in your affairs.

First, we shall show how to enter a trade (*barato*). Trades are usually of three kinds, as we said in Section 9 of Treatise III, Pages 161 to 167, where it is stated fully and you can refer to it.

I say, therefore, that no matter how you make a record of the trade in your books, you shall first enter it in the memorandum book, stating in detail all about it, its terms and conditions and whether it was made through a broker. After you have so described it, you then at the end shall put a money value on it; and you shall put down such price in accordance with the current value which the things that you have traded have; reckoning in any kind of money in the memorandum book. Afterwards the bookkeeper, when he transfers the entry to the Journal and Ledger, will reduce that money to the standard money that you have adopted.

This is done because, without entering the value of the things that you have traded, you could not, from your books and accounts, learn, except with great

제20장
물물교환 거래 및 조합 거래 등을 일지, 분개장, 원장에 기록하는 방법

이제는 상업에서 가장 중요하고 널리 알려진 거래를 기록하는 방법에 대하여 설명하고자 한다. 이러한 거래는 이 거래에 따른 손익을 별도로 파악하기 위하여 분리되어 기장되어야 한다. 이러한 거래에는 물물교환 거래, 조합 거래, 공동 여행, 공동 벤처사업, 다른 사람에게 받은 수수료, 환어음, 어음, 실물 거래, 상점계정 등이 포함된다. 이러한 계정에 대하여 간단히 언급하고자 한다. 장부 기록시에는 개인사업과 혼동되지 않도록 유의해야 한다.

먼저 물물교환 거래에 대하여 설명하고자 한다. 물물교환에는 세 가지 유형이 있으며 이에 대하여는 본 글의 제9장에서 충분히 설명했다.

물물교환 거래도 먼저 일지에 거래 내역을 상세하게 기록해야 한다. 브로커가 누구였는지를 포함하여. 그렇게 한 다음에 최종적으로 해야 할 일은 금액적인 평가다. 즉, 현재 가격을 참고하여 그 금액을 기록하되, 일지에는 어떤 종류의 화폐로 기록하여도 무방하다. 그러고 나서 일지 기록을 분개장과 원장으로 전기할 때에는 자신이 사용하는 화폐 단위로 수정하면 된다.

이것으로 다 된 것이다. 왜냐하면 금액을 기록하지 않고는 거래에 따른 손익을 알 수 없기 때문이다. 상품은 항상 실제 화폐로 평가되어야 한다.

교환으로 수취한 상품을 별도의 계정으로 기록해도 된다. 상인이 이미 보유하고 있던 것과는 별도의 계정을 만들어 기록하면 각각의 손익을 파악하여 어느 것이 더 수익률이 높은 거래인지 파악할 수 있기 때문이다. 물론 모든 상품을 하나의 계정으로 처리해도 된

difficulty, what your profit or loss is. The merchandise must always be reduced to actual money value in order to take care of it (in the books).

You may keep a separate account of the goods received in trade, if you wish to do that, in order to know how much you make out of them separate from those of the same kind that you might already have at home, or separate from those that you might get after that, in order to know which was the best transaction. You also may keep only one account of all the goods—for instance, if you have already some ginger, and you get some more ginger through a trade. In this case you shall make the entries in the Journal as follows:

Per Ginger in bulk or in packages // A sugar, such and such kind, so many packages, weighing so many pounds. Received from a trade for sugar in this manner: I valued the sugar 24 ducats per hundred, of which I should receive one-third in cash, and I valued the ginger at so many ducats per hundred. The said sugar is in so many loaves weighing so many pounds, worth 20 ducats per hundred, and for the said ginger I received so many pounds of sugar and so many loaves, and their value is: L____, S____, G____, P____

And if you do not know exactly how many loaves of sugar you have received for the said ginger, it does not matter, because you may correct the mistake in the following entry, whether the mistake was made plus or minus, or correct it through the cash entry. On the contrary, you know exactly the weight and money value, and you lose nothing in either by not knowing the number of loaves. It is not always possible to keep an account of all small details.

Now you will debit cash for whatever cash you received, and you shall credit sugar in the following manner:

Per Cash // A ditto. In the said trade I received cash from so and so for so many loaves of sugar weighing so many pounds; value:

L____, S____, G____, P____

You shall record in the Journal direct all these different items soon after the trade is made, and should take the name of the merchandise if you do not want to keep a separate account; but if you want to keep them in a separate account, you will write this way in the Journal:

Per ginger *bellidi* received by trade from so and so, etc. // A sugar, etc., stating

다. 상인이 이미 생강을 보유하고 있는 상태에서 교환으로 생강을 추가로 취득하는 경우 분개장 기록은 다음과 같다.

Per 생강(벌크 또는 패키지 단위) // A 설탕, 종류, 패키지 수, 무게. 내가 보유하던 설탕과 교환하여 생강을 취득하다. 설탕은 단위당 24더컷이다. 설탕 총액의 1/3은 현금으로 받았고, 생강은 단위당 20더컷이다. 내가 준 설탕의 덩어리 수, 무게는 얼마였고, 내가 받은 생강의 덩어리 수, 무게는 얼마였다. 금액은 얼마이다.

L____, S____, G____, P____

| 분개 해설 | 차변 생강 ○○○ // 대변 설탕 ○○○ (생강은 취득, 설탕은 제공)

교환으로 취득한 생강 덩어리의 수를 모른다 해도 문제가 되지는 않는다. 그러한 실수는 다음의 현금 분개를 통하여 교정할 수 있기 때문이다. 반면에 무게와 금액은 정확히 파악해야 한다. 덩어리 수를 모른다 해도 상인이 잃을 것은 없다. 그리고 세세한 사항 모두를 추적하여 기록하는 것이 언제나 가능한 것은 아니기 때문이다.

이제 다음과 같이 받은 현금을 차변에, 설탕을 대변에 기록하면 된다.

Per 현금 // A 설탕. 물물교환으로 아무개 씨로부터 현금을 받다.

L____, S____, G____, P____

| 분개 해설 | 차변 현금 ○○○ // 대변 설탕 ○○○ (현금 취득분)

상기의 분개는 먼저 교환으로 취득한 생강가액으로 1차 분개를 실시한 후, 웃돈으로 받은 것을 2차로 분개한 것이다. 따라서 교환으로 제공한 설탕의 가액은 취득한 생강가액 ＋ 현찰로 수취한 금액이 된다.

이러한 기록은 거래가 이루어지자마자 바로 분개장에 기록되어야 한다. 물물교환으로 취득한 상품을 별도 계정으로 처리하지 않고자 하는 경우에는 상품의 이름만을 계정 명칭으로 기록하면 된다. 그러나 별도로 처리하고자 하는 경우에는 다음과 같이 분개한다.

everything as shown above. In the Ledger then they will have separate accounts. This will be sufficient for you for all kinds of trades.

Per 생강 bellidi(교환으로 취득한 것) // A 설탕, 기타 세부사항 설명.

그리고 나서 원장에는 이 계정으로 전기하면 된다. 물물교환거래 기록방법에 대하여는 이것으로 충분할 것이다.

CHAPTER 21

THE OTHER WELL-KNOWN ENTRY CALLED PARTNERSHIP. HOW IT SHOULD BE WRITTEN IN EACH BOOK IN THE PROPER MANNER

The other well-known entry is the buying of anything in partnership (*compra* or *compagnie*—may also mean joint venture but not corporation) with other people, such as silks, spices, cotton, dyes, or money exchanges, etc. These accounts must all be entered in all three books separately from your own. In the first, that is, the memorandum book, after writing down the date at the top, you shall state in a simple way all the purchases with terms and conditions, referring to papers or other instruments that you might have made, stating for how long it was made and what were its objects, mentioning the employes and apprentices that you should keep, etc., and the share, and how much each of you puts in the business, whether in goods or cash, etc., who are the debtors and who are the creditors. You should credit the partners (*compratori*) for the amount which each of them contributes, and you shall debit cash with the same if you keep the account with your own. But it is better for the business if you keep this cash account separate from your private one when you are the one at the head of the business, in which case you should have a separate set of books in the same order and way we have shown previously. This will facilitate things for you. However, you might keep all these accounts in your own personal books opening new accounts which, as we have said, are referred to as well-known accounts because they are kept separate from all the others, and I will show here how to enter them in your Day Book and then in the Journal and Ledger—but if you keep separate books, I will not give you any further instruction, because what I have said so far will be sufficient for you—you shall do as follows: On this day we have made a contract with so and so, and so and so, jointly, to buy

제21장
조합거래 기록방법

또 다른 방법은 조합 구매에 대한 것이다. 조합 구매는 비법인 공동구매를 의미한다. 이 거래는 자신의 장부와 다른 별도의 장부에 기록되어야 한다. 먼저 일지에 기록하되, 상단에 날짜를 기록한 후 관련 문서를 참조하여 사업기간, 목적, 피고용인, 도제, 지분, 현금 또는 현물 출자액 등 거래 내역을 간결하게 기록하고, 아울러 누가 채무자이고 채권자인지도 기록한다. 조합원으로부터 출자금을 받으면 조합원(이름)을 대변으로, 현금을 차변으로 분개한다. 그러나 당신이 조합 경영진인 경우에는 별도로 현금 원장을 운영하는 것이 더 바람직하며, 아예 조합 자체의 장부체계를 갖추는 것이 더 좋다. 이렇게 하면 일이 쉬워질 것이다. 물론 이 모든 원장을 자신의 장부체계 속에 포함시켜 운영해도 된다. 어차피 기존에 운영하던 원장과는 분리될 것이기 때문이다. 이제 간략하게 장부 작성법을 설명하고자 한다.

이날 우리는 모피 등을 공동 구매하기로 계약을 체결했고, 계약문서는 작성되어 있다. 아무개가 현금으로 출자했고, 나머지는 프랑스산 모직을 현물로 출자했다. 평가액은 얼마이다. 또 다른 사람은 채권을 출자했다.

그리고 나서 분개장에 분개한다. 여기서는 당신이 현금과 조합원의 자본을 갖고 있다고 가정한다. 분개장 기록시에는 조합계정과 자신의 사적인 계정이 혼동되지 않도록 계정 명칭에 조합이라는 단어를 추가해야 한다. 먼저 현금 출자부터 분개하고 나머지는 순서대로 분개한다.

Per 조합 현금 // A 조합원의 이름 — 이렇게 하면 다른 계정과 혼동되지 않을 것이

(*facto compra*) wool, etc., under terms and conditions, etc., as appears from such and such paper or such and such instrument, for so many years, etc. So and so put in as his share, so much in cash; the other put so many bales of French wool, weighing net so many pounds, etc., estimated at so many ducats per, etc. The third, so and so, put in so many credits, namely, one for so many ducats, etc.

Then, in the Journal, putting everything in its own place, you shall imagine that you have a partnership's cash (*cassa de compagnia*) and a partnership's capital (*cavedale de compagnia*); so that in each entry you make, you shall always name the accounts of the partnership so that you can distinguish them from your own entries. First, you make the cash entry, and then follow it systematically by the other entries:

Per Partnership cash // A such and such partner's account—so that if you have other accounts, you will not get confused—so and so put in on this day as his share according to our agreement as appears from the contract, etc. value: L____, S____, G____, P____

Then you shall mention the other things that they have contributed:

Per French wool // A partner's account, for so many bales weighing in total, net, so many pounds, as examined by all of us, at so many ducats per bushel, according to the terms of the contract we have made, etc., worth in total so many ducats; value: L____, S____, G____, P____

And so on for the other different items, and as to the due bills which have been put in the Company, you shall state this way:

Per Mr. So and So, Partnership's account // A so and so, according to our agreement, which so and so transferred to the Partnership as good due bill of so many ducats: L____, S____, G____, P____

Now that I have given you a kind of introduction to these new entries, I won't go any further, as it would be a very tiresome thing to repeat all I have said.

And I will not say anything as to the way in which to make these entries in the Ledger, as I know it will be easy for you to know what should be entered as debit and what as credit from the Journal. You shall enter them accordingly as I have told you at Chapter 15, and shall cancel these entries in the Journal as I told you at Chapter 12, always writing in the margin just opposite them the number of the debit and credit pages of the Ledger, and as you enter them in the Ledger you shall also enter them in the index, as I have told you repeatedly before.

다 — 이날 계약에 따라 지분에 해당되는 현금을 출자하다.

L___, S___, G___, P___

다음에는 두 번째 출자분을 분개한다.

Per 프랑스산 모직 // A 조합원의 이름, 무게와 단가는 얼마이며, 조합원 모두의 확인을 거친 것이다. 금액은 얼마다.　　　　　L___, S___, G___, P___

조합으로 그 권리가 이전된 채권에 대하여는 다음과 같이 분개한다.

Per 채무자의 이름 // A 조합원의 이름, 계약에 따라 채권이 조합으로 이전되다.

L___, S___, G___, P___

이제 조합 구성에 따른 세 가지 출자에 대하여 설명하였으므로, 더 이상의 설명은 생략하겠다. 반복하는 것은 지루한 일이기 때문이다.

또한 이 분개를 원장의 차변과 대변에 전기하는 것에 대하여도 더 이상 언급하지 않겠다. 그리고 원장으로 전기한 후에는 분개장 기사를 소인해야 한다. 즉 원장 페이지를 기록한 옆에 소인을 하고, 다음에는 원장의 목차를 작성해야 한다.

| 해설 |
① 안토니오가 현금으로 조합에 출자한 경우: 차변 현금 ○○○ // 대변 안토니오 ○○○
② 마르쿠스가 상품으로 조합에 출자한 경우: 차변 상품 명칭 ○○○ // 대변 마르쿠스 ○○○
③ 로도비코가 채권을 조합에 출자한 경우: 차변 채무자 명칭 ○○○ // 대변 로도비코 ○○○

③에서의 채무자는 로도비코가 아니라 조합에 상환해야 하므로, 채권 출자는 현금 또는 현물 출자와 같은 효과를 가진다.

CHAPTER 22

REGARDING THE ENTRIES OF EVERY KIND OF EXPENSE, AS FOR INSTANCE HOUSEHOLD EXPENSES, ORDINARY OR EXTRAORDINARY, MERCANTILE EXPENSES, WAGES OF CLERKS AND APPRENTICES. HOW THEY SHOULD BE ENTERED IN THE BOOKS

Besides the entries so far mentioned, you shall open these accounts in your books: that is, mercantile expenses, ordinary household expenses, extraordinary expenses, and account for what is cashed in (*entrata*) and what is paid out (*uscita*) : one for profits and loss (*pro e danno*—favor and damages) or (*avanzi e desavanzi*—increase and deficit), or (*utile e danno*—profit and damage) or (*guadagno e perdita*—gain and loss), which accounts are very necessary at any time so that the merchant can always know what is his capital and at the end when he figures up the closing (*saldo*), how his business is going.

I will show here clearly enough how these accounts should be kept in the books. The account named "small business expenses" is kept because we can not enter every little thing in the account of the merchandise that you sell or buy. For instance, it may happen that after a few days, for these goods that you sell or buy, you will have to pay the porter, the weigher, the packer, the shipper and the driver, and others, paying to this one one penny. to the other one two pennies, etc.; if you want to keep a separate account for each of these transactions, it would be too long and too expensive. As the proverb says: *De minimis non curat Praetor* (Officials do not bother with details). And it may be that you will have to employ those same people—drivers, porters, shippers and packers—for different things, as, for instance, you may need them for loading the several merchandises in a seaport, and you will employ them and will have to pay them for all these services at one time, and you could not charge the several kinds of merchandises with its proportion of

제22장
가계비 및 경상비, 영업비, 임금 등의 기록방법

지금까지 설명한 것 외에 다음에 언급하는 계정 원장도 설정해야 한다. 즉, 상업비용, 경상적인 가계비, 비경상비 계정 및 현금출납장 등이다. 이는 손익계산을 하기 위한 것이다. 그리고 이들 계정은 매우 필요하다. 상인은 어느 시점에서나 자신의 자본 상태를 알고 있어야 하고, 결산을 통하여 손익을 알아야 하기 때문이다.

지금부터는 이들 계정 기록방법에 대하여 설명하고자 한다. 소사업비 계정은 사고파는 상품계정에 모든 거래를 기록하기 어려울 때 작성되는 것이다. 사고파는 상품들로 인하여 짐꾼, 계근자, 포장자, 운송자, 마부 등에게 소액을 지급하는 경우가 있다. 이 거래 각각에 대하여 독립적인 계정을 설정하여 운영하는 것은 너무 길고 그 대가가 크다. 관리자는 세세한 것에 지나치게 신경 쓰지 않는다. 다시 말해 "대강 철저히 한다."라는 속담이 있다. 그리고 상품의 하역과 관련하여 여러 사람을 고용하고 이들에게 그 비용을 지급해야 하는 경우가 있는데, 이때 이들에게 지급한 금액에 비례하여 그 금액을 하역된 각각의 상품에 차변 기입, 즉 상품 원가로 가산 기록하는 것은 매우 어려운 일이다. 따라서 먼저 소사업비 계정을 개설하고, 거기에 발생한 비용을 차기하면 된다. 그러고는 이 계정 원장에 직원급여를 기록하면 된다. 물론 어떤 사람들은 급여라는 별도 계정을 설정하여 운영하기도 한다. 그들이 1년에 직원급여로 얼마나 지출하는지를 알기 위해서지만, 여기서는 직원급여를 별도 계정으로 설정하지 말고, 소사업비라는 통합계정에 기록하라는 의미이다. 그리고 이 계정은 차변 잔액이다. 만약 잔액이 대변에 나타나면 그것은 뭔가 오류가 있는 것이다. 먼저 일지는 다음과 같이 기록한다.

these expenses. Therefore you open this account which is called "small business expenses," which is always used in the debit as are all the other expenses. You enter in this account the salaries of your store employes, although some keep a separate account of the salaries that they pay so that they know how much they pay for salaries every year, etc. This should also always appear as a debit. If the account should be in credit, this would show that there is a mistake. Therefore you shall say as follows in the memorandum book:

On this day we have paid to drivers, shippers, packers, weighers, etc., who loaded and unloaded such and such goods, so many ducats, etc.; then in the Journal you shall say as follows:

Per small business expenses // A cash. Cash paid for boats, ropes, etc., for such and such goods in total, so many ducats; value;   L____, S____, G____, P____

In the Ledger, you shall state as follows:

Small business expenses (*dee dare*—shall give) debit per cash on this day, etc., value; page, etc.   L____, S____, G____, P____

We can not do without the account of ordinary household expenses. By these expenses we mean expenses for grains, wine, wood, oil, salt, meat, shoes, hats, stockings, cloths, tips, expenses for tailors, barbers, bakers, cleaners, etc., kitchen utensils, vases, glasses, casks, etc.

Many keep different accounts for all these different things, so that they can see at a glance how each account stands, and you may do so and open all these different accounts, and any accounts that you like, but I am talking to you about what the merchant can not do without. And you shall keep this account in the way I have told you to keep the small business expense account, and make each entry day by day as you have such expenses, as for grain, wine, wool, etc. Many open special accounts for these different things so that at the end of the year or at any time they may know how much they are paying out; but for the small accounts, as meat, fish, boat fares, etc., you shall set aside in a little bag one or two ducats and make small payments out of this amount. It will be impossible to keep an account of all these small things.

In the Journal you shall state so:

Per household expenses // A cash. Cash set aside in a little bag for small

이날 마부, 하역자, 계근자 등에게 상하차 노임을 지급하다로 기록하고, 분개장에 다음과 같이 분개한다.

Per 소사업비 // A 현금. 하역노임을 지불한 현금

L____, S____, G____, P____

| 분개 해설 | 차변 소사업비 ○○○ // 대변 현금 ○○○

원장에는 다음과 같이 전기한다.
소사업비 차변, 대변은 현금, 날짜 및 금액, 분개장 페이지 등

L____, S____, G____, P____

또한 경상적인 가계비 계정도 필수다. 이 비용은 식품비, 와인비, 땔감, 소금, 고기, 모자, 양말, 식기 등 가계를 유지하기 위한 모든 비용을 의미한다.

많은 사람들이 이 모든 항목에 대하여 별도 계정을 설정하여 기록한다. 한눈에 각 항목별 잔액이 얼마인지를 파악하기 위해서다. 그러므로 당신도 그런 방식으로 장부를 기록해도 된다. 그러나 내가 여기서 강조하고자 하는 것은 상인에게 가장 필수적인 것에 대한 것들이므로, 내가 설명하는 방식으로 이 계정을 운영하기 바란다. 즉, 상기 항목들에 대한 지출을 매일 이 계정 원장에 기록하라. 그러면 연말 또는 어느 시점에서라도 그 지급 총액을 쉽게 알 수 있다. 그리고 식비 및 보트 사용료 등의 소액 지출을 위하여 얼마간의 금액을 별도의 주머니에 비축해야 하고, 실제로 그런 사건이 발생하면 주머니에 비축한 돈으로 지급하는 것이 좋다. 소소한 항목 모두에 대하여 계정을 설정하는 것은 불가능하기 때문이다.

분개장에는 이렇게 기록한다.

Per 가계비 // A 현금, 주머니에 비축해둔 현금

L____, S____, G____, P____

| 해설 | ① 소액자금 비축시: 차변 소액자금 ○○○ // 대변 현금 ○○○
② 소액자금 결산시: 차변 식비 ○○○ // 대변 소액자금 ○○○
차변 보트비 ○○○ // 대변 소액자금 ○○○

영어 원문에서는 household expenses, 즉 가계비로 번역하였으나, 소액자금 비축분이므로 가계비보다는 소액자금(비축액)으로 번역하는 것이 올바른 번역으로 보인다.

expenses, so many ducats, value: L____, S____, G____, P____

If you wish, you can include in the household expenses the extraordinary expenses, as those that you make for amusements or that you lose in some game, or for things or money that you might lose, or that might be stolen or lost in a wreck or through fire, etc., for all are classified as extraordinary expenses. If you want to keep a seperate account for them, you may do so, as many do, in order to know at the end of the year how much you have expended for extraordinary expenses, under which title you should include also gifts and presents that you might make to any one for any reason. Of these expenses, I will not speak any longer, because I am sure that you, keeping in mind what we have said so far, will know how to manage yourself. And leaving this subject, I will tell you of the way to open your store accounts in the Ledger and in the other books as if you wanted to conduct a store for your own account. I shall tell you that you must pay good attention, for it is very nice thing for you to know.

그리고 가계비 계정에 비경상비를 기록해도 무방하다. 비경상비란 도박손실액, 도난손실액, 난파손실액, 화재손실액 등을 의미한다. 또한 상기 각 항목을 별도 계정으로 운영해도 된다. 그리고 선물 증정에 따른 비용도 비경상비로 처리해도 된다. 이제 이들 비용에 대하여는 더 이상 설명하지 않으려 한다. 끝으로 지점을 내는 경우의 장부 기록방법을 설명하고자 한다. 이에 대하여는 충분한 주의를 기울이는 것이 좋을 것이다.

CHAPTER 23

IN WHAT MANNER THE ACCOUNTS OF A STORE SHOULD BE KEPT. WHETHER THE STORE IS UNDER YOUR CARE OR UNDER THE CARE OF OTHER PEOPLE. HOW THE ACCOUNTS SHOULD BE ENTERED IN THE AUTHENTIC BOOKS OF THE OWNER SEPARATE FROM THOSE OF THE STORE ITSELF

I say then that if you should have a store outside of your house (branch store) and not in the same building with your house, but which you have fully equipped, then for the sake of order you should keep the accounts in this way: You should charge it in your books with all the different things that you put into it, day by day, and should credit all the different merchandise that you put in it also each one by itself, and you must imagine that this store is just like a person who should be your debtor for all the things that you may give (*dai*) it or spend for it for any reason. And so on the contrary you shall credit it with all that you take out of it and receive from it (*cavi e recevi*) as if it were a debtor who would pay you gradually. Thus at any time that you so desire, you may see how the store is running—that is, at a profit or at a loss—so you will know what you will have to do and how you will have to manage it. There are many who in their books charge everything to the manager of the store. This, however, can not be done properly without the consent of that person, because you can never enter in your books as a debtor any person without his knowing it, nor put him as a creditor under certain conditions without his consent. If you should do these things, it would not be right and your books would be considered wrong.

As to all the fixtures which you might put in said store necessary to the running of it according to the circumstances—if you had for instance a drug-store, you would have to furnish it with vases, boiling pots, copper utensils, with which to work—you shall charge your store with all this furniture. So all of these things you

제23장
지점을 직접운영 또는 위탁운영하는 경우의 거래 기록방법

　상인이 자신의 집, 즉 본점 이외의 장소에 완전한 설비를 갖춘 또 하나의 가게(지점)를 내는 경우에는, 다음과 같이 해야 체계적인 회계기록이 될 것이다. 상인이 매일 지점으로 보내는 것은 분개장에 차기(차변 기입)하고, 지점으로 보내는 상품은 대기(대변 기입)해야 한다. 상인은 지점을 여러 이유로 상인에게 재화를 차입하는 채무자로 간주해야 한다. 반대로 지점으로부터 수취하는 경우에는 채무자로부터 대여금을 회수하는 경우에 해당되므로 이를 대기해야 한다. 이러한 방식으로 기록하면 상인은 필요 시 언제든지 지점의 운영상태, 즉 손익을 파악할 수 있고, 이로써 향후 무엇을 어떻게 관리해야 하는가를 파악할 수 있다. 많은 상인들이 지점의 지배인을 장부상의 채무자로 기록하고 있다. 그러나 이것은 그 사람의 동의가 없이 기록한 것이므로 타당한 회계기록이 아니다. 어떤 사람의 동의 없이 그 사람을 채무자로 기록해서는 안 되기 때문이다. 또한, 동의 없이 아무나 채권자로 기록해서도 안 된다. 이런 식으로 기록한 장부는 올바른 장부가 아니다.

　약국을 설립하게 되면, 꽃병, 작은 솥, 구리 용기 등이 필요한데, 이러한 집기비품을 지점약국에 보낸 경우, 상인은 이 모든 집기비품과 관련하여 지점약국을 차기해야 한다. 즉, 상인은 지점에 보낸 모든 것을 차기해야 하고, 지점의 지배인은 자필 또는 대필로 이 모든 물품에 대한 리스트를 작성해야 하고, 이렇게 하면 모든 것이 명백하게 될 것이다. 이렇게 하면 상인이 그 지점의 경영권을 타인 또는 다른 고용인에게 넘겨도 지장이 없을 것이다. 그러나 상인이 직접 경영을 하고자 하는 경우에는 내가 설명하는 대로 처리하면 아무런 지장이 없을 것이다. 상인이 다른 사업은 하지 않고 앞에서 언급한 지점을 통해서

shall charge, and he who is at the head of store shall make a proper inventory of all these things in his own handwriting or in the handwriting of somebody else, at his pleasure, so that everything should be clear. And this will be sufficient for a store whose management you may have turned over to somebody or to some of your employes. But if you want to run the store yourself, you shall do as I will tell you and it will be all right. Let us suppose that you buy and do all of your business through the said store and do not have to take care of any other business, then you shall keep the books as I have said before, whether you buy or sell. You shall credit all those that sell goods to you on time, if you buy on time, or credit cash if you buy for cash, and charge the store; and if you should sell at retail, as when the sale should not amount to four or six ducats, and so on, then you shall keep all these moneys in a small drawer or box from which you shall take it after eight or ten days, and then you shall charge this amount to cash and shall credit the store: and you shall make this entry as follows:

Per various merchandise sold—for which you shall have kept an account—and so on. I shall not talk at length about this because I have given you sufficient explanation previously and you know how to go ahead by this time. For accounts are nothing else than the expression in writing of the arrangement of his affairs, which the merchant keeps in his mind, and if he follow this system always he will know all about his business and will know exactly whether his business goes well or not. Therefore the proverb: If you are in business and do not know all about it, your money will go like flies—That is, you will lose it. And according to the circumstances you can remedy what is to be remedied; for instance, if necessary, you might open other accounts. And this will be sufficient for you.

만 사업을 하는 경우에도 상인은 그가 물건을 팔든 사든 내가 전에 말한 바대로 장부를 기록해야 한다. 즉, 외상으로 구매하는 경우 상인에게 외상을 준 사람을 대기하고, 현금으로 구매한 경우에는 현금을 대기해야 하고, 지점은 차기해야 한다. 그리고 4~6 더캇 이하의 소액으로 소매 판매하는 경우에는 그 돈을 작은 서랍 또는 상자에 일단 보관한다. 그리고 8일 내지 10일 후에 이를 꺼내어 이 금액을 차기하고, 지점은 대기한다. 즉, 아래와 같이 분개기록한다.

차변 여러 상품의 매출원가―상인은 원장을 기록해야 한다―등. 나는 이에 대하여 자세히 설명하지 않고자 한다. 내가 이미 충분히 설명을 하였으므로 이제는 처리방법을 알고 있기 때문이다. 원장 또는 회계라는 것은 거래를 체계적으로 정리 기록하는 것이 불과하다는 것을 상인은 항상 명심하고 있어야 한다. 상인이 이러한 시스템을 따르면 그는 그의 사업 전부에 대하여 알게 되고, 그의 사업이 잘 진행되는지 아닌지를 정확히 알 수 있게 된다. "사업을 하는 자가 그 사업 전부를 알지 못하면 그의 돈은 날아가 버린다. 즉, 그는 모든 돈을 잃게 된다."라는 격언이 있다. 우리는 고쳐질 수 있는 것만을 고칠 수 있다. 따라서 필요하면 다른 원장을 개설해도 된다. 이 정도면 충분한 설명이 되었을 것이다.

| 해설 |
상기의 영역문 중 차대 분개와 관련된 것은 사실상 요령부득의 문장이다. 다만, 지점을 채무자와 같은 성격의 인명으로 간주하라는 것은 지점 및 사업부를 인명으로 간주하는 송도부기와 같은 개념이다. 상기의 문장에서 그런대로 해석이 가능한 것을 추려서 분개를 하면 아래와 같다.
① 지점의 외상매입: 차변 상품명칭 ○○○ // 대변 외상제공자 명칭 ○○○
② 지점의 현금매입: 차변 상품명칭 ○○○ // 대변 현금 ○○○

| 분개해설 | 정상적인 지점거래 분개
① 지점에 대한 현금출자: 차변 지점명칭 ○○○ // 대변 현금 ○○○
② 지점에 상품발송: 차변 지점명칭 ○○○ // 대변 상품명칭 ○○○
③ 지점으로부터 현금수취: 차변 현금 ○○○ // 대변 지점명칭 ○○○
본 장의 문장을 의역하여 분개하면 상기와 같다. 나폴리 지점, 아테네 지점, 런던 지점 등과 같이 지점이 다수인 경우에는 계정을 "지점"으로 기록해서는 안 되고, 본점과 실제로 거래를 실시한 지점의 명칭으로 기록해야 한다.

CHAPTER 24

HOW YOU SHOULD KEEP IN THE JOURNAL AND LEDGER. THE ACCOUNTS WITH THE BANK. WHAT IS UNDERSTOOD BY THEM. BILLS OF EXCHANGE—WHETHER YOU DEAL WITH A BANK OR YOURSELF ARE A BANKER. RECEIPTS FOR DRAFTS—WHAT IS UNDERSTOOD BY THEM AND WHY THEY ARE MADE OUT IN DUPLICATE

In respect to banks, which you can find nowadays in Venice, in Bruges, in Antwerp, Barcelona, and other places well known to the commercial world, you must keep your accounts with them with the greatest diligence.

You can generally establish connections with a bank. For instance, you may leave your money with the bank as a place of greater safety, or you may keep your money in the bank as a deposit in order to make therefrom your daily payments to Peter, John and Martin, for a bank draft is like a public notarial instrument, because they are controlled by the state.

If you put money in the bank, then you shall charge the bank or the owner or partners of the bank and shall credit your cash and make the entries in the Journal as follows:

For Bank of Lipamani // A cash. Cash deposited with so and so by me, or others, for my account, on this day counting gold and other money, etc., in all so many ducats; value: L___, S___, G___, P___

And you will have the banker give you some kind of a written record for your surety; if you make other deposits you shall do the same. In case you should withdraw money, the banker shall have you write a receipt; in this way, things will be kept always clear.

It is true that at times this kind of receipt is not given, because, as we said, the books of the bank are always public and authentic; but it is better to require this writing, because, as I have told you, things can't be too clear for the merchant.

제24장

은행과의 거래를 분개장 및 원장에 기록하는 방법과 그 의미. 독자가 은행의 고객인 경우와 은행인 경우의 기록방법. 각종 증빙을 복본화해야 하는 이유

　은행은 베니스, 브뤼셀, 앤트워프, 바르셀로나 등의 유럽 각 도시에 있는데, 이 은행들과 거래할 때는 기록을 신중하게 해야 한다. 은행과 거래를 시작하는 것은 쉽다. 즉, 은행을 안전한 금고로 여겨 여유자금을 예치할 수도 있고, 이 사람 저 사람에게 지불을 하기 위한 금고로 사용하기 위하여 예치할 수도 있다. 은행은 국가에 의해 통제받는 기관이므로 은행이 발행하는 어음 등은 일종의 공정증서와 같은 효력을 갖기 때문이다.

　상인이 은행에 현금을 예치하면, 은행 또는 그 소유자 또는 그 조합원명(즉, 주주)을 차기하고, 현금을 대기하면 된다. 분개장에는 다음과 같이 기록한다.

　Per 리파마니 은행 // A 현금. 나 또는 대리인이 내 계좌로 현금과 금화를 합쳐서 얼마를 은행에 예치하다.　　　　　　　　L＿＿, S＿＿, G＿＿, P＿＿

| 분개 해설 |
① 숨마 부기: 차변 은행 명칭 ○○○ // 대변 현금 ○○○
② 현행 부기: 차변 보통예금 ○○○ // 대변 현금 ○○○

　은행에 예치한 후에는 은행으로부터 이를 증빙하는 문서를 받아야 한다. 반대로 예금을 인출하는 경우에는 예금자가 은행에 영수증을 써서 주어야 한다. 이런 식으로 하면 모든 것이 명쾌해질 것이다. 가끔 이러한 영수증을 주고받지 않는 경우가 있다. 은행의 장부가 상당한 공신력이 있기 때문에 은행의 기록만 믿고 관련 문서의 수수를 등한히 하는 경우가 있는 것이다. 그러나 이러한 경우에도 문서를 받아두는 것이 더 좋다. 전에 말한 바

If you want to keep this account in the name of the owners or partners of the bank, you may do so, as it is the same thing, because, if you open the account under the name of the bank, by the bank you mean the owners or the partners. If you keep it under the name of the owners, you shall say this way:

Per Mr. Girolimo Lipamani, banker, and associates—if there are many—// A cash—and here you write as above. In your books you shall always mention all agreements, terms, conditions that there might be; also instruments of writing and places where you keep them, whether file box, pouch or trunk, so that you may easily find them, as these papers should be diligently kept for an everlasting memorial of the transaction (*ad perpetuam memoriam*) on account of dangers.

As you may have several different business relations with the bankers for yourself, or for others, you must keep various accounts with them so that you won't mix one thing with another, and avoid confusion, and in your entries you shall say: On account of such and such thing, or on account of so and so, or on account of goods, or on account of cash deposited in your name or in the name of others, as we have said. You will know yourself how to make these entries. In the same way you will proceed in case others should turn money over to you for some account; you shall charge that account in your book—that is, you shall charge the bank, stating whether it was in part payment or in full, etc., and you shall credit the person that gave you the money. This will be all right.

When you should withdraw money from a bank either to pay somebody else as part payment or payment in full, or to make a remittance to parties in other countries, you shall do in this case just the opposite of what we just said—that is, if you withdraw money you shall charge your cash and credit the bank or owners of the bank for the amount withdrawn; and if you should give an order on the bank for somebody else, you shall charge this party and credit the bank or owners of the bank for that much, stating the reasons. You shall enter the cash item in your Journal as follows:

Per cash // A bank, or Mr. Girolimo Lipamani, for cash which on this day or on such and such day I withdrew for my need, in all so many ducats, value:

L____, S____, G____, P____

And if you should issue an order in favor of Mr. Martino, for instance, you shall

와 같이 상인은 매사를 분명하게 해야 하기 때문이다. 분개장 분개시 은행명 대신에 은행의 소유자 또는 주주명으로 기록을 해도 되는데, 그 이유는 은행명이라는 것이 결국은 은행의 소유자 또는 주주를 의미하기 때문이다. 그리고 소유자명으로 분개를 하려면 다음과 같이 하면 된다.

Per 지롤리모 리파마니 씨, 은행 소유자 또는 주주들(다른 주주가 있는 경우) // A 현금

그리고 나머지 적요 사항들, 예금자는 반드시 자신의 장부에 예금조건 등을 기록해야 한다. 그리고 그 증빙문서를 파일박스, 파우치, 트렁크 등 어디에 보관하고 있는지도 기록해야 나중에 쉽게 찾을 수 있다. 그리고 이 문서들은 영구보존 대상이므로 신중하고도 주의 깊게 보관해야 한다.

은행과는 예금거래뿐만 아니라 상품거래를 비롯하여 자신 또는 다른 사람과 관련된 여러 종류의 다른 거래도 할 수 있는데, 이 경우 혼동되지 않도록 계정을 별도로 설정해야 한다. 그리고 이런 경우 장부에 자신 또는 다른 사람의 이름으로 예치된 현금 때문에 발생한 거래인지, 상품 때문에 발생한 거래인지 거래에 해당하는 사유를 기록해야 한다. 즉, 각 경우에 따른 기록방법을 알아야 한다. 같은 방식으로 다른 사람이 상인에게 은행이체 방식으로 돈을 지급할 수도 있는데, 이 경우 수취한 은행계좌를 차기하고, 상인에게 돈을 지급한 사람을 대기하면 된다. 즉, 은행통장으로 대금을 받았으므로 은행명을 차기하되, 전액지급인지 부분지급인지의 여부를 기록하고, 자신에게 돈을 지급한 사람을 대기해야 한다.

| **분개 해설** | 차변 은행 명칭 ○○○ // 대변 지급자 명칭 ○○○ (타인으로부터 이체 수취한 경우)

다른 사람에게 지급하기 위하여 또는 외국에 송금하기 위하여 은행에서 예금을 인출할 때에는 예금할 때와 반대로 분개하면 된다. 즉, 현금을 차기하고 은행명 또는 그 소유자를 대기하면 된다. 그리고 은행으로 하여금 다른 사람에게 지급하도록 지불명령을 하는 경우에는 받은 사람을 차기하고, 은행명 또는 그 소유자를 대기하면 된다. 물론 거기에 지불명령 사유 등도 기록해야 한다. 이 경우의 분개장 분개는 다음과 같다.

Per 현금 // A 은행 명칭 또는 소유자 지롤리모 리파마니 씨. 어느 날 나는 어떤 사유로 현금을 인출하다.   L____, S____, G____, P____ say thus:

Per Martino on such and such a day // A ditto for ditto for cash, etc., for so many ducats, for which I gave an order, in part payment or in full payment, or for a loan, etc., on this day; value: L____, S____, G____, P____

Every time you transfer these entries from the Journal into the Ledger, you shall also record them in the index and cancel them, as I have shown you, adding more or less words according to the facts in the case.

You must do the same in case you want to send drafts elsewhere, as to London, Bruges, Rome, Lyons, etc. You shall mention in the letter the terms, conditions, etc., whether these drafts are at sight or at a certain date or at pleasure of the payor, as it is customary, mentioning also whether it is a first, second, third draft, etc., so that no misunderstanding can occur between you and your correspondent, mentioning also the kind of money in which you draw or transmit, their value, the commission, the costs and interest that might follow a protest—in a word, everything must be mentioned, why and how.

I have told you how you have to proceed in dealing with a bank. If on the contrary you are the banker you have to do in the opposite way (*mutatis mutandis*); when you pay you charge the man to whom you pay and credit cash. If one of your creditors, without withdrawing money, should issue a draft to somebody else, you shall say in the Journal as follows: Per that special creditor of yours // A the man to whom the money was assigned. In this way you just make the transfer from one creditor to another and you still remain as debtor and act as a go-between, as witness or agent of the two parties. For ink, paper, rent, trouble and time you get a commission, which is always lawful, even though through a draft there is no risk of travel, or the risk when money should be transferred to third parties, etc., as in actual exchanges, of which we have spoken in its place. If you are a banker, whenever you close an account with your creditors always remember to get back all the papers, documents or other writings in your own handwriting that they might have. When you issue any such paper always mention it in your books so that when the time comes you will remember to ask for them and to destroy them so that nobody else should appear with these papers and ask money for the second time. You must always require good receipts as those do who are accustomed to

| **분개 해설** | 차변 현금 ○○○ // 대변 은행 명칭 ○○○ (예금 인출시의 분개)

그리고 마르티노 씨에게 지급하라고 은행에 요청한 경우에는 다음과 같이 분개한다.
Per 마르티노 // A 은행 명칭 또는 그 소유자명. 채무변제 등을 위하여 은행으로 하여금 마르티노 씨에게 지급하도록 요청했다.   L____, S____, G____, P____

| **분개 해설** | 차변 마르티노 ○○○ // 대변 은행 명칭 ○○○ (마르티노에게 이체지급 분개)

분개장 기록을 원장에 전기할 때마다 원장의 목차를 작성하고 아울러 분개장에 소인을 해야 한다. 물론 다소간의 설명도 덧붙여야 한다.
런던, 로마, 리용 등에 환어음을 보낼 때에도 같은 방식으로 기록해야 한다. 거래조건, 몇 번째 이서인지, 일람불 어음인지, 확정일자 지급어음인지, 요구시점 지급어음인지 등도 기록해야 한다. 이는 상인과 그 대리인 사이에 오해가 발생하지 않게 하기 위한 것이므로 인출 또는 송금하는 화폐의 종류, 금액, 중개료, 수수료 및 이자 등을 기록해야 한다. 한마디로 말하자면 모든 것을 기록해야 한다.
이제까지는 예금자 입장에서의 은행거래 기록방법에 대하여 설명했다. 반대로 당신이 은행가인 경우에는 정반대로 분개하면 된다. 지급할 때는 당신에게 받은 사람을 차기하고 당신의 현금을 대기하면 된다. 그리고 당신의 채권자, 즉 예금자가 자신의 예금채권을 다른 사람에게 돌리라고 요청한 경우에는 다음과 같이 분개하면 된다.
Per 요청한 채권자 명칭 // A 돌려지는 사람의 이름

| **분개 해설** | 차변 요청한 예금자 명칭_A ○○○ // 대변 돌려지는 사람의 이름_B ○○○

상기의 분개에서 차변 분개는 예금채무의 감액 분개이고, 대변 분개는 신규 예금채무의 증가 분개다. 즉, 예금(채권)자의 명칭이 A에서 B로 바뀐 것으로 보면 된다.
이렇게 하여 한 채권자에서 다른 채권자로 이체가 완료된다.
물론 당신은 아직도 채무자다. 채권자의 이름만 바뀌었기 때문이다. 여기서 당신의 역할은 두 채권자 사이의 중개인 또는 대리인, 증인에 해당된다. 잉크비, 종이값, 집세, 수고비, 시간비 등 때문에 당신은 수수료를 받는데, 이것은 합법적인 것이다. 이러한 이체거

this kind of business. For the custom is this: If you, for instance, come from Geneva to Venice with a draft on Messrs. Giovanni Frescobaldi & Co., of Florence, which draft might be at sight or on a certain date or at your pleasure, and the amount were for a hundred ducats, that is, for as many ducats as you have paid to the drawer of the draft, then the said Messrs. Giovanni & Co., when they honor the draft and give you the cash will require you to give two receipts written in your own handwriting, and if you should not know how to write, a third party or a notary public will make them out. He will not be satisfied with one because he has to send one to the banker at Geneva, who wrote him to pay the hundred ducats to you for his account just to show that he honored his request, and for this purpose he will send to the other banker a letter enclosing your receipt written in your handwriting. The other receipt he will keep for himself on file so that in balancing with the other banker, the banker could not deny the transaction, and if you should go to Geneva you could not complain of him or of Mr. Giovanni for if you should complain he would show you your receipt written by yourself and you would not play a beautiful part in it. All these precautions ought to be taken by necessity on account of the bad faith of the present times. Out of these transactions two entries ought to be made in the Ledger, one entry in the account with Mr. Giovanni, in which you shall charge the drawer of the draft, (*letter de cambio*) the other entry in the account of your correspondent at Geneva, crediting Mr. Giovanni with that hundred ducats paid through a draft. This is the method that the bankers of all the world keep so that their transaction may appear clear; therefore you will have to take some trouble on your part and try to enter everything in its own place with great care.

래를 통하여 현금의 직접운송에 따른 위험과 여행의 위험 등이 제거되기 때문이다. 그리고 당신이 은행가인 경우, 채권자들과 거래를 종결하는 때는 반드시 당신이 그 전에 발행한 모든 문서를 회수해야 한다. 문서를 발행할 때는 반드시 장부에 내역을 기록해야 하고, 때가 되면 채권자들에게 문서를 요구하여 그것들을 폐기해야 한다. 아무도 그 문서를 갖고 두 번 세 번 청구하지 않도록 하기 위해서다. 상거래에 정통한 사람들이 하는 것처럼 당신도 항상 증빙문서를 확보해야 한다. 상거래 관습은 다음과 같다.

예를 들면, 당신이 제네바에서 베니스로 지오반니가 이서한 어음을 들고 가는 경우도 있다. 이 어음은 일람불 또는 확정일자 지급조건 등의 어음으로서 그 금액은 100더컷일 수도 있다. 당신은 이미 어음 발행인인 지오반니에게 그 금액을 지급했다. 그들이 그 어음을 인정하여 당신에게 현금을 지급할 때는 당신에게 두 장의 문서를 작성해달라고 요청할 것이다. 만약 당신이 작성법을 모르는 경우에는 제3자 또는 공증인이 작성하게 될 것이다. 그는 한 장으로 만족하지 않을 것이다. 한 장은 제네바의 은행가에게 보내야 하기 때문이다. 이 은행가는 그가 당신에게 그의 계좌에서 100더컷을 지급하라고 쓴 사람이다. 이러한 이유로 그는 다른 은행가에게 당신이 쓴 영수증을 보내어 거래를 종결할 것이다. 다른 영수증은 다른 은행가와 대조하여 그 거래를 부인하지 못하게 할 목적으로 그가 직접 보관한다. 만약 제네바로 가야 하는 경우 당신은 그 또는 지오반니에게 불평해서는 안 된다. 당신이 불평하면 그는 당신이 직접 쓴 영수증을 제시할 것이고, 이 경우 당신의 모습은 그리 아름답지 않을 것이다. 이렇게 절차가 복잡한 것은 모두 현재의 불신풍조 때문이다. 이 거래로 두 건의 기사가 원장에 전기되어야 한다. 즉, 지오반니 계정에 어음발행인을 차기하고, 제네바에 있는 당신의 대리인 계정에 지오반니를 대기해야 한다. 금액은 어음을 통하여 지급된 100더컷이다. 이것이 온 세상의 은행들이 거래를 명확히 하기 위하여 처리하는 방법이다. 따라서 당신도 그와 똑같은 노력을 기울여야 하고, 모든 것을 항상 제자리에 기록하도록 노력해야 한다.

| 해설 | ① 어음대여 시점: 차변 지오반니 100 // 대변 현금 100 (지오반니 채권 증가, 현금 감소)
② 대여금 회수 시점: 차변 대리인 100 // 대변 지오반니 100 (대리인 채권 증가, 지오반니 채권 감소)
③ 대리인으로부터 수취 시점: 차변 현금 100 // 대변 대리인 100 (현금 증가, 대리인 채권 감소)

CHAPTER 25

ANOTHER ACCOUNT WHICH IS USUALLY KEPT IN THE LEDGER, CALLED INCOME AND EXPENSES, FOR WHICH OFTEN A SEPARATE BOOK IS USED, AND WHY

There are some who, in their books, are accustomed to keep an account called Income and Expense (*Entrata e uscita*), in which they enter extraordinary things, or any other thing that they deem proper; others keep an account called extraordinary expenses and in it they record gifts, which they receive or give. They keep it as a credit and debit account, and then at the end of the year they ascertain the remainder (*resto*) which is either a profit or a loss and transfer it to capital as you will understand when we talk about the balance. But really the account we have called "household expenses" is sufficient for all this unless someone should like to keep a separate account for his own curiosity, but it would be of no great value because things should be arranged as briefly as possible. In other places it is customary to keep the income and expense account in a separate book which is balanced when they balance the authenticated books and all other affairs. This custom is not to be criticized but it requires more work.

제25장

손실과 이익이라는 계정의 의미와
이를 별도의 원장으로 개설하는 이유

    어떤 사람들은 손실과 이익이라는 계정에 비경상비 혹은 적당한 비용을 기록한다. 또 다른 사람들은 비경상비 계정에 그들이 주고받는 선물가액을 기록한다. 그들은 그 계정을 차변과 대변으로 분리하여 기록하고, 연말에 (대차) 잔액을 산출하여 그 잔액을 자본금계정으로 이체한다. 이에 대하여는 후술한 것을 보면 이해할 수 있을 것이다. 그러나 실제로는 우리가 가계비라고 칭하는 계정을 운영하는 것으로 충분하다. 물론 각자의 취향에 따라 상기의 방식으로 기록해도 무방하다. 그러나 이것은 별로 가치가 없는 일이다. 기록이란 가능한 한 간결해야 하기 때문이다. 또 어떤 곳에서는 손익계정 원장을 별도의 장부로 만들기도 한다. 이는 관인장부와 다른 모든 거래를 대조하여 결산할 때 작성된다. 이것은 비판할 일은 아니나, 업무량이 많다는 단점이 있다.

    | **해설** | 상기의 번역에서는 'household expenses'를 가계비로 번역하였으나 가계비(家計費)는 원래 상인의 사업비에 포함될 수 없는 것이다. 이 부분을 가계비로 번역한 것은 영어 원문을 존중했기 때문이다. 제대로 번역한다면 '가게비'가 옳은 번역일 것이다.

CHAPTER 26

HOW ENTRIES SHOULD BE MADE IN MERCANTILE BOOKS RELATIVE TO TRIPS WHICH YOU CONDUCT YOURSELF OR YOU ENTRUST TO OTHER PEOPLE, AND THE TWO LEDGERS RESULTING THEREFROM

Trips are made usually in two ways, either personally or through somebody else; therefore two are the ways to keep their accounts and the book always ought to be in duplicate whether the trip is made by you personally or it is in charge of somebody else. One ledger is kept at home and the other one is taken along and kept on the trip. If you conduct the trip yourself, for the sake of order and system, you must take a new inventory also a small Ledger and small Journal among the things you take with you and follow the instruction above given. If you sell or buy or exchange, you must charge and credit according to the facts, persons, goods, cash, traveling capital, traveling profit and loss, etc. This is the best way, no matter what other people may say. You might keep an account with the mercantile house which furnishes you with the goods which you take on the trip. In this case you shall credit the said house in your little Ledger and charge the different goods one by one. In this way you would open your mercantile house accounts, capital account, etc., as in your main books, and coming back safe and sound you would return to the mercantile house either other goods in exchange for those that you took or money, and you would close the accounts with the entering in your big Ledger the respective profit or loss item. In this way your business will be clear. If, however, you entrust the trip to some other party, then you should charge this party with all the goods that you entrust with him, saying: Per trip entrusted to so and so, etc., and you should keep an account with him, as if he were one of your customers, for all goods and moneys, keeping separate accounts, etc., and he on

제26장
직접출장 또는 위탁출장 관련 거래의 기록방법

출장은 직접 가는 방법이나 대리인이 가는 방법 두 가지에 의해 이루어질 수 있다. 따라서 두 가지 기록방법이 있고, 장부는 직접출장이든 간접출장이든 간에 두 벌이 준비되어야 한다. 하나는 집에 보관하기 위한 용도이고, 또 하나는 휴대용이다. 직접출장을 가는 경우에는 먼저 새로이 재물기를 작성해야 한다. 그리고 분개장, 원장 등을 휴대해야 하고 기록은 앞에서 설명한 대로 실시해야 한다. 즉, 팔거나 사거나 교환을 하게 되면 인명, 상품, 현금, 여비 등을 차기 또는 대기해야 한다. 누가 무슨 말을 하든 이것이 최선의 방법이다. 출장 중에 상품을 외상으로 구매하는 경우, 상품제공자를 대기하고 각 상품을 하나씩 차기하면 된다.

| **분개 해설** | 차변 상품 명칭 ○○○ // 대변 외상제공자 명칭 ○○○

이런 방식으로 외상제공자 계정, 자본금계정 등을 개설하고, 집에 돌아와서 그 상품 대가를 자신의 상품 또는 현금으로 결제하는 경우에는, 원래의 원장에 기록하여 관련 거래를 종결하고 손익을 산출해야 한다. 이렇게 하면 모든 것이 명쾌할 것이다. 반면에 대리인을 출장 보내는 경우에는 자신에게 상품을 받은 그 대리인을 차기하면 된다. 즉, Per 누구에게 맡긴 여행, 기타 등등과 같이 그가 고객인 것처럼 생각하고 그와의 거래를 기록해야 한다. 즉, 그에게 제공한 모든 상품과 돈에 대하여 별도로 계정을 설정하여 그와의 거래를 기록하면 되는 것이다. 그리고 대리인 자신도 자신의 원장을 준비해야 한다. 대리인의 원장에는 출장 위탁자인 주인이 항상 채권자(대변)로 기록되어야 한다. 그리고 그가

his part will set up a little Ledger in which he makes you creditor for everything. When he comes back he will balance with you; and if your traveling salesman were in fetters (sentence remains unfinished in the original)

여행에서 돌아오면 그때 결산하면 된다. 만일 그 대리인이 현지에 구속되어 있는 경우에는 (이하는 원문 없음)

CHAPTER 27

ANOTHER WELL-KNOWN ACCOUNT NAMED PROFIT AND LOSS, OR PROFIT AND DEFICIT. HOW IT SHOULD BE KEPT IN THE LEDGER AND WHY IT IS NOT KEPT IN THE JOURNAL AS THE OTHER ACCOUNTS

After the other accounts, there must follow one which is named variously, according to different localities, Favor and Damage (*Pro a Danno*), or Profit and Damage (*Utile a Danno*), or Increase and Deficit (*Avanzi e Desavanzi*). Into this other accounts in the Ledger have their remainders, as we will show when we speak of the trial balance. You should not put these entries in the Journal, but only in the Ledger, as they originate from overs or shorts in the debits and credits, and not from actual transactions. You shall open the account this way:

Profit and Loss debit (*dee dare*—shall give), and Profit and Loss credit (*dee havere*—shall have).

That is, if you have sustained a loss in a special line of merchandise and in this account in your Ledger would show less in the credit than the debit, then you will add the difference (*saldo*) to the credit so as to make it balance, and you shall enter as follows:

Credit (*dee havere*—shall have), per Profit and Loss, so much, which I enter here in order to balance on account of loss sustained—and so on, and you will mark the page of the Profit and Loss account where you write down the entry. Then you go to the Profit and Loss account and in the debit column you shall enter as follows:

Profit and Loss debit (*dee dare*—shall give), on this day, to such and such loss sustained, so much—which has been entered in the credit of said merchandise account in order to balance it at page so and so. If the account of this special merchandise would show a profit instead of loss—that is, more in the credit than

제27장
손익계정과 손익이 원장에만 기록되어야 하는 이유

여러 계정 원장의 뒤에는 지역에 따라 다양하게 명명되는 계정 원장, 즉 손익계정 원장을 설치해야 한다. 각 계정의 잔액은 이 계정으로 이체, 즉 전기되어야 한다. 이에 대하여는 시산표편에서 설명하고자 한다. 이 계정은 분개장에 설치해서는 안 된다. 원장에서 발생한 과부족액에 불과하고 실제 거래가 아니기 때문이다. 손익계정 원장은 다음과 같이 개설한다.

손익 차변, 그리고 손익 대변: 즉, 어떤 상품에서 손실이 발생한 경우, 차변(매입액)이 대변(매출액)보다 크므로 차변 잔액이 발생한다(해설: 기말재고액이 없는 경우). 이 경우 대차를 일치시키기 위하여 그 계정의 대변에 차액을 기록하는데, 그 방법은 다음과 같다.

상품계정 대변, 이체는 손익계정, 손실로 인한 차액을 여기에 기록하여 상품계정의 차대변 잔액을 일치시킨다. 그리고 이체되는 손익계정의 페이지 번호를 기록한다. 그리고 손익계정 원장으로 이동하여 손익계정의 차변(비용란)에 다음과 같이 기록한다.

손익계정 차변, 날짜, 상품계정의 대변 금액, 즉 손실액을 여기로 전기하다. 상품계정의 페이지 번호는 제 몇 페이지다. 만약 상품에서 이익이 난 경우에는 위와 반대로 기록하면 된다. 잔액이 좋은 쪽이든 나쁜 쪽이든 모든 계정에 대하여 상기의 절차를 반복해야 한다. 이렇게 하면 모든 계정의 대차 잔액이 일치하게 된다. 이것이 장부의 정확성을 보여주는 조건이다. 이에 대하여는 시산표 편에서 설명하고자 한다. 그리고 이렇게 하면 한눈에 손익 여부와 그 금액을 파악할 수 있다. 그리고 손익계정의 잔액은 자본금계정으로 이체되어야 하는데, 자본금계정은 모든 계정의 종착지라고 할 수 있다.

in the debit—then you will proceed in the opposite way. The same you shall do one by one for all accounts with merchandise or different things, whether they show good or bad results, so that your Ledger always shows the accounts in balance—that is, as much in the debit as in the credit. This is the condition the Ledger will be in if it is correct, as I will explain to you when I am talking of the balance. In this way you will see at a glance whether you are gaining or losing, and how much. And this account must then be transferred for its closing (*saldo*) into the capital account, which is always the last in all the ledgers and is consequently the receptacle of all other accounts, as you will understand.

| 해설 | 원장만을 이용한 마감

- 마감 전 상품계정 차변 800, 대변 500, 잔액 300(기초, 기말재고는 없다고 가정)
- 상품계정의 마감과 손익계정, 자본금계정 전기 및 마감 절차
① 상품계정의 대변에 300을 기록하여, 대차를 각각 800으로 일치시킨다.
② 손익계정의 차변에 상품계정 손실액을 상품 건별로 전기한다.
③ 상품이 한 가지인 경우, 손익계정은 차변 잔액 300이 된다.
④ 손익계정 대변에 300을 기입하여 손익계정의 대차를 일치, 마감한다.
⑤ 상기의 300을 자본금계정 차변에 전기하여, 자본금계정의 잔액을 산출한다.
　당기손익 이체 전의 자본금 잔액이 1,000인 경우, 이 이체로 인하여 당기 말 자본금 잔액, 즉 상인의 순재산 잔액은 700으로 줄어들고, 이것으로 당기의 회계는 종료된다.
⑥ 상품손실 외에 다른 일반 관리비용이 가산되면 자본금은 더 줄어들 것이다.

| 해설 | 분개장을 이용한 마감
① 차변 손익_상품손실 300 // 대변 상품 300
② 차변 자본금 300 // 손익_상품손실 300
③ 상기의 분개와 원장 잔액
　상품계정: 차변 800, 대변 800 → 잔액 0
　손익계정: 차변 300, 대변 300 → 잔액 0
　자본금계정: 차변 300, 대변 1000 → 잔액 700

〈상품 원장〉

	차변	대변
당기 매입	800	
당기 매출		500
손익으로		300
합계	800	800

〈손익(계산서) 원장〉

	차변	대변
상품에서	300	
자본주로		300
합계	300	300

〈자본주 원장〉

	차변	대변
기초 잔액		1000
손익에서	300	
차기 이월	700	
합계	1000	1000

CHAPTER 28

HOW FULL ACCOUNTS IN THE LEDGER SHOULD BE CARRIED FORWARD AND THE PLACE TO WHICH THEY MUST BE TRANSFERRED SO THAT NO CROOKEDNESS CAN BE PRACTICED IN THE LEDGER

You should know that when an account has been filled out, either in the debit or in the credit, and you cannot make any more entries in the space reserved for such an account, you must at once carry this account forward to a page after all your other accounts, so that there is no space left in the Ledger between this transferred account and the last of the other accounts. Otherwise it would be considered a fraud. It must be carried forward in the manner which we have given above when writing about the balancing of profit and loss. In making the transfers, you should make entries on the debit and credit sides only, without making any entry in the Journal. Transfers are not made in the Journal; still, if you so desired, you might do that and it would be all right; but it is not necessary, because it would be that much more trouble without any necessity. All that need be done is to increase the smaller quantity—that is, if the account shows more in the debit than in the credit, you ought to add the difference to the credit. I will give you, now, an example of one of these transfers:

Let us suppose that Martino has had a long account with you of several transactions, so that his account should be transferred from ledger page 30. Suppose further that the last account of your book is at page 60, and is at the top of said page, so that on the same page there is space enough to transfer the Martino account. Suppose that there is on debit side, L 80, S 15, G 15, P 24; and the credit shows that he has given you, L 72, S 9, G 3, P 17. Deducting the credit from the debit, there is a remainder (*resta*) of: L 8, S 6, G 5, P 7. This is the amount that

제28장
원장의 공간을 다 사용한 경우 새 원장을 만드는 방법

어느 계정 원장의 공간을 다 사용한 경우, 즉 어느 계정 원장의 차변이든 대변이든 그 어느 한쪽을 다 사용하여 여백이 없는 경우에는 그 나머지 한쪽의 여백에 그 어떤 기록도 해서는 안 된다. 즉시 맨 뒤 페이지로 이동하여 기록해야 한다. 현재의 계정 원장과 다른 계정 원장 사이에 여백이 없기 때문이다. 이렇게 하지 않으면 그것은 사기 또는 가짜 장부가 될 것이다. 그것은 손익결산편에서 설명한 방식으로 이동해야 한다. 이동, 즉 이월할 때에는 원장에만 기록하고, 분개장에는 그 어떤 기록도 해서는 안 된다. 이월은 분개장에서 이루어지는 것이 아니기 때문이다. 취향에 따라 분개장에 기록해도 무방하나 그것은 불필요한 일이다. 쓸데없이 고생만 많기 때문이다. 해야 할 일은 차변과 대변 잔액 중 작은 쪽을 더해주면 된다. 즉, 차변이 크면 그 차액을 대변에 가산하여 대차를 일치시키면 되는 것이다. 예시는 다음과 같다.

마르티노 씨와의 거래가 많다 보니, 그의 계정 원장은 30페이지로부터 이월되어야 한다고 가정한다. 그리고 현재 원장의 마지막 페이지는 60페이지라고 가정한다. 즉 60페이지에 마르티노 계정 잔액을 이월할 수 있다고 가정한다. 현재 차변 금액은 L 80, S 15, G 15, P 24이고, 대변 금액은 L 72, S 9, G 3, P 17이다. 따라서 차액은 L 8, S 6, G 5, P 7이다. 이 금액이 새로운 페이지의 차변에 기록될 금액이다. 그리고 30페이지에는 대변에 이 금액을 기록하여 다음과 같이 대차를 일치시켜야 한다.

날짜, 기타 사항, 나는 차변 잔액을 이월하고, 이 금액을 여기, 즉 대변에 기록하여 대차를 일치시킨다. 금액은 L 8, S 6, G 5, P 7이고, 이월은 60페이지다.

you should bring forward to the debit side of the new page, and on the old page you must add the same amount in the credit column to make it balance, saying as follows:

On such and such day, etc., per himself, I bring forward (*porta avanti*) this amount to the debit side as a remainder (*resta*), and the same amount I enter here per closing (*saldo*), that is: L 8, S 6, G 5, P 7. see at page 60:

L____, S____, G____, P____

And you shall cancel the account both on the debit and credit side with a diagonal line. After that, you will go to page 60 and shall enter in the debit column the said remainder, always writing down at the top of the page the year, if none already has been mentioned, as has been said above. You shall enter there as follows:

Martino debit on such and such day per himself, as per remainder (*resta*) taken from the page of his old account and therein entered per closing (*saldo*), see page 30:

This is the way for you to proceed with all accounts that you should transfer: Place them, as I have told you, without leaving any space in between. The accounts should be opened in the order in which they originate in such place and at such time, so that nobody can speak evil of you.

                                                    L____, S____, G____, P____

 그리고 구 계정 원장의 차변과 대변에 대각선을 긋고, 즉 소인을 한 후에 60페이지로 가서 차변에 위의 금액을 다음과 같이 기록해야 한다.
 마르티노 계정 차변, 마르티노의 구 계정 원장의 마지막 페이지에서 이월된 금액이며, 구 계정 원장의 페이지는 30이다.

                                                    L____, S____, G____, P____

 이것이 계정 잔액을 이월하는 방법이다. 그리고 사이에 아무런 공간도 남기지 말고 기록해야 한다. 새로운 계정 원장은 사유가 발생한 곳과 시간 순서에 따라 개설되어야 한다. 그러면 아무도 당신을 비방하지 않을 것이다.

 | 해설 | 원장의 이월(잔액 넘기기)방법

 〈마르티노 원장, 30페이지〉

	차변	대변
기중 거래분	80,000	72,000
새 원장으로 이월		8,000
합계	80,000	80,000

 〈마르티노 원장, 60페이지〉

	차변	대변
구 원장에서 이월	8,000	
합계	8,000	

 원장의 잔액 이월방법은 은행의 예금통장 이월방법과 같다.

CHAPTER 29

HOW TO CHANGE THE YEAR IN THE LEDGER BETWEEN TWO SUCCESSIVE ENTRIES IN CASE THE BOOKS ARE NOT CLOSED EVERY YEAR

It might be that you must change the year in your ledger accounts before you balance it. In this case, you should write the year in the margin before the first entry of the new year, as has been previously said at Chapter 15; all the following entries should be understood as having occurred during that year.

But it is always good to close the books each year, especially if you are in partnership with others. The proverb says: Frequent accounting makes for long friendship. Thus you will do in similar cases.

제29장

원장을 매년 갱신하지 않는 경우 원장의 연도를 바꾸는 방법

결산을 하기 전에 계정 원장의 연도를 바꾸어야 하는 경우도 있다. 이때는 15장에서 설명한 바와 같이 새로운 연도의 거래를 기록하기 전에 여백에 연도를 기록하면 된다. 모든 거래는 그해에 발생한 것으로 이해될 수 있도록 기록되어야 하기 때문이다.

그러나 같은 장부를 수년간 사용하는 것보다는 매년 마감하는 것, 즉 매년 새로운 장부를 사용하는 것이 더 좋은 방법인데, 특히 공동 사업을 할 경우에 그렇다. 계산이 우정을 지속시킨다는 속담이 있다. 이 속담은 당신 그리고 당신의 사업에도 적용될 것이다.

CHAPTER 30

HOW AN ABSTRACT OR STATEMENT OF AN ACCOUNT SHOULD BE MADE TO A DEBTOR WHO MIGHT REQUEST IT, OR FOR YOUR EMPLOYER IN CASE YOU ARE MANAGER OR COMMISSIONER OF THE ADMINISTRATION OF HIS PROPERTY

In addition, you must know how to make an abstract or a statement of an account if your debtor requests it. This is a favor that can not be refused, especially if your debtor has had an account with you for years or months, etc. In this case you should go away back to the time when you began to have transactions with him, or back to the time from which he desires to have his statement, in case you have had previous settlements. And you should do this willingly. You should copy all his account on a sheet of paper large enough to contain it all. If it should not be large enough, you will draw a balance at the end of the page and shall carry the latter, in debit or credit, forward to the other side of the sheet, as I told you at Chapter 28. And so on, until the end of the account, and at the end you must reduce the whole account to the net remainder in a single entry in debit or credit, according to the facts. These statements must be made out very carefully.

The following is the way you have to proceed in adjusting your own business with the business of your employer. But if you should act for others as an agent or commissioner, then you will make out a statement for your employer just as it appears in the ledger, crediting yourself from time to time with your commissions according to your agreements. Then at the end you shall charge yourself with the net remainder, or you shall credit yourself if you had to put in any money of your own. Your employer will then go through this statement, compare it with his own book, and if he finds it correct, he will like you better and trust you more. For this reason, of all the things that he gave or sent you, you should with your

제30장

채무자 또는 고용주를 위하여 계정 요약서를 작성하는 방법

　채무자가 내역서를 요구하는 경우도 있으므로 요약서를 작성하는 방법도 알아야 한다. 채무자가 당신과 아주 오랫동안 거래한 사람인 경우에는 이러한 요구를 거절하지 않는 것이 정도다. 이 경우 당신은 거래의 개시 시점 또는 채무자가 요구하는 시점으로 거슬러 올라가서 이러한 업무를 기꺼이 해주어야 한다. 먼저 큰 종이를 준비하여 거래 내역을 복사해야 한다. 종이가 크지 않은 경우에는 각 페이지의 끝에 차변과 대변 각각의 합계를 기록하고, 그 합계를 다음 페이지로 이월하면 된다. 그리고 맨 마지막에는 대차 어느 한쪽의 잔액, 즉 순잔액(이 경우에는 미회수액)을 기록하여 정리해야 한다. 그리고 이 작업은 신중하게 이루어져야 한다.

　다음은 당신을 고용한 사람과 관련된 업무를 처리하는 데 사용하는 방법이다. 그러나 당신이 다른 사람의 대리인으로 활동하는 경우에는 원장의 기록을 근거로 하여 보고서를 작성해야 할 것이다. 또한 때때로 계약에 따른 커미션으로 인하여 대리인 자신을 대기해야 하는 경우도 있을 것이다. 보통은 보고서의 끝에 대리인 자신을 차기하는 것으로 마무리되지만, 대리인이 자신의 돈을 투입하는 경우에는 자신의 이름을 대기해야 한다. 그러면 고용주는 이 보고서를 훑어볼 것이고, 자신의 장부와 비교하여 오류가 없는 것을 확인하고 나면 당신을 더 좋아하고 신뢰하게 될 것이다. 이러한 이유로 고용주로부터 어떤 것을 받을 때는 그 내역을 체계적으로 기록해두어야 한다. 이 점 명심하기 바란다.

own handwriting keep an orderly account when you receive them. Observe this carefully.

On the contrary, if you are the employer, you may have your managers or commissioners make out these statements for you. But before these statements are delivered they ought to be compared carefully with each entry in the Ledger, Journal and Memorandum Book, or with any other paper relative thereto, so that no mistake could be made between the parties.

반대로 당신이 고용주인 경우에는 대리인들로 하여금 보고서를 작성, 제출하도록 요구하게 된다. 이 보고서는 반드시 원장, 분개장 및 일지 등의 기록과 관련 증빙과 대조되어야 하고, 이렇게 해야 당사자 간에 실수가 발생하지 않는다.

CHAPTER 31

HOW TO TAKE OUT ONE OR MORE ENTRIES WHICH BY MISTAKE YOU MIGHT HAVE ENTERED IN A DIFFERENT PLACE FROM THE RIGHT ONE, WHICH MAY HAPPEN THROUGH ABSENTMINDEDNESS

The good bookkeeper should also know how to take out—or as they call it in Florence "*stornare*"—an entry which by mistake you might have written down in the wrong place as, for instance, if you had entered it as a debit instead of a credit entry; or when you have to enter it in the account of Mr. Martino and you put it in the account of Mr. Giovanni.

For at times you cannot be so diligent that you are unable to make mistakes. The proverb says: He who does nothing, makes no mistakes: he who makes no mistakes, learns nothing.

And you shall correct this entry as follows: If you had placed this entry in the debit column while you should have put it in the credit column, in order to correct this, you shall make another entry opposite this one in the credit for the same amount. And you shall say thus: On such and such day for the amount which has been entered opposite here under the debit and should have been put in the credit, see page, etc., and you shall write down in the column of figures:

L____, S____, G____, P____

which you wrote down by mistake in the other column. In front of these two entries you shall mark a cross or any other mark so that when you make out an abstract or statement of the account you should leave these entries out. After you have made this correction it is just as if you had written nothing in the debit column. You then make the entry in the credit column as it should have been and everything will be as it should have been.

제31장
실수로 다른 곳에 기록한 것을 교정하는 방법

유능한 부기자는 실수를 교정할 줄 알아야 한다. 플로렌스에서는 이를 'stornare'라고 하는데, 기록상의 오류라는 것은 대기해야 할 것을 차기한다든가, 마르티노 원장에 기록해야 할 것을 지오반니 원장에 기록하는 따위 등이다.

가끔은 아무리 주의해도 어쩔 수 없이 실수를 하는 경우가 있다. 아무것도 하지 않는 사람은 실수가 없다. 그러나 실수하지 않는 자는 아무것도 배우지 못한다는 속담도 있다.

교정은 다음과 같이 한다. 대기해야 할 것을 차기한 경우에는 같은 금액을 차기한 반대편, 즉 대변에 기록한 후 다음과 같이 주를 단다. 몇 월 몇 일에 대기해야 할 것을 차기하였다. 분개장 페이지는 몇 페이지이고, 실수로 다른 칸에 쓴 금액은 얼마다. 실수분과 교정분 기록이라는 두 기사의 앞에 십자가 기호 등을 부가하여야 한다. 보고서 등을 작성할 때 이 기록은 제외해야 하기 때문이다. 이렇게 교정을 하면 차변에는 아무것도 기록하지 않은 것처럼 된다. 그리고 나서 원래의 자리인 대변에 기록을 하면 모든 것이 제자리에 기록되는 것이다.

| 해설 | 잘못된 분개의 교정시 그 잘못된 분개를 삭제 또는 수정해서는 안 된다는 뜻이다. 조선왕조실록처럼 원본은 그대로 둔 채, 추가본을 부가하는 방식이어야 한다는 뜻이다. 즉, 분개의 교정은 덧대기 방식이어야 한다.

① 오류 분개: 입금 차입금 1,000
- 오류 원인: 차입한 사실이 없음

② 수정 분개: 출금 차입금 1,000
- 분개 결과: 이 분개로 차입금 잔액은 0원이 된다.
- 이러한 분개를 반대 분개 또는 덧대기 분개라고 한다.

CHAPTER 32

HOW THE BALANCE OF THE LEDGER IS MADE AND HOW THE ACCOUNTS OF AN OLD LEDGER ARE TRANSFERRED TO A NEW ONE

After all we have said you must know now how to carry forward the accounts from one Ledger to another if you want to have a new Ledger for the reason that the old one is all filled up or because another year begins, as is customary in the best known places, especially at Milan where the big merchants renew every year their Ledgers.

This operation, together with the operations of which we will speak, is called the balancing (*bilancio*) of the Ledger, and if you want to do this well you shall do it with great diligence and order. That is, first you shall get a helper as you could hardly do it alone. You give him the Journal for greater precaution and you shall keep the Ledger. Then you tell him, beginning with the first entry in the Journal, to call the numbers of the pages of your Ledger where that entry has been made, first in debit and then in credit. Accordingly in turn you shall obey him and shall always find the page in the Ledger that he calls and you shall ask him what kind of an entry it is, that is, for what and for whom, and you shall look at the pages to which he refers to see if you find that item and that account. If the amount is the same, call it out. If you find it there the same as in the journal, check it (*lanzarala*—mark it with a lance Λ or V) or dot it (*pontarala*), or any proper mark over the lire mark, or in some other place, so that you can readily see it. You ask your helper to make a similar mark or check—as we are used to call it in some places—in the Journal at the same entry. Care must be taken that no entry will be dotted (*pontata*) either by you without him, or by him without you, as great mistakes might be made

제32장

원장 기록의 검증, 즉 시산표 작성방법과 구 장부의 계정 잔액을 새 장부로 넘기는 방법

상인은 원장의 잔액을 이월하는 방법을 알아야 한다. 장부에 더 이상의 기록공간이 없거나 새해가 되었거나 하는 이유로 새 장부를 사용해야 하는 경우가 있기 때문이고, 특히 밀라노에서는 매년 장부를 갱신하는 관습이 있다.

이 작업을 balancing(bilancio)이라고 한다. 이 작업을 잘 하려면 신중함이 요구된다. 먼저 이 작업을 혼자서 하기는 어려우므로 협조자를 구해야 한다. 협조자에게 분개장을 주고 당신은 원장을 갖는다. 그리고 분개장의 첫 기사부터 시작하여 전기된 원장의 페이지 번호를 차변과 대변 순으로 불러달라고 요구해야 한다. 즉, 분개장 좌단에 기록된 페이지 번호를 소리쳐 외치라고 요구해야 한다. 당신은 그가 부른 페이지를 찾은 후, 그에게 거래 내역을 물어야 한다. 그리고 금액이 같으면 대조필 또는 확인완료 신호를 보낸다. 원장과 분개장을 대조하여 양자가 일치함을 확인하면, 창(∧ 또는 ∨) 표시 또는 점, 기타 적당한 표시, 즉 소인을 해야 하며 그 위치는 lire 마크 또는 다른 적당한 위치에 하면 된다. 이는 나중에 쉽게 위치를 찾기 위함이다. 그리고 협조자에게도 그가 갖고 있는 분개장에 확인필 표시를 하도록 해야 한다. 그러나 어느 한쪽의 동의 없이 소인을 해서는 안 된다. 소인은 그 기사가 정상적인 기록이라는 것을 인증하는 것이므로 동의 없는 소인이나 임의적 소인은 중대한 오류를 초래할 수도 있기 때문이다. 채무자에게 제공하는 내역도 같은 방식으로 확인 절차를 거친 후에 제공해야 한다. 즉, 분개장과 원장 양자를 대조하고 아울러 관련 문서까지 조사하여 확인한 후에 채무자에게 제공해야 한다는 의미이다.

이런 식으로 모든 원장과 분개장을 처리하여 두 장부의 대차가 일치하면, 그것은 모

otherwise, for once the entry is dotted it means that it is correct. The same is done in making out statements of accounts for your debtors before you deliver them. They should have been compared with the Ledger and Journal, or with any other writing in which the entries of the transaction have been recorded, as we have said at Chapter 30.

After you have proceeded in this way through all the accounts of the Ledger and Journal and found that the two books correspond in debit and credit, it will mean that all the accounts are correct and the entries entered correctly. Take care that your helper shall mark each entry in the Journal with two dots or little lances; in the ledger you mark down only one for each entry because you know that for each entry in the journal there are two made in the Ledger, therefore, the two dots or lances.

In making this balance it is good if you mark in the Journal two dots or lances under the lire, one under the other. This will mean that the entry is correct in debit and credit in the Ledger. Some use these marks in the Journal: They put a mark before the per for the debit and after the lire for the credit. Any way both customs are good, however, one single mark in the Journal might be enough, that is, only the debit mark, because you can then mark yourself the credit side on the page of the Ledger where that entry is as this page is mentioned in the debit entry in your ledger. It will then not be necessary for your helper to call to you this credit page. So that by comparing only the debit side with him you could yourself check the credit side. But it would be more convenient for you if you proceed with your helper in the manner above said.

After you have finished checking off the Journal, if you find in the Ledger some account or entry which has not been checked off in debit or credit, this would indicate that there has been some mistake in the Ledger, that is, that that entry is superfluous whether in the debit or credit, and you shall correct this error by making an entry for the same amount in the opposite side—that is, if the superfluous entry was in the debit, you make an entry on the credit side, or *vice versa*. And how you should proceed to correct the error I have told you in the preceding chapter. The same would be done in case your helper finds some entry which your ledger did not show whether in the debit or credit column, which also

든 분개와 전기가 정확하게 기록되었음을 의미한다. 협조자로 하여금 분개장에 소인케 하고 원장은 당신이 소인을 하되, 분개장의 한 분개가 두 개의 원장에 기록되므로 원장의 소인을 두 번 해야 한다는 것을 알고 있어야 한다.

　분개장 소인은 lire 마크 밑 또는 다른 적당한 장소에 점 또는 창 표시를 하는 것이 좋다. 분개장 소인은 그 기사가 원장의 대차변으로 정확하게 전기되었음을 의미한다. 어떤 사람들은 차기 소인은 Per 근처에, 대기 소인은 lire 다음에 하기도 한다. 어느 방법이든 좋으나 분개장 소인은 차변에 한 번만 해도 충분하다. 이 페이지가 원장의 차변에 언급되어 있으므로 대변에는 당신이 직접 소인하면 되기 때문이다. 협조자로 하여금 대변 페이지를 소리쳐 부르게 하는 것은 불필요하다. 차변을 그와 대조하여 당신이 대변을 소인할 수 있기 때문이다. 그러나 협조자와 상기의 방식으로 진행하는 것이 편리할 것이다.

　분개장 소인을 완료한 후, 원장의 특정 계정 또는 기록에서 대차 어느 한쪽이 소인되지 않은 것이 발견될 수도 있는데, 이것은 원장에 오류가 있었음을 의미한다. 이 경우 대차가 일치하지 않으므로 이를 수정해야 한다. 이 오류는 반대편에 동액을 기록하면 된다. 즉, 차변이 대변보다 크면 대변에 차액을 기록하여 양자를 일치시킨다. 그리고 협조자가 원장의 대차 어느 쪽에도 안 보이는 분개를 발견할 수도 있는데, 이것은 원장의 오류이므로, 그 교정은 좀 다른 방법으로 이루어져야 한다. 즉, 전기를 하거나 새로운 계정을 개설하고, 실제 날짜보다 늦게 전기되었음을 언급하면 된다. 유능한 부기자는 왜 이러한 차이가 발생하는지를 항상 설명할 수 있어야 한다. 그렇게 하면 장부에 대한 불신을 제거할 수 있기 때문이다. 그리고 공증인은 그 문서에서 추가 또는 생략된 것을 언급할 필요가 없다. 유능한 부기자는 그 상업적 신뢰도가 제고되도록 처신해야 한다.

　만일 앞에서 언급한 기사가 대차 어느 한쪽에만 전기된 경우에는 빠진 것만 보충하여 기록하고, 그 이유를 언급해주면 된다. 이런 식으로 모든 계정을 확인한 후 그들이 이에 대하여 동의하면 당신은 당신의 장부가 정확하고 잘 관리된 것으로 확신할 수 있다.

　또 분개장에 없거나 분개장에서 발견되지 않는 기록이 원장에 나타날 수도 있다. 이것은 잔액을 이월할 때, 다른 계정 원장을 마감하기 위하여 기록한 대차 차액이다. 이 잔액의 원인이 되는 기사를 원장에서 찾아 그것이 제자리에 있으면, 그 원장은 정확하게 기록된 것으로 간주하여도 무방하다.

would indicate an error in the ledger and should be corrected in a different way. That is, you should make that entry or open that account in the debit or credit, mentioning the different dates, as the entry would be made later than it should have been. A good bookkeeper should always mention why such differences arise, so that the books are above suspicion; thus the notary public in his instruments need not mention what has been added or omitted. Thus the good bookkeeper must act so that the mercantile reputation be kept up.

But if the said entry should have been entered on only one side, debit or credit, then it would be sufficient for you to put it where it is missing, mentioning how it happened through mistake, etc. So you will go on through all your accounts and, if they agree, you know that your Ledger is right and well kept.

You must know that there may be found in the Ledger some entries which are not in the Journal and cannot be found in the Journal. These are the difference between the debit and credit placed there to close (*per saldi*) the different accounts when they are carried forward, as we have said in Chapter 28. Of these balances or remainders, you will find their correlative entries in the Ledger, whether in debit or credit, on the page indicated in these accounts. When you find each correlative entry in its proper place, you may conclude that your Ledger is in proper order.

What we have said so far about comparing the Ledger with the Journal, should be observed also in comparing the memorandum book or scrap book with the Journal, day by day, if you use the memorandum book, in the manner I spoke about at the beginning of this treatise. If you have other books, you should do the same. The last book to be compared should be the Ledger, the next to the last the Journal.

지금까지 설명한 것은 원장과 분개장의 대조에 관한 것이며, 일지를 기록하는 경우에는 일지와 분개장의 대조시에도 상기의 방법이 적용 준수되어야 한다. 그리고 그 외의 다른 장부를 기록하는 경우에도 역시 같은 방법이 적용되어야 한다. 가장 마지막으로 대조해야 할 것은 원장이고, 그 다음은 분개장이다.

CHAPTER 33

HOW THE TRANSACTIONS WHICH MIGHT OCCUR WHILE YOU BALANCE YOUR BOOKS SHOULD BE RECORDED, AND HOW IN THE OLD BOOKS NO ENTRY SHOULD BE MADE OR CHANGED DURING THAT TIME, AND REASONS WHY

After you have regularly done and observed all these things, see that no new entry is made in any book which comes before the Ledger—that is, in the memorandum book and Journal—because the equalizing or closing (*el saldo*) of all the books should be understood to take place on the same day. But if, while you are balancing your books, some transactions should occur, you shall enter them in the new books to which you intend to carry forward the old ones—that is, in the memorandum book or Journal, but not in the Ledger, until you have carried forward all the different accounts of the old Ledger. If you have not yet a new set of books, then you will record these transactions and their respective explanations on a separate sheet of paper until the books are ready. When the new books are ready, you enter them in these books which shall bear new marks—that is, if the old ones that you are balancing now were marked with a cross, then you should mark these new ones with the capital letter A.

제33장

결산 도중에 발생하는 거래의 기록방법, 그리고 결산 도중 구 장부에 어떠한 기록도 해서는 안 되는 이유

상기의 작업을 완료한 후에는 분개장과 일지에 새로운 기록이 없는지 살펴보아야 한다. 모든 계정 원장의 대차 일치 작업은 그날에 모두 끝내야 하기 때문이다. 일치 작업 도중에 거래가 발생할 수도 있고, 이 경우 거래는 새 일지와 새 분개장에 기록해야 한다. 즉, 모든 계정의 잔액을 이월할 때까지는 원장에 기록할 수 없고, 분개장과 일지에만 기록할 수 있기 때문이다. 새로운 장부를 아직 준비하지 못한 경우에는 별도의 종이에 기록했다가 새 장부에 기록하면 된다. 헌 장부의 기호가 십자가 표시인 경우에 새 장부의 기호는 문자 A로 해야 한다.

CHAPTER 34

HOW ALL THE ACCOUNTS OF THE OLD LEDGER SHOULD BE CLOSED AND WHY. ABOUT THE GRAND TOTALS OF THE DEBITS AND CREDITS, WHICH IS THE PREPARATION OF THE TRIAL BALANCE

After you have done this carefully, you shall close your Ledger accounts in this way: You should commence first with cash account, then the different debtors, then the merchandise, and then your customers. Transfer the remainders in Ledger A, that is, in the new Ledger. You should not, as I have said above, transfer the remainders in the new Journal.

You shall add all the different entries in debit and in credit, always adding to the smaller side the difference, as I have told you above when explaining the carrying forward of the remainder. These two accounts are practically the same thing; the only difference is that in the first case the remainder was carried forward to another page of the same Ledger, while in this instance it is carried forward from one Ledger to another. While in the first instance you would mark down the new page of the same Ledger, in this case you mark down the page of the new Ledger; making the transfer from one ledger to another, any account should appear only once in each ledger. This is a peculiarity of the last entry of the accounts of the Ledgers.

In making the transfer, you should proceed as follows: Let us suppose that the account of Mr. Martino has a debit remainder (*resto*) in your "Cross" Ledger at page 60 of L 12, S. 15, G 10. P. 26, and you want to transfer it to Ledger A at page 8 in debit; in the "Cross" Ledger you have to add to the credit column and you shall put the following at the end of all the other entries: On such and such day—putting down always the same day in which you do the balancing (*bilancio*)—per himself as

제34장

구 장부 각 계정의 마감과 그 이유. 원장의 차변과 대변 각각의 합계로 결산 및 장부기록을 검증하는 것에 대하여

　　각 계정의 대차 일치작업을 한 후 계정 원장은 다음과 같이 마감한다. 먼저 현금계정, 채무자계정, 상품계정 그리고 고객계정 순으로 진행한다. A원장, 즉 새 원장에 잔액을 기록하라. 전술한 바와 같이 분개장에 이월하는 것이 아니라 원장에 이월한다는 것을 명심해야 한다.

　　이제 차변과 대변 각변 금액의 총액을 산출해야 하고, 내가 앞에서 잔액의 이월에 대하여 설명한 것처럼 대차 차액을 작은 쪽에 가산해야 한다. 신구 두 계정은 실질적으로 동일한 것이다. 차이가 있다면, 하나는 원장의 다른 페이지로 잔액을 넘긴 계정이고, 다른 하나는 다른 페이지에서 잔액을 넘겨받았다는 것뿐이다. 이월작업을 하면 같은 원장의 새 페이지 번호를 기록해야 하는데, 여기서는 새 원장에 이월하는 것이므로 새 원장의 페이지를 기록하면 될 것이다. 새 원장으로 이월할 때, 어떤 계정이든 원장에 한 번만 출현해야 한다. 이것이 원장에서 마지막 기록을 할 때의 특성이다.

　　이월은 다음과 같이 실시한다. 먼저 마르티노 씨의 잔액이 차변 잔액이고 금액이 L 12, S 15, G 10, P 26이고, 그 내역이 60페이지에 기록되어 있다고 가정한다. 이를 새 원장(A원장)의 8페이지 대변으로 이월하고자 하는 경우, 십자가 원장, 즉 구 원장의 대변에 더하기를 하고, 원장의 마지막 부분에 다음과 같이 설명문을 추가한다. 몇 월 몇 일, 즉 대차 일치 작업하는 날에 — 항상 대차 일치 작업일자와 같은 날짜를 기록해야 한다 — 새 원장의 차변에 잔액을 이월하기 위하여 여기, 즉 대변에 L 12, S 15, G 10, P 26의 금액을 가산한다. 그리고 참조 페이지는 새 원장의 8페이지 등의 적요를 기입해야 한다.

posted to Ledger A to the debit, per remainder (*resto*), which amount I add here in order to close (*saldo*)—value; see page 8: L 12, S 15, G 10, P 26.

And then you shall cancel the account in the debit and credit diagonally, as I have told you in talking about the bringing forward of the accounts. Then put down the total of all the entries, in the debit as well as in the credit, so that the eye can see at a glance that it is all even. You shall also write down at the new page in Ledger A, in the debit column, as follows: First you put down at the top of the page the year, and you put the day in front of the place where you make the entry for the reason mentioned in Chapter 15, then you say, Mr. Martino so and so, debit (*dee dare*—shall give) on such and such day per himself as per remainder (*resto*) carried from "Cross" Ledger, which has been added in the credit column in order to close (*saldo*), see page 60, value: L 12, S 15, G 10, P 26.

Thus you will proceed with all the accounts of the Cross Ledger which you want to transfer to Ledger A: cash account, capital account, merchandise, personal property, real property, debtors, creditors, public officers, brokers, public weighmen, etc., with whom we have sometimes very long accounts. But as to those accounts which you should not care to transfer to Ledger A, as, for instance, your own personal accounts of which you are not obliged to give an account to another, as, for instance, small mercantile expenses, household expenses, income and expenses and all extraordinary expenses—rentals, *pescioni*, *feudi* or *livelli*, etc. All these accounts should be closed (*saldore*) in the Cross Ledger into the favor and damage account, or increase and deficit, or profit and damage account, as it is sometimes called. You shall enter them in the debit column, as it is rare that these expense accounts should show anything in the credit side. As I often have told you, add the difference to the column, either debit or credit, which shows a smaller total, saying: Per profit and loss in this account, see page, etc. By doing so, you shall have closed (*saldore*) all these different accounts in the profit and loss account through which then, by adding all the debit and all the credit entries, you will be able to know what is your gain or loss, for with this balance all entries are equalized; the things that had to be deducted were deducted, and the things that had to be added were added proportionately in their respective places. If this account shows more in the debit than in the credit, that means that you have lost

그리고 나서 앞에서 계정 이월에 대하여 설명한 것처럼 차변과 대변에 대각선을 긋는다. 즉 소인을 한다. 그리고 대차 각각의 합계를 기록하여 한눈에 대차가 일치함을 확인할 수 있게 한다. 다음에 새 원장의 차변에 다음과 같이 기록해야 한다. 먼저 상단에 연도를 기입하고 제15장에서 설명한 이유를 기록하는 곳의 앞쪽에 일자를 기입한다. 그리고 마르티노 씨, 차변(그가 어느 날짜에 나에게 주어야 한다), 마감을 위하여 내가 구 원장의 대변에 기록된 잔액을 여기로 이월했다. 참조 페이지는 60페이지다. 금액 L 12, S 15, G 10, P 26과 같이 기록한다.

구 원장에서 새 원장으로 이월을 원하는 모든 계정에 대하여 이와 같은 작업을 실시해야 한다. 현금 원장, 출자자 원장, 상품 원장, 유동자산 원장, 부동산 원장, 채무자 원장, 채권자 원장, 공공 감독자 원장, 브로커 원장, 공공 계측사 원장 등 모든 계정에 대하여 상기의 작업을 실시한다. 그러나 새 원장으로 이월할 필요가 없는 계정도 있다. 이는 다른 사람에게 제출 또는 알려야 할 필요가 없는 사적인 계정들이다. 사적인 원장이란 소사업비, 가계비, 수익과 비용 및 모든 비경상비 원장 ― 임대료 원장 등 ― 이다. 이 계정 원장의 잔액은 새 원장이 아니라 구 원장의 손익계정으로 이월되어야 한다. 이 손익계정은 손해와 이익, 증가와 결손, 이익과 손해 원장 등으로 불리기도 한다. 이 잔액은 손익계정의 차변에 전기되어야 한다. 비용계정 잔액이 대변에 전기될 수도 있지만 이것은 매우 드문 일이다. 내가 여러 번 언급한 것처럼, 대차 차액을 작은 쪽에 더해주고, 다음과 같이 설명을 추가하면 된다. 이 잔액을 손익계정으로 이체하고, 손익계정의 몇 페이지에 이월한다. 이렇게 손익계정으로 이체한 후, 손익계정의 차변 합계와 대변 합계를 산출한 후 이를 비교하면 손익 여부를 쉽게 파악할 수 있다. 손익계정의 차변 금액이 더 크면 사업기간 중에 손실이 발생한 것이고, 반대의 경우에는 순이익이 발생한 것이다.

이들 계정을 마감하여 순손실인지 순이익인지를 파악한 후에는 이 잔액, 즉 순이익 또는 순손실을 사업 개시 시점에 재물 내역을 기록했던 자본금 계정으로 이체하여 손익계정을 마감해야 한다. 손익계정은 다음과 같이 마감한다. 손실이 발생하면 ― 하나님은 성실한 기독교인으로 생활하는 사람이라면 그가 어떠한 상황에 있을지라도 지켜주신다 ― 그 순손실액을 대변에 가산하며, 몇 월 몇 일에 손실을 자본금 계정으로 이체하며, 그 금액과 참조 페이지는 ~이다. 그리고 손익계정의 대차 양방을 대각선을 그어 소인한 후,

that much in your business since you began, If the credit is more than the debit, that means that in the same period of time you have gained.

After you know by the closing (*saldorai*) of this account what your profit or loss is, then you shall close this account into the capital account in which, at the beginning of your management of your business, you entered the inventory of all your worldly goods. You shall close the account in this way: If the losses are in excess—from which state of affairs may God keep every one who really lives as a good Christian—then you have to add to the credit in the usual manner, saying: On such and such day, Per capital on account of losses in this account, see page so and so, value, etc. Then you shall cancel the account with a diagonal line in debit and credit, and put in the total amount of all the debit entries, as well as of the credit entries, which should be equal. And then in the capital account, you shall write in the debit column: Capital debit (*dee dare*—shall give) on such and such day, per profit and loss account on account of losses as marked down in the credit column of said account in order to close (*per saldo*), value, etc.:   L____, S____, G____, P____

If instead there should be a profit, which will happen when the profit and loss account would show more in the credit than in the debit, then you should add the difference to the debit side to make the equalization, referring to the capital account and respective page. You should credit the same amount to the capital account, making the entry on the credit side where all the other goods of yours have been entered, personal or real. Therefore, from the capital account, which always must be the last account in the entire Ledger, you may always learn what your fortune is, by adding together all the debits and all the credits, which you have transferred in Ledger A.

Then this capital account should be closed and carried forward with the other accounts to Ledger A, either in total or entry by entry. You can do either way, but it is customary to transfer only the total amount, so that the entire value of your inventory (*inventario*) is shown at a glance. Don't forget to number the pages, after which you will enter all the different accounts in the alphabet of Ledger A, each at its own place, as I have said Chapter 5, so that you may find very easily the account you want. In this way the entire first Ledger, and with it the Journal and memorandum book, are closed and closed up.

대차 각각의 합계를 기록하여 대차가 일치하는지 확인한다. 그러고 나서 자본금계정 원장의 차변에 다음과 같이 기록한다. 자본금계정 차변, 손익계정을 마감하여 그 대변에 기록된 금액을 어느 날짜에 여기로 이체한다. 금액은 얼마이다.

반대로 순이익이 발생하면, 손익계정 원장의 대변 금액이 차변 금액보다 더 클 것이다. 그러면 그 차액을 차변에 가산하여 대차를 일치시킨다. 그러고는 자본금계정의 대변에 순이익을 이체기록한다. 자본금계정에는 재물기에서 전기한 동산, 부동산 및 상품 기록들이 보일 것이다. 자본금계정은 계정 중에서 가장 마지막 계정이며, 이 계정에서 사업자의 순재산 상태를 파악할 수 있다. 즉, 자본금계정에 기록된 대차 각각의 합계를 산출한 후 잔액을 산출함으로써 자본, 즉 순재산을 파악할 수 있는 것이다. 그리고 이 잔액이 새 원장으로 이월되는 것이다.

자본금 원장의 잔액도 새 원장으로 이월되는 동시에 마감되어야 한다. 이월은 총액으로 할 수도 있고, 출자 건별로 이월할 수도 있으며, 어느 방식이든 무방하다. 그러나 오직 총액만 이월하는 것이 관행이다. 그렇게 해야 재산 총액을 한눈에 파악할 수 있기 때문이다. 그리고 새 원장에 기록한 후에는 페이지 번호를 매기는 것을 명심해야 한다. 이미 제5장에서 언급한 바와 같이 그렇게 해야 계정 원장 찾기가 수월하기 때문이다. 이런 식으로 먼저 원장이 마감되고, 다음에는 분개장, 일지순으로 마감된다.

마감 전에 각 원장기록의 정확성을 제고하려면, 한 장의 종이를 준비한 다음, 구 원장에 나타난 모든 (계정의) 차변 총액을 그 종이의 좌측에, 대변 총액은 모두 우측에 기록해야 한다. 차변 총액을 합계한 대총액(숨마숨마룸)을 산출한다. 마찬가지로 대변 총액의 숨마숨마룸도 산출하여야 한다. 즉, 차변과 대변 총합계가 산출된 것이다. 이 두 금액이 일치하면, 내가 제14장에서 설명한 바에 의하여 당신의 장부가 제대로 기록 및 마감되었다고 결론 내려도 된다. 그러나 차이가 나면, 원장에 오류가 있는 것이므로 하나님이 주신 지혜와 여태까지 배운 것의 도움으로 오류를 찾아내야 한다. 이러한 능력은 서두에 말한 바와 같이 상인에게 매우 필요한 것이다. 사업을 하는 자가 장부 기록방법을 모르는 것은 눈을 감고 헤매는 격이고, 결국은 거대한 손실로 귀착되기 때문이다.

그러므로 상인은 내가 이 훌륭한 책에서 충분히 설명한 방법에 따라 유능한 부기자가 되도록 모든 노력을 기울여야 한다. 나는 모든 규칙을 설명했고, 이 책의 서두에서 제

In order that it may be clearer that the books were correct before the said closing, you shall summarize on a sheet of paper all the debit totals that appear in the Cross Ledger and place them at the left, then you shall write down all the credit totals at the right. Of all these debit totals you make one sum total which is called grand total (*summa summarum*), and likewise you shall make a sum total of all the credit totals, which is also called grand total (*summa summarum*). The first is the grand total of the debits, and the second is the grand total of the credits. Now, if these two grand totals are equal—that is, if one is just as much as the other—that is, if those of the debit and those of the credit are alike—then you shall conclude that your Ledger was very well kept and closed, for the reason that I gave you in Chapter 14. But if one of the grand totals is bigger than the other, that would indicate a mistake in your Ledger, which mistake you will have to look for diligently with the industry and the intelligence God gave you and with the help of what you have learned. This part of the work, as we said at the beginning, is highly necessary to the good merchant, for, if you are not a good bookkeeper in your business, you will go on groping like a blind man and may meet great losses.

Therefore, take good care and make all efforts to be a good bookkeeper, such as I have shown you fully in this sublime work how to become one. I have given you all the rules and indicated the places where everything can be found, in the table of contents which I have placed at the beginning of this work.

Of all the things thus far treated, as I promised you in Chapter 12, I will now give you a summary of the most essential things for your own recollection, which no doubt will be very useful to you.

And remember to pray God for me so that to His praise and glory I may always go on doing good.

시한 순서에 따라 모든 내용을 찾을 수 있는 곳도 설명했다.

　내가 제12장에서 약속한 바와 같이, 지금까지 다루어진 모든 것 중에서 복습을 위하여 가장 핵심적인 내용을 요약하여 알려주고자 한다. 이것이 당신들에게 매우 유익할 것이라는 것에 대하여 나는 의심하지 않는다.

　그리고 내가 하나님의 영광과 그에 대한 찬양을 위하여 언제나 선한 일을 할 수 있도록 나를 위하여 하나님께 기도해주기를 바란다.

CHAPTER 35

HOW AND IN WHAT ORDER PAPERS SHOULD BE KEPT, SUCH AS MANUSCRIPTS, FAMILY LETTERS, POLICIES, PROCESSES, JUDGEMENTS AND OTHER INSTRUMENTS OF WRITING AND THE RECORD BOOK OF IMPORTANT LETTERS

Here follow the manner and rules for keeping documents and manuscripts, such as papers relative to payments made, receipts for drafts, or gifts of merchandise, confidential letters, which things are very important for merchants and if they are lost, may cause great danger.

First, we shall talk of confidential letters which you may write to or receive from your customers. You should always keep these in a little desk until the end of the month. At the end of the month tie them together in a bunch and put them away and write on the outside of each the date of receipt and the date of reply, and do this month by month, then, at the end of the year, of all these papers make one big bundle and write on it the year, and put it away. Any time you need a letter, go to these bundles.

Keep in your desk pouches in which to place the letters that your friends may give you to be sent away with your own letters. If the letter should be sent to Rome, put it in the Rome pouch, and if to Florence, put it in the Florence pouch, etc. And then when you send your messenger, put these letters with yours and send them to your correspondent in that particular town. To be of service is always a good thing, and it is customary also to give a gratuity for that good service.

You should have several little compartments, or little bags, as many as there are places or cities in which you do business, as, for instance, Rome, Florence, Naples, Milan, Genoa, Lyon, London, Bruges, and on each little bag you shall write its proper name—that is, you will write on one "Rome," on another "Florence," etc.,

제35장

편지, 증서 및 판결문 등의
보관방법과 문서 수발부 작성에 대하여

여기에서는 지출증빙, 어음수취증, 상품을 선물로 제공한 내역 및 기타 비밀문서 등의 각종 서류 보전방법에 대하여 설명한다. 서류는 상인에게 매우 중요하고, 만일 이것을 분실하면 큰 위험이 닥칠 수도 있다.

고객들과 주고받는 사적인 문서에 대하여 설명한다. 월말까지는 작은 책상에 이 문서들을 보관한다. 월말이 되면 묶어서 다른 곳에 옮겨두며, 그 표면에 수신일자와 발신일자를 기록한다. 매월 이렇게 하다가 연말에 다시 월 단위 묶음을 크게 묶어서 문서고 등에 보전하되, 표면에 연도를 기록해둔다. 필요하면 이 묶음을 찾으면 된다.

그대가 편지를 보낼 때, 친구의 편지도 같이 보내고자 하는 경우에는 그 친구의 편지를 보관하기 위한 주머니를 그대의 책상 위에 준비해두어야 한다. 로마로 보낼 것은 로마 주머니에, 플로렌스에 보낼 것은 플로렌스 주머니에 보관한다. 그러고는 메신저를 불러 이 편지를 그에게 주어, 각 도시에 주재하는 대리인에게 보내면 된다. 남에게 도움이 되는 것은 좋은 일이고, 좋은 서비스에 대하여 감사의 인사를 하는 것이 관례이다.

또한 개설된 사업장 수만큼 작은 가방을 마련하여 거기에 적당한 이름을 쓴 후, 각 사업장에 보낼 문서를 보관해두면 좋다.

and in these bags you shall put the letters that somebody might send you to be forwarded to those places.

When you have answered a letter and sent the answer away, you shall mention on the outside of the said letter the answer, by whom you sent it and the day, just as you did when you received the letter.

As to the day, you shall never forget to mark it in any of your transactions, whether small or large, and especially in writing letters in which these things must be mentioned, namely: the year, the day, the place, and your name. It is customary to put the name at the end of the right side in a corner. It is customary among merchants to write the year and the day and the place at the top at the beginning of the letter. But first, like a good Christian, you shall always remember to write down the glorious name of our Savior—that is, the name of Jesus, or in its place the sign of the Holy Cross, in whose name our transactions must always be made, and you shall do as follows: Cross 1494. On this 17th day of April in Venice.

And then go on with what you want to say—that is, "My very dear," etc. But the students and other people, like the monks or priests, etc., who are not in business, are used to writing the day and year at the end after writing the letter. The merchants are accustomed to put at the top as we have said. If you should do otherwise and not write the day, there will be confusion and you will be made fun of because we say the letter which does not bear the day was written during the night, and the letter which does not bear the place we say that it was written in the other world, not in this one; and besides the fun made of you there would be vexations, which is worse, as I have said.

After you have sent your answer away, you put your letter in its proper place; and what we have said of one letter will apply to all the other letters. It must be observed that when the letters you send away are of importance, you should first make a record of them in a book which is kept for this special purpose. In this book the letter should be copied, word for word, if it is of great importance—as, for instance, the letters of exchange, or letters of goods sent, etc., otherwise only a record of the substantial part should be made similarly as we do in the memorandum book, saying: On this day, etc., we have written to so and so, etc., and we send him the following things, etc., as per his letter of such and such date

어떤 편지에 답장을 보낼 때는 받은 편지의 표면에 답한 내용, 배달자의 이름, 날짜 등을 기록해야 하고 편지를 받았을 때도 마찬가지다.

크든 작든 어떤 거래든 날짜를 잊지 말고 반드시 기록해야 한다. 편지를 쓸 때는 특히 그렇고, 연월일 그리고 주소, 당신의 이름을 잊지 말고 기록해야 한다. 이름은 오른쪽 구석에 쓰며, 연월일, 주소는 상단에 쓰는 것이 상인들의 관습이다. 그러나 무엇보다 중요한 것은 당신이 크리스천이라면 모든 거래는 그의 이름으로 이루어지기 때문에 우리의 구원자이신 예수님의 이름을 반드시 다음과 같이 기록해야 한다.

† 1494년 4월 17일, 베니스.

그러고 나서 'My very dear'로 하고 싶은 이야기를 시작하면 된다. 사업을 하지 않는 성직자나 학생 등은 편지를 다 쓴 후 그 끝에 날짜를 쓴다. 반면에 상인은 편지의 첫 머리에 날짜를 쓴다. 남들과 다르게 하고 싶어서 날짜를 쓰지 않으면 혼란만 일으키고, 남의 조롱거리만 될 뿐이다. 날짜가 없는 편지는 밤에 쓰인 것으로 여기고, 주소가 없는 편지는 이 세상이 아니라 저승에서 쓴 편지로 여기기 때문이다. 게다가 조롱을 받으면 화가 치밀고 그러면 일은 더 악화된다.

어떤 편지에 대하여 답장을 보낸 후에는 그 답장의 원인이 되는 편지를 적절한 장소에 보관해야 한다. 그리고 이것은 다른 모든 편지에도 적용된다. 그것이 중요한 편지인 경우에는 편지기록부에 기록해두어야 한다. 그리고 아주 중요한 편지는 이 기록부에 글자 그대로 복사해두어야 한다. 일반적인 편지는 일지에 기록하듯 핵심 내용만 다음과 같이 기록하면 된다. 날짜, 아무개에게 편지를 쓰고, 다음의 것들을 그에게 보냈다. 이 편지는 그가 어느 날짜에 보낸 것에 대한 답장이고, 이 편지는 어느 파우치에 보관되어 있다.

he requested or gave commission for, etc., which letter we have placed in such and such pouch.

After you have sealed the letter on the outside and addressed it, it is custom of many to mark on the outside your special mark, so that they may know that it is correspondence of a merchant, because great attention is given to merchants, for they are the ones, as we said at the beginning of this treatise, who support our republics.

For this purpose, the Most Reverend Cardinals do likewise, by writing their name on the outside of their correspondence so that nobody could claim as an excuse that he did not know from whom it was. The correspondence of the Holy Father remains open so that its contents may be known, like bulls, privileges, etc., although for things which are more personal or confidential the seal representing the Fisherman (*Pescatore*—St. Peter) is used to seal them.

All these letters, then, month by month, year by year, you shall put together in a bundle and you will keep them in an orderly way in a chest, wardrobe or cupboard. As you receive them during the day, put them aside in the same order, so that if necessary you might find them more easily; and I won't talk any longer about this, as I know that you have understood it.

You shall keep in a more secret place, as private boxes and chests, all manuscripts of your debtors who have not paid you, as I said in Chapter 17. Likewise keep the receipts in a safe place for any emergency. But when you should pay others, have the other party write the receipt in a receipt book, as I told you at the beginning, so that a receipt cannot be easily lost or go astray.

You shall do the same as to important writing, as, for instance, memoranda of the brokers, or of merchants, or of weighmen, or relative to goods placed in or taken out of the custom house, either land or sea custom houses, and judgments or decrees of the consuls or of other public officials, or all kinds of notarial instruments written on parchments which ought to be kept in a place apart. The same should be said of the copies of instruments and papers of attorneys or counselors at law relative to lawsuits.

It is also wise to have a separate book for memoranda, which we call memoranda book, in which day by day you shall keep a record of the things that you might

편지를 봉하고 주소를 쓴 다음에 자신만의 특별한 기호를 표시하는 것이 관습이다. 그러면 그것이 어느 상인의 편지인지 누구나 쉽게 알 수 있다. 이 글의 서두에서 말한 것처럼 상인은 이 나라를 지탱하는 존재이기 때문에 상인에게 많은 관심과 주의가 집중되기 때문이다.

이러한 이유로 영예로운 추기경들은 편지 겉면에 이름을 쓴다. 이렇게 하면 아무도 그 편지가 누구의 것인지 몰랐다는 변명을 하지 못하기 때문이다. 보통 추기경들의 편지나 교황의 교서 등은 그 안의 내용이 알려질 수 있도록 하기 위하여 봉함을 하지는 않는다. 그러나 그 내용이 사적인 것이거나 비밀스러운 것의 경우에는 어부, 즉 성 베드로를 의미하는 인장으로 봉함을 하는 것이 관례이다.

모든 편지는 월 또는 연 단위로 묶어서 문서고 등에 체계적으로 보관해야 한다. 근무시간 중에 편지를 받는 경우 같은 순서로 임시 보관한다. 그러면 필요시 편지들을 쉽게 찾을 수 있다.

미회수 채권 내역서 등은 좀 더 비밀스러운 장소에 보관할 수도 있다. 비상시를 대비하여 안전한 곳에 보관해야 한다. 그러나 타인에게 현금을 지급할 때는 수취자로 하여금 지불대장에 영수필이라는 의미의 글을 쓰게 해야 한다. 영수증이라는 것은 쉽게 분실되기 때문이다.

각종 중요 문서, 즉 브로커의 각서, 송장, 세관의 상품반출증, 판결문 등은 별도의 장소에 보관해야 하며, 공증서 및 판결문 등도 역시 복사해두어야 한다.

be afraid of forgetting and, if you forget them, may prove to be dangerous to you. Every day, the last thing in the evening, just before going to bed, you shall glance over this book to see whether everything which should have been done has been done, etc., and you shall cancel with your pen the things that have been done, and in this book you shall make a record of the things that you have lent to your neighbor or friend for one or two days, as, for instance, store, vases, caldrons, or any other thing.

These rules, and the other very useful rules of which I have spoken before, you shall follow and, according to the the localities and times, you shall be more or less particular, adding or omitting as it seems best to you, because it is impossible to give rules for every little thing in the mercantile business, as we have already said. The proverb says that we need more bridges to make a merchant than a doctor of laws can make.

If you understand well all the things that I have spoken of so far, I am sure you with your intelligence will carry on your business well.

그리고 비망록을 별도로 작성하는 것도 좋은 일이다. 비망록은 잊어서는 안 될 것, 잊으면 큰 위험이 되는 것 등을 기록하는 장부다. 매일 저녁 잠들기 바로 전에 해야 할 일은, 이 책을 보고 할 일을 제대로 마쳤는지를 확인하는 일이다. 이 장부에는 이웃에게 잠시 빌려준 꽃병, 냄비, 솥 등을 기록해도 된다.

여기서 제시한 규칙을 상인은 준수해야 하며, 지역과 시대적 특성에 따라 가감하여 적용하는 것도 가능한 일이다. 여기서 상업상의 행위규칙에 대한 모든 것을 일일이 다 설명할 수는 없기 때문이다. 법률가보다 상인이 더 많은 능력을 필요로 한다는 속담이 있다.

지금까지 내가 설명한 것을 제대로 이해한다면, 여태까지 배운 것으로 그대의 사업을 성공적으로 수행할 수 있을 것이라 확신한다.

CHAPTER 36

SUMMARY OF THE RULES AND WAYS FOR KEEPING A LEDGER

All the creditors must appear in the Ledger at the right hand side, and all the debtors at the left.

All entries made in the ledger have to be double entries—that is, if you make one creditor, you must make some one debtor.

Each debit (shall give—*dee dare*) and credit (shall have—*dee havere*) entry must contain three things, namely: the day, the amount and the reason for the entry.

The last name in the entry of the debit (in the Ledger) must be the first name in the entry of the credit. On the same day that you make the debit entry, you should make the credit entry.

By a trial balance (*bilancio*) of the Ledger we mean a sheet of paper folded lengthwise in the middle, on which we write down all the creditors of the Ledger at the right side and the debtors at the left side. We see whether the total of the debits is equal to that of the credits, and if so, the Ledger is in order.

The trial balance of the Ledger should be equal—that is, the total of the credits—I do not say creditors—should be equal to the total of the debits—I do not say debtors. If they were not equal there would be a mistake in the Ledger.

The cash account should always be a debtor or equal. If it were different, there would be a mistake in the ledger.

You must not and cannot make any one debtor in your book without permission or consent of the person that has to appear as a debtor; if you should, that account would be considered false. Likewise you cannot add terms or

제36장
장부 기록방법과 그 규칙의 요약

(나 또는 회사의) 채권자는 원장의 우측에, (나 또는 회사의) 채무자는 좌측에 기록한다.

| 해설 | 왜 좌측 또는 우측에 기록해야 하는지에 대한 언급은 없다.

원장으로의 전기는 반드시 두 번 실시해야 한다. 채권자를 기록하면, 반드시 채무자도 기록해주어야 한다.

모든 대차는 세 가지를 기록해야 한다. 날짜, 금액, 거래 이유 등이다.

원장의 차변에 기록된 마지막 인명은 대변 기록의 첫 인명이어야 한다. 즉, 차변과 대변은 같은 날에 기록되어야 한다.

| 해설 | "원장의 차변에 기록된 마지막 인명은 대변기록의 첫 인명이어야 한다."라는 원문의 의미는 미상이다. 하지만, 원장에 기록된 모든 명칭이 인명이라는 것만은 확실하다. 따라서 숨마부기의 pepper(후추), wool(양털) 등의 상품명칭 계정도 송도부기처럼 인명이다.

시산표는 가운데를 중심으로 세로로 접은 종이다. 이 종이의 오른편에 채권자를, 왼편에 채무자를 기록한다. 양방의 합계가 같으면 제대로 기록된 장부로 인정한다.

시산표는 한 장의 큰 종이를 세로로 접은 종이이고, 거기에 원장의 대변과 차변에 기록된 모든 것을 대변은 우측에, 차변은 좌측에 기록해야 한다. 이 시산표에서 차변 총액과 대변 총액을 비교했을 때 같으면 그 원장은 제대로 기록된 것이다.

conditions to a credit without permission and consent of the creditor. If you should, that statement would be untrue.

The values in the Ledger must be reckoned in one kind of money. In the explanation of the entries, you may name all sorts of money, either *ducats*, or *lire*, or *Florence*, or gold *scudi*, or anything else; but in writing the amount in the column, you should always use the same kind of money throughout—that is, the money that you reckon by at the beginning should be the same all through the Ledger.

The debit or credit entries of the cash account may be shortened, if you desire, by not giving the reason for the entry; you may simply say from so and so, for so and so, because the reason for the entry is stated in the opposite entry.

If a new account should be opened, you must use a new page and must not go back even if there was room enough to place the new account. You should not write backward, but always forward—that is, go forward as the days go, which never come back. If you do otherwise, the book would be untrue.

If you should make an entry in the Ledger by mistake which should not have been made, as it happens at times through absentmindedness, and if you wanted to correct it, you shall do as follows: Mark with a cross or with an "II" that special entry, and then make an entry on the opposite side under the same account. That is, if the errorneous entry was on the credit side—say, for instance, for L 50, S 10, D 6—you make an entry in the debit side, saying: Debit (*dee dare*) L 50, S 10, D 6, for the opposite entry cross marked which is hereby corrected, because it was put in through a mistake and should not have been made. Then mark with a cross this new entry. This is all.

When the spaces given to any particular account are all filled so that no more entries can be made and you want to carry forward that account, do in this way: Figure out the remainder of the said account—that is, whether it is debit or credit remainder. Now let us say that there is a credit remainder of L 20, S 4, D 2. You should write on the opposite side, without mentioning any date, as follows: Debit L 28, S 4, D 2, per remainder (*per resto*) of this account carried forward in the credit at page so and so. And it is done. The said entry is to be marked in the margin so, namely: *Ro,* Which means "*resto*"(remainder), but this does not mean that it is a true debit entry although it is on the debit side. It is rather the credit which is transferred

시산표에서 대변 총액과 차변 총액은 같아야 한다. 양변의 금액이 다르면, 원장에 오류가 있는 것이다. 여기서 대변과 차변은 채권자와 채무자라는 의미가 아니라는 것을 밝혀둔다.

현금계정은 반드시 채무자(차변 잔액) 또는 0잔액이어야 한다. 그렇지 않으면 원장에 오류가 있는 것이다.

타인의 동의 없이 장부에 그 사람을 채무자로 기록할 수도 없고 해서도 안 된다. 임의로 기록되면 그 장부는 가짜 장부로 간주된다. 마찬가지로 채권자의 동의 없이 채무를 기록해서도 안 된다. 이런 장부 역시 가짜 장부다.

원장의 금액은 한 가지 화폐로 기록 계산되어야 한다. 하지만 적요란에는 다양한 화폐로 설명문을 달아도 된다. 다시 말하면, 금액란에 기입되는 금액은 장부 전체에 걸쳐 처음부터 끝까지 동일한 화폐로 기록되어야 한다.

현금계정의 입출 내역은 입출사유 없이 간단하게 기록해도 된다. 간단하게 누구에게 주었고 받았다 정도로 기록해도 된다. 상대계정 원장에 그 상세 내역이 기록되기 때문이다.

계정 원장을 개설하려면 새 종이에 해야 한다. 새 계정 원장을 설치하기 위한 여백이 충분히 있어도 되돌아가서는 안 된다. 그리고 소급 또는 후진하여 기록해서는 안 된다. 날짜가 전진은 있어도 후진은 없고, 한번 가면 결코 돌아오지 않는 것과 같다. 만일 후진 또는 소급하여 기록한다면 그 장부는 가짜로 간주된다.

무심결에 또는 고의가 아닌 실수로 원장을 잘못 기록하였고, 이를 교정하고자 하는 경우에는 다음과 같이 한다. 먼저 십자가 표시 또는 H(Holy) 표시를 한 후, 반대편에 기록하면 된다. 실수로 대변에 L 50, S 10, D 6으로 기록된 경우, 반대편에 다음과 같이 기록한다.

차변 L 50, S 10, D 6, 실수로 기록된 것을 교정하기 위하여 여기에 반대기입을 한다. 그러고 나서 새 기록에 십자가 표시를 하면 된다. 이것이 전부다.

현 계정 원장의 공간이 다 채워져 새로운 계정 원장을 개설하고 잔액을 이월해야 하는 경우에는 다음과 같이 한다.

먼저 구 계정 원장의 잔액이 차변인지 대변인지를 산출한다. 대변 잔액 L 20, S 4,

through the debit side. Now you must turn the pages and keep on turning them until you find a new page where you shall credit that account by naming the account and making a new entry without putting down any day. And you shall say in the following manner: So and so is credit (*dee havere*) L 28, S 4, D 2, per remainder (*per resto*) of account transferred from page so and so, and you should mark this entry in the margin by *Ro,* which means "*resto*" remainder, and that is done.

In the same way, as I have shown you, you shall proceed if the account has a debit remainder—that is, what you enter on the credit side you should transfer to the debit side.

When the ledger is all filled up, or old, and you want to transfer it into a new one, you proceed in the following manner: First you must see whether your old book bears a mark on its cover—for instance, an A. In this case you must mark the new Ledger in which you want to transfer the old one by B, because the books of the merchants go by order, one after the other, according to the letters of the alphabet. Then you have to take the trial balance of the old book and see that it is equal. From the trial balance sheet you must copy in the new Ledger all the creditors and debtors all in order just as they appear in the trial balance sheet, but make a separate account for each amount;
and leave to each account all the space that you think you may need. And in each debit account you shall say: Per so much as per debit remainder (*resta a dare*) in the old book marked A, at page so and so. And in each credit account you shall say: Per so much as per credit remainder (*resta a havere*) in the old book marked A, at page so and so. In this way you transfer the old Ledger into the new one. Now, in order to cancel the old book, you must cancel each account by making it balance of which we have spoken—that is, if an account of the old Ledger shows a credit remainder as the trial balance would show you, you shall debit this account for the same amount, saying, so much remains in the credit of this account, carried forward in the credit in the new Ledger marked B, at page so and so. In this way you shall have closed the old Ledger and opened the new one for, as I have shown you how to do for a creditor, the same you shall do for a debtor, with this difference, that while you debit an account, which may show a credit remainder, you shall credit the account which may show a debit remainder. This is all.

D 2인 경우, 반대편에 날짜를 생략하고 다음과 같이 기록한다.

차변 L 28(20의 오기), S 4, D 2, 이 계정의 잔액을 새 계정 원장의 몇 페이지로 이월한다. 이것으로 된 것이다.

이 기사는 여백에 기록되며, 다시 말하면 여기서 Ro는 resoto(잔액)의 약자이나, 그것은 차변에 기록되지만 진정한 차변 기록은 아니라는 의미이다. 오히려 차변을 통하여 이월되는 대변 잔액이라고 할 수 있다. 그리고 페이지를 넘겨서 이 잔액을 기록해야 할 새로운 페이지를 찾는다. 그리고 거기에 날짜는 기록하지 않고 바로 대변에 다음과 같이 기록한다.

대변 L 28(20의 오기), S 4, D 2. 이 금액은 제 몇 페이지로부터 이월된 잔액이다. 그리고 여백에 'Ro'라는 기호를 표시해야 하는데, 이는 잔액이라는 의미이다. 즉, 구 계정 원장으로부터의 이월 잔액이라는 의미이다. 그러면 된 것이다.

마찬가지로 차변 잔액이면, 그 계정 원장의 대변에 잔액을 기록 후, 이를 새 계정 원장의 차변으로 이월하면 된다.

원장을 다 사용하거나 오래되어서 이를 새 원장으로 이월하고자 하는 경우에는 다음과 같이 한다.

먼저 구 원장의 표지 마크가 A 등인지를 확인한다. A이면 새 원장의 명칭은 B원장이 된다. 상인은 항상 일을 순서에 맞추어 해야 하고, 원장은 특히 알파벳 순서로 만들어야 하기 때문이다. 그리고 나서 구 원장의 시산표를 작성하여 대차가 일치하는지를 확인해야 한다. 이 시산표를 보면서 새 원장에 모든 차변과 대변을 순서대로 복사기입하고, 금액을 기록할 계정 원장을 만들되, 각 계정 원장의 공간은 개설자의 판단에 따라 할당한다.

그리고 차변 잔액인 계정에는 구 원장, 즉 A원장의 몇 페이지에 기록된 차변 잔액(resta a dare: 채무자가 회사에 주어야 할 잔액)이라고 기록한다. 그리고 대변 잔액인 계정에는 구 원장, 즉 A원장의 몇 페이지에 기록된 대변 잔액(resta a havere: 채권자가 가져야 할 잔액)이라고 기록한다. 이런 식으로 구 원장의 잔액을 새로운 원장으로 이월한다. 다음에는 시산표를 작성하고 장부를 소인해야 한다. 즉, 구 계정 원장의 잔액이 시산표에 나타나는 것처럼 대변 잔액이면, 이 잔액을 차변에 기록한다. 그러나 이것은 새 계정 원장의 대변으로 이월하기 위한 것이다.

THINGS WHICH SHOULD BE ENTERED IN THE BOOKS OF THE MERCHANTS

Of all the cash that you might have, if it is your own—that is, that you might have earned at different times in the past, or which might have been bequeathed to you by your dead relatives or given you as a gift from some Prince, you shall make yourself a creditor (*creditore te medesima*), and make cash debitor. As to all jewelry or goods which might be your own—that is, that you may have got through business or that might have been left you through a will or given to you as a present, you must value them in cash and make as many accounts as there are things and make each debitor by saying: For so many, etc., of which I find myself possessed on this day, so many *denari*, posted credit entry at such and such page; and then you make creditor your account (*tuo conto*), that is yourself (*medesimo*), with the amount of each of these entries. But remember these entries should not be for less than ten ducats each, as small things of little value are not entered in the Ledger.

Of all the real property that you might own, as houses, lands, stores, you make the cash debitor and estimate their value at your discretion in cash, and you make creditor yourself or your personal account (*tuo sopradette conto*). Then you make debitor an account of that special property by giving the value, as I have said above, and make yourself creditor because, as I have told you, all entries must have three things: The date, the value in cash, and the reason.

If you should buy merchandise or anything else for cash, you should make a debtor of that special merchandise or thing and like creditor cash, and if you should say, I bought that merchandise for cash, but a bank will furnish the cash, or a friend of mine will do so, I will answer you that any way, you must make a debitor of that special merchandise; but where I told you to credit cash, you should, instead, credit that special bank, or that special friend who furnished the money.

If you should buy merchandise or anything else, partly for cash and partly on time, you shall make that special merchandise debitor, and make a creditor of the party from whom you bought it on time and under the conditions that you might have agreed upon; as, for instance, one-third in cash and the rest in six months. After this you will have to make another entry—that is, make a debitor of the party from whom you bought it for the amount of the cash that you have given him for that one-third, and make creditor cash or the bank which might have paid that

이런 식으로 구 원장을 마감하고 새 원장을 개설하는 것이다. 대차 각 변의 잔액 처리 방법은 차변 잔액이면 대기하고 대변 잔액이면 차기하여 계정 원장의 양방 금액을 일치시킨다는 차이밖에 없다는 점은 이미 설명하였으며, 이것이 전부다.

상인의 장부에 기록되어야 하는 것들

사업으로 취득하였거나 죽은 친척에게 상속받거나 또는 귀족에게 증여받은 현금은 출자상인 자신(의 이름)을 대여자로 기록(대기)하고, 현금을 채무자로 기록(차기)한다.

| 분개 해설 | 차변 현금 ○○○ // 대변 출자자 명칭(자기 이름) ○○○
| 해설 | 채무자, 채권자(대여자) 등은 '자신의' 또는 '회사의'라는 수식어가 생략된 것이다.

사업, 수증 및 상속 등에 의하여 자신의 소유가 된 상품 또는 보석이 있으면, 먼저 이들을 현금가액으로 평가하고, 이들 각각을, 즉 그 종류대로 계정으로 설정하여 이들 각각을 채무자로 기록해야 한다. 그리고 자기 자신을 대여자로 기록해야 한다. 그리고 이 날짜로 이를 (출자자) 원장의 대변 몇 페이지에 전기하였는지도 기록해야 한다. 그러나 10더컷 이하의 재산은 기록해서는 안 된다는 것에 유의해야 한다. 소소한 것이 원장에 기록되어서는 안 되기 때문이다.

| 분개 해설 | 차변 상품 또는 보석 ○○○ // 대변 출자자 명칭 ○○○

가옥, 토지, 상점 등의 부동산의 경우에도 각 재산을 현금으로 평가하여 이들을 채무자로 기록해야 한다. 그리고 나서 자기 자신을 대여자로 기록해야 한다. 그리고 기록시에는 반드시 날짜, 금액, 이유, 이 세 가지를 기록해야 한다.

| 분개 해설 | 차변 토지 ○○○ // 대변 출자자 명칭 ○○○

상품 등을 현금으로 구입하는 경우에는 그 특정 상품을 채무자로 기록하고, 현금을 대여자로 기록해야 한다. 현금으로 상품을 구입하였으나 그 대금을 은행 또는 친구가 지급하기로 한 경우에는 역시 상품을 채무자로 기록하고, 그리고 현금을 대여자로 기록하

much for you.

If you should sell any merchandise or anything else, you should proceed as above with the exception that you should proceed in the opposite way—that is, where I told you that when you bought you should make the merchandise debitor, when you sell you will have to make your merchandise a creditor and charge the cash account if it is sold for cash, or charge the bank that might have promised the payment. And if you make a sale on time, you will have to charge the party to whom you sold it on time, and if you make the sale partly for cash and partly on time, you shall proceed as I have shown you in explaining about the buying.

If you should give merchandise in exchange, for instance, let us say I have sold 1,000 pounds of English wool in exchange for pepper—that is, for 2,000 pounds of pepper—I ask, how shall we make this entry in the Ledger? You shall do as follows: Estimate what the value of pepper is, at your discretion, in cash. Now let us say that you estimated 12 ducats per hundred; the 2,000 pounds would be worth 240 ducats. Therefore, you shall make the wool a creditor with 240 ducats, for which amount you have sold it. This is the manner that you should follow in all the trade entries. If you have received 2,000 pounds of pepper valued at 240 ducats, you shall make the pepper a debitor and say: Said pepper debtor on this day, see page, etc., etc.

If you should loan cash to some of your friends, you shall charge the friend to whom you have given it and credit cash. If you should borrow cash from some friend, you will have to debit cash and credit your friend.

If you have received 8 or 10 or 20 ducats in order to insure a ship or galley, or anything else, you should credit the account "ship insurance," and explain all about it—how, when and where, and how much per cent.; and shall charge the cash account.

는 대신에 은행 또는 친구를 대여자로 기록하면 된다.

| 분개 해설 | 차변 상품 명칭 ○○○ // 대변 은행 명칭 또는 친구 이름 ○○○

일부 현금, 일부 외상으로 구입한 경우에는 그 상품을 채무자로 기록하고, 외상제공자를 대여자로 기록한다. 예를 들어 1/3은 현금, 나머지는 6개월 외상으로 구입한 경우에는 한 번 더 분개해야 한다. 즉 물건값의 1/3을 현금으로 지급하였으므로 이 현금을 받은 자, 즉 외상제공자를 채무자로 기록하고, 현금 또는 은행을 대여자로 기록해야 하는 것이다.

| 분개 해설 |
① 전액 외상매입 가정 분개: 차변 상품 명칭 ○○○// 대변 외상제공자 명칭 ○○○
② 현금 지급분의 추가 분개: 차변 외상제공자 명칭 ○○○// 대변 현금 ○○○

상품을 판매하는 경우에는 상기와 반대로 해야 한다는 것만 제외하면 나머지는 같다. 즉 살 때는 상품을 채무자로 기록하고, 판매한 경우에는 상품을 대여자로 기록하되, 현금판매의 경우에는 현금을 채무자로 기록한다. 이 경우 은행이 상품대금을 지급하기로 한 경우에는 은행을 채무자로 기록한다. 외상으로 판매하는 경우에는 외상구매자를 채무자로 기록하고 상품을 대여자로 기록한다. 일부 현금, 일부 외상으로 판매한 경우에는 일부 현금, 일부 외상 구매의 경우를 참조하기 바란다.

| 분개 해설 |
① 현금판매: 차변 현금 ○○○ // 대변 상품 명칭 ○○○
② 외상판매: 차변 외상구매자 명칭 ○○○ // 대변 상품 명칭 ○○○
③ 은행지급 외상판매: 차변 은행 명칭 ○○○ // 대변 상품 명칭 ○○○

물물교환의 경우, 즉 보유하던 양모를 후추와 교환하는 경우에는 어떻게 기록해야 하는가? 먼저 교환으로 취득하게 되는 후추를 현금가액으로 평가해야 한다. 후추가 100파운드에 12더컷이면, 2,000파운드의 후추는 240더컷이 된다. 따라서 양모를 240더컷의 금액으로 대여자로 기록한다. 즉 그 금액으로 양모를 팔았다고 가정하는 것이다. 이것이 물물교환 거래를 기록하는 방법이다. 그리고 2,000파운드의 후추를 240더컷에 취득한

If anybody should send you any goods with instructions to sell them or exchange them on commission, I say that you have to charge in the Ledger that special merchandise belonging to so and so with the freight, or duty, or for storage, and credit the cash account. You shall credit the cash for all cash that you have to pay on account of goods: for instance, cash paid for transportation or duty, or brokerage, etc., and charge the account of that special goods for that which you have paid in money.

것이므로 그 금액으로 후추를 채무자로 기록하면 된다. 즉 원장에 전술한 후추를 차변으로 몇 월 몇 일에 기록하며, 분개장 페이지는 ~이다라고 기록하면 되는 것이다.

| 분개 해설 |
① 양모의 현금판매 가정: 차변 현금 240 // 대변 양모 240
② 후추의 현금구매 가정: 차변 후추 240 // 대변 현금 240
③ 통합 분개: 차변 후추 240 // 대변 양모 240 (후추 취득, 양모 제공)

친구에게 현금을 대여해주는 경우에는 친구를 채무자로 기록하고, 현금을 대여자로 기록한다. 친구에게 현금을 차입하는 경우에는 현금을 채무자로 기록하고, 친구를 대여자로 기록한다.

| 분개 해설 |
① 현금 대여: 차변 친구 이름 ○○○ // 대변 현금 ○○○
② 현금 차입: 차변 현금 ○○○ // 대변 친구 이름 ○○○

그리고 보험료를 현금으로 수취한 경우에는, 보험료 수익계정을 대여자로 기록하고, 그에 대한 설명을 추가한다. 그리고 현금을 채무자로 기록한다.

| 분개 해설 | 차변 현금 ○○○ // 대변 보험료수익 ○○○

판매 등의 목적으로 상품을 발송하면서 발생하는 운반비, 관세, 보관료 등을 현금으로 지급하는 경우에는 현금을 대여자로 기록한다. 즉, 상품으로 인하여 지불하게 되는 경비는 현금을 대여자로 기록해야 한다. 그리고 그 경비지급의 원인이 되는 특정 상품을 채무자로 기록해야 한다.

| 분개 해설 | 차변 상품 명칭 ○○○ // 대변 현금 ○○○ (적요: 운반비, 관세 등)

THINGS THAT SHOULD BE RECORDED IN A RECORD BOOK (*RECORDANZE*) OF THE MERCHANT

All the house and store goods that you may find yourself possessed of—these should be put down in order—that is, all the things made of iron by itself, leaving space enough to make additions if necessary; also leaving room to mark in the margin the things that might be lost or sold or given as presents or spoiled. But I don't mean small things of little value.

Make a record of all the brass things separately, as I have said, and then a record of the tin things, and then the wooden things, and copper things, and then the silver things and gold things, always leaving enough space between each class so that you may add something if necessary, and to put down a memorandum of any object that might be missing.

All sureties or obligations or promises of payment that you might make for some friend, explaining clearly everything.

All goods or other things that might be left with you in custody, or that you might borrow from some friend, as well as all the things that other friends of yours might borrow from you.

All conditional transactions—that is, purchases and sales, as, for instance, a contract that you shall send me by the next ship coming from England, so many *cantara* of *woll di li mistri*, on condition that it is good; and when I receive it I will pay you so much per *cantara* or by the hundred, or otherwise; I will send you in exchange so many *cantara* of cotton.

All houses, lands, stores or jewels that you might rent at so many ducats and so many lire per year. And when you collect the rent, then the money should be entered in the Ledger, as I have told you.

If you should lend some jewels, silver or gold vase to some friend, say, for instance, for eight or fifteen days, things like this should not be entered in the Ledger, but should be recorded in this record book, because in a few days, you will get them back. In the same way, if somebody should lend you something like the things mentioned, you should not make any entry in the Ledger, but put down a little memorandum in the record book, because in a short time you will have to give it back.

How *Lire*, *Soldi*, *Denari* and *Picioli*, etc., should be written down as abbreviations.

상인의 일지에 기록되어야 하는 것들

상인이 보유하는 가옥 및 상품 등은 순차적으로 기록되어야 한다. 즉, 철제 물건은 철제 물건 그룹에 기록해야 하고, 필요시 철제 물건의 추가에 대비하여 여분의 공간을 확보해두어야 한다. 아울러 분실, 매각, 선물로 제공 및 부식 등과 같은 사태가 발생할 수도 있으므로 이를 기록할 여백도 확보해야 한다. 그러나 이것은 가치가 적은 물건에는 적용되지 아니한다.

그리고 놋 제품, 주석 제품, 은 제품 등도 그룹별로 각각 기록하고, 역시 물건의 추가에 대비하여 여분의 공간도 확보하고, 분실 등의 상황을 기록할 수 있도록 메모란도 확보해두어야 한다.

그리고 친구들에 대하여 행한 지급약속 등도 명쾌하게 정리해두어야 한다.

아울러 친구들이 빌려가는 것뿐만 아니라 친구에게 빌리는 것, 일시적으로 보관하는 것 등에 대하여도 그렇다.

모든 조건부 거래, 즉 영국에서 오는 다음 배편으로 보내면 이의 수취시 얼마를 지급하거나 얼마의 면섬유를 보내겠다는 계약 등도 마찬가지다.

유상으로 가옥, 토지, 상점 등을 임대하는 경우 임대료를 수취하게 되면 이를 장부에 기록해야 한다.

예를 들어 보석, 금 꽃병 등을 친구에게 며칠 빌려준 경우 이런 것은 원장에 기록해서는 안 되지만, 비망록 등에는 기록해야 한다. 며칠 후 돌려받아야 하기 때문이다. 마찬가지로 친구에게 상기의 것들을 빌린 경우에도 원장에 기록해서는 안 되고, 비망록에는 기록해야 한다. 며칠 후에 돌려주어야 하기 때문이다.

Lire, Soldi 등은 약어로 기록할 수도 있다(각각의 약어는 다른 면을 참고하기 바란다).

Lire; Soldi; Denari; Picioli; Libbre; Once; Danarpesi; Grani; Carati; Ducati; Florin larghi.
(See other side for their abbreviations.)

HOW THE DEBIT AND THE CREDIT (LEDGER) ENTRIES ARE MADE

HOW THE DEBIT (LEDGER) ENTRIES ARE MADE (차변)	(금액)	HOW THE CREDIT (LEDGER) ENTRIES ARE MADE (대변)	(금액)
MCCCCLXXXXIII, Lodovico, son of Piero Forestani, shall give on the 14th day of November, 1493, L 44, S 1, D 8, for cash loaned, posted cash shall have at page 2:	L 44, S 1, D 8	MCCCCLXXXXIII, Lodovico, son of Piero Forestani, shall have on Nov. 22, 1493, L 20, S 4, D 2, for part payment. And for him Francesco, son of Antonio Cavalcanti, promised to pay it to us at our pleasure; posted shall give at page 2:	L 20, S 4, D 2
And on the 18th ditto, L 18, S 11, D 6, which we promised to pay for him to Martino, son of Piero Foraboschi at his pleasure, posted said shall have at page 2:	L 18, S 11, D 6		
Cash in hands of Simone, son of Alessio Bombeni, shall give on Nov. 14, 1493, for L 62, S 13, D 2, for Francesco, son of Antonio Cavalcanti, page 2:	L 62, S 13, D 6	Cash in hands of Simone, son of Alessio Bombeni, shall have, on Nov. 14, 1493, for L 44, S 1, D 8, from Lodovico Piero Forestani, L 44, S 1, D 8; and on Nov. 22, 1493, L 18, S 11, D 6, to Martino, son of Piero Forabaschi, page 2:	L 44, S 1, D 8 (좌측의 밑줄친 금액은 영역 시 타이핑 오류) L 18, S 11, D 6

원장의 차변과 대변에 기록하는 방법

■ 로도비코 원장

차변(대여 출금)	대변(대여회수 입금)
1493. 11.14 로도비코에게 현금 L 44, S 1, D 8을 대여하다. 상대계정은 현금이고, 원면(원장 페이지 번호)은 2이다. L 44, S 1, D 8 | 해설 | 현금원장 대변 1번 기사와 대응된다. 1493. 11.18 로도비코를 대신하여 마르티노에게 지급하기로 하다. 상대계정은 마르티노이고, 원면은 2이다. | 해설 | 로도비코가 마르티노에게 진 빚을 내가 대신 갚기로 하다. 따라서 로도비코에 대한 채권은 증가한다. 이 기사는 마르티노 원장 대변과 대응된다. L 18, S 11, D 6	1493.11.22 로도비코, 로도비코가 나에게 진 채무를 프란체스코가 인수하다. 상대계정은 프란체스코이고, 원면은 2이다. L 20, S 4, D 2 | 해설 | 따라서 로도비코에 대한 채권을 회수한 것으로 처리한 것이다. 프란체스코 원장 차변과 대응된다.

■ 현금 원장

차변(입금)	대변(출금)

1493. 11.14 현금(나, 시모네의 것), 프란체스코가 예치한 금액이다. 상대계정은 프란체스코이고, 원면은 2이다.   L 62, S 13, D 6
| 해설 | 프란체스코로부터 차입금 수취에 해당된다. 프란체스코 원장 대변과 대응된다.
	1493. 11.14 현금, 로도비코에게 L 44, S 1, D 8을 대여하다. 상대계정은 로도비코이다.
	                  L 44, S 1, D 8
	| 해설 | 영어 원문에서는 현금 원장 대변의 기사가 1건이지만, 실제로는 2건이므로, 이를 분리하여 표시하였다. 상기의 기사는 로도비코 원장 차변 1번 기사와 대응된다.
	
	1493.11.20(22는 오기) 현금, 마르티노에게 지급한 현금이고, 이는 로도비코를 대신하여 지급한 것이다. 상대계정은 마르티노이고, 원면은 2이다.
	| 해설 | 마르티노 원장 차변과 대응된다.
	                  L 18, S 11, D 6

Martino, son of Piero Foraboschi, shall give on Nov. 20, 1493, for L 18, S 11, D 6, taken by him in cash, posted Cash at page 2:	L 18, S 11, D 6	Martino, son of Piero Foraboschi, shall have on Nov. 18, 1493, for L 18, S 11, D 6, which we promised to pay him at his pleasure for Lodovico, son of Pietro Forestani; posted shall give entry at p. 8:	L 18, S 11, D 6
Francesco, son of Antonio Cavalcanti, shall give, on Nov. 12, 1493, L 20, S 4, D 2, which he promised to pay to us at our pleasure for Lodovico, son of Pietro Forestani; page 2:	L 20, S 4, D 2	Francesco, son of Antonio Cavalcanti, shall have on Nov. 14, 1493, for L 62, S 13, D 6, which he brought himself in cash; posted cash shall give at page 2:	L 62, S 13, D 6

■ 마르티노 원장

차변(차입 상환출금)	대변(차입 입금)
1493.11.20 마르티노에게 (앞에서 지급 약속한 금액) L 18, S 11, D 6을 현금으로 지급하다. 상대 계정은 현금이고, 원면은 2이다.　　　　L 18, S 11, D 6 | 해설 |　현금원장 대변 2번째 기사와 대응된다.	1493.11.18 마르티노에게 로도비코의 채무(L 18, S 11, D 6)를 대신 갚기로 약속하다. 　　　　　　　　　　　　L 18, S 11, D 6 | 해설 |　로도비코 원장 차변 두 번째 기사와 연결된다.

■ 프란체스코 원장

차변(차입 상환출금)	대변(차입 입금)
1493.11.22(12는 오타) 프란체스코가 로도비코를 대신하여 우리에게 지급하기로 하다. 상대계정은 로도비코이고, 원면은 2이다.　　　L 20, S 4, D 2 | 해설 |　로도비코가 나에게 진 채무를 프란체스코가 인수하다. 로도비코 원장 대변과 대응된다.	1493. 11.14 프란체스코가 현금 L 62, S 13, D 6을 예치하다. 상대계정은 현금이고, 원면은 2이다. 　　　　　　　　　　　　L 62, S 13, D 6 | 해설 |　현금 원장 차변과 대응된다.

\| 해설 \|　숨마의 마지막 부분인 상기의 원장에 대하여 히라이 야스타로는 숨마에서 가장 난해한 부분이라고 하였으나, 복식부기의 근본원리인 대차 일치의 원칙을 충실히 따르고 적용하면 그리 어렵지 않은 내용이다. 먼저 영역문의 현금 원장 기록 오류를 찾은 후, 상기의 원장기사로 원래의 분개를 역으로 추정하면 다음의 분개를 도출해낼 수 있다. 즉, 아래의 분개를 원장으로 전기한 것이 상기의 예시 원장이라고 할 수 있다.

〈거래 내역과 추정 분개〉

11/14 차변 로도비코 L 44, S 1, D 8 // 대변 현금 L 44, S 1, D 8
　　　　내가 로도비코에게 현금을 대여하다.
　　　　영어 원문의 현금 원장에서는 상기의 금액이 금액란이 아니라 적요란에 기록되었다.
　　　　따라서 이 금액은 오기이므로 금액란으로 옮겨 적어야 한다.

11/14 차변 현금 L 62, S 13, D 6 // 대변 프란체스코 L 62, S 13, D 6
　　　　프란체스코가 현금을 나에게 예치하다(프란체스코에게 현금으로 차입하다).

11/18 차변 로도비코 L 18, S 11, D 6 // 대변 마르티노 L 18, S 11, D 6
　　　　로도비코가 마르티노에게 진 빚을 내가 대신 지급하기로 하다.
　　　　이 분개로 로도비코에 대한 채권은 증가하고,
　　　　마르티노에 대하여 새로이 L 18, S 11, D 6 의 채무가 발생하게 된다.

11/20 차변 마르티노 L 18, S 11, D 6 // 대변 현금 L 18, S 11, D 6
　　　　마르티노에게 진 로도비코의 빚을 내가 현금으로 지급하다.
　　　　이 분개로 마르티노에 대한 채무 잔액은 0이 된다.

11/22 차변 프란체스코 L 20, S 4, D 2 // 대변 로도비코 L 20, S 4, D 2

프란체스코가 로도비코의 채무를 인수하다.
이 분개로 프란체스코에 대한 채무는 감소하고,
동시에 로도비코에 대한 채권도 L 20, S 4, D 2만큼 감소하게 된다.
프란체스코에 대한 채무가 감소하는 이유는 그 전에 프란체스코에 대한 채무가 있었기 때문이다. 만일 프란체스코에 대한 채무가 없었다면, 이 거래는 프란체스코에 대한 대여금 증가로 표시되어야 한다.

* 원문에는 이 거래가 11/12로 기록되어 있으나, 프란체스코가 현금을 예치한 것이 11/14이므로, 프란체스코가 로도비코의 채무를 인수 또는 대급할 수 있는 것은 그 이후로 추론되므로, 본 번역에서는 11/12를 11/22로 수정하였다.

상기의 분개와 사건을 표로 나타내면 다음과 같다.

■ 분개 해설표

날짜	차변	금액	대변	사건의 내용
14일	로도비코	L 44, S 1, D 8	현금	로도비코에게 현금으로 대여하다. ※ 로도비코에 대한 채권 증가, 현금 감소
14일	현금	L 62, S 13, D 6	프란체스코	프란체스코가 나(시모네)에게 현금을 예치하다. ※ 현금 증가, 프란체스코에 대한 채무 증가
18일	로도비코	L 18, S 11, D 6	마르티노	로도비코가 마르티노에게 진 빚을 내가 마르티노에게 지급하기로 약정하다. ※ 로도비코에 대한 채권 증가, 마르티노에 대한 채무 증가
20일	마르티노	L 18, S 11, D 6	현금	로도비코 대신 지급 약속하기로 한 금액을 마르티노에게 실제로 지급하다. ※ 마르티노에 대한 채무 감소, 현금 감소
22일	프란체스코	L 20, S 4, D 2	로도비코	로도비코가 나에게 진 빚을 프란체스코가 대신 갚기로 약속하다. ※ 프란체스코에 대한 채무 감소, 로도비코에 대한 채권 감소

rança, e de gran pericolo in perderle e smarrirle. E però, dele lettere familiari quali spesso fra te e li toi amici potino acadere, quelle sequitendo serba in un banchetto ala tua veneritie. E finito di ricevute legale tuyn maço e riposte dapte segnando ogniuna de fore delo che la receuuti di che li respondi. E così si fa amice p inde. E poi ala fin de l'anno de tutti qlli maçi citarai un maço grade, e segna suo CP̄°. E quando voi aiamastra a qi ricorri. haverai il tuo studio overo scritoio una casta nela ql reporrai e ob ioura se vessero sp̄ in co lo reu mandate. doue sedici che la mandasti. metela tú tasca di roma. e se a firença in qlla venireua &c. E poi nel spaçare del fante pigliale con le tuoi al tuo rispodere in quel tal luogo la uoi. pbe ci scriuere sempre e buono e anche tu sa' par suo beneragio per eer seruito &c. atorno eso quito copura cioe si fa i piu casehette, cioe in tante q̄ te sonno le terre luogh̄ li de quali fare le toe faccide cō dicíamo. Roma. Fir̄e. Napoli. Milano. Inoa. Lion. Loura Buca &c. E sopa ditte casehette p ordine scriuerai illusione, cioe a l'una dira' Roma. al tra' Fir̄ca &c, in le quali poi reporarai le l'e che p qlli luoghi te fossero mandate da quals aico che la mandassi. E fatta che li b̄arai coperta e mandarla pure in pitta la de foia. e se se li del suo recevere e p chi. Cosi similiter poraī mentione del ar̄cp. fra. E però sta mandasi con lo suo giorno. El qual pī ma' in materia tua facenda ta che sia, o piccola o grade chi sia maione in tre in te q̄ti lēpe li deue porre simile siuno ci dire luogo. el nome tuo si qa' ua me si costuma mettendo da pede auanti destra de la fra' ip un cāthone. et CP̄°. cioè el dē luogo fra mercātanti se usa ponere di sopra nel principio de la l'a. Da poi a' modo bon x̄piano doutrai sēpre amēte de ponere el glorioso nome de n̄ra salute cioe el don nome de IHS. overo in suo scābio la figura de la ſcā croce. nel cui nome sēp tutte le nr̄e opationi debano eer pricipiate. E farai el scritto coi. 1494 a dì .x. di maggio i Venegia. E poi segua tuo dire. cioe cariffimo &c. ma li studiati e altre gēti cōe sonno religioſi &c che non trafficano. usano del luogo do ue la l'ettera e fatta ponere di sotto con lo di è CP̄°. E li mercati costumano di sopra a modo ditto al tāmēte non vi ponendoci di scribe costumano. E di te seria fatto bene pche se dici la l'a che non ha el pricipio che se fatta ce nome. E qlla che no' ha notato el luogo se ocs che se fatta. Ital̄° modo e non in qlto. e oltra le beffe che peggio e ne legue scandalo vt dixi. Expedita che b̄arai sua respost̄a posela al deputato luogo la poni cōe b̄ar detto. E qlto che dito habiamo de l'ā sola intēdi p āme. Unde ancora da notare che q̄do lettere che tu mā di fossero d'importāça. alle tale se voglīano p registrare in p̄listīco da presolo a qsto dou rato nel qlregistro si deue ponere tutta da verso ad verbū sella fuse grande iporaça cōe sonno li cōe cambio. o de robe mandate o ō. &c. o vero i ē gliare ſolo a substança. cōe moaie direbossi disse cfs. &c. habiamo scritto al tale &c. cioe p la tale del mandamo le tal co le &c. sop̄a sua de dutti &c. o colm̄le e richiestī &c. la qual poacimo in tasca &c. E di tuo se figlīara che b̄arai la tua che inadi e fatto la sopa scrita sīsa. p molti ponerai el suo sēgno et suo nō. acio si cognosca che sia de mercāti i quali molto se deuebauere risuardo p che sondalīcōe i pricipio pi qlto tractato diccmo che mancagūo le repub̄. E a qsto tūe de reuerentia el simile li p.mi Cardinali pongano defor el suo pstīero nome acio niū se posia re fore de non sape de chi la soli. E molto piu apraftere el sātisp padre sī le sue patēce &c. apre cōe fona tutte le suefar c. Altri chi altre cose piu inde che poca lāue ci signo' de pescatore &c. Le lettre poi inite. e p incie. o vero sino p anno recarrai i maçi, overo sice da pole poni ordinariamēti uito arbutro o iularcāto scuro. E cioe nascuto al comora ove se la tieni ācio posa più pīsto a tue occurrēze retrovarle dī laqlcosa ne curo più dire p̄lso so

제2편
1494 베니스 회계 요약

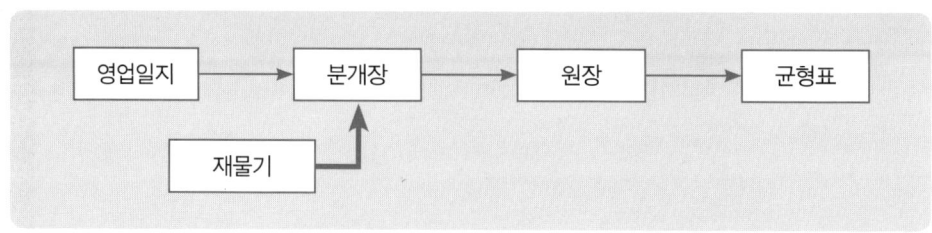

| 영업일지 |

- 모든 거래 사실을 기록하는 장부다.
- 차대 방식이 아니라 사실을 사실대로만 기록하면 되는 기록부이다.
- 이 일지는 기장을 생략할 수 있다.

| 재물기 |

- 기초 대차대조표에 해당되는 기록부이다.
- 부기를 시작하기에 앞서 기록하는 장부이다.
- 사업개시 시점의 재산과 채무를 기록하는 장부이다.
- 등재되는 재산은 소소한 것 이외의 모든 재산이다.
  - 동산, 부동산, 상품, 기타 채권 등 재산적 가치가 있는 모든 것이 기록대상이다.
  - 따라서 이 재산 각각은 화폐로, 즉 금액으로 환산 기록되어야 한다.
- 채권과 채무는 인명별로 기록되어야 한다.
- 이렇게 작성된 재물기는 분개장으로 전기되어야 한다.
  - 즉, 기초 대차대조표를 분개장에 기록하는 것이 된다.
  - 이 전기 작업 이후부터 판매, 구매 등의 일반적인 거래를 분개하는 것이다.

| 분개장 |

- 거래라는 사건을 채무자와 채권자(차변과 대변)로 분해하여 기록하는 장부이다.
- 분개는 반드시 대차 양변 동액으로 기록해야 한다.
- 차변은 Per, 대변은 A로 표시한다.
  - Per는 회사의 채무자, A는 회사의 채권자를 의미한다.
  - Per, A 다음에는 주고받은 인명을 기록해야 한다.
- 차대 분리기호 '//' 는 등호 '='과 같다.
  - 분개시 차변과 대변의 금액은 언제나 같아야 하기 때문이다.

| 분개 예시 |
현금 차입: Per 현금 1,000 // A 로도비코(인명) 1,000
현금 대여: Per 마르티노(인명) 700 // A 현금 700

| 원장 |

- 원장은 분개장 기록을 전기하여 작성되는 장부이다.
- 원장은 각 계정, 즉 인명별로 설정한다.
- 각 인명별 원장은 차변과 대변으로 2분된다.
- 분개된 것 중에서
  - Per는 원장의 Debitori(Debit, 차변)로 전기하고
  - A는 원장의 Creditori(Credit, 대변)로 전기한다.

| 분개장과 원장의 전기와 연결관계 |
(분개)
1일 현금 차입: Per 현금 1,000 // A 프란체스코(인명) 1,000
2일 현금 대여: Per 마르티노(인명) 700 // A 현금 700
3일 현금 회수: Per 현금 400 // A 마르티노 400
4일 현금 상환: Per 프란체스코 400 // A 현금 400

■ 현금원장

차변(Debit)	대변(Credit)
1일 프란체스코에게 차입 1,000	2일 마르티노에게 대여 700
3일 마르티노에게 대여금 회수 400	4일 프란체스코에게 상환 400

■ 프란체스코 원장

차변(Debit)	대변(Credit)
2일 현금으로 차입금 상환 400	1일 현금으로 차입금 수취 1,000

■ 마르티노 원장

차변(Debit)	대변(Credit)
2일 현금으로 대여 700	3일 현금으로 회수 400

- 상기의 원장은 각 분개를 전기하여 작성된 것이다.
- 원장의 좌측에는 채무자, 우측에는 채권자를 기록하며, 잔액란은 없다.

거래 유형별 분개 예시

| 재물기와 그 분개 |

재산, 채무 내역	분개
현금 500만 원	Per 현금 500 // A 현병주 500만 원 (현병주는 출자자의 명칭이다.)
비단 100필, 총액 100만 원	Per 비단 100 // A 현병주 100
무명 200필, 총액 30만 원	Per 무명 30 // A 현병주 30 (비단, 무명 등과 같이 상품 명칭을 기록한다.)
베니스 은행예치금 600만 원	Per 베니스은행 600 // A 현병주 600
토지 1,000만 원	Per 토지 100 // A 현병주 1,000
이태로에 대한 채무 700만 원	Per 현병주 700 // A 이태로 700
한필교에 대한 채권 400만 원	Per 한필교 400 // A 현병주 400

　재물기는 현금출자, 현물출자, 채권출자, 채무출자 내역서에 해당된다. 이 재물기는 그 내역 그대로 분개장에 전기되어야 하고, 이는 출자 분개에 해당된다. 그리고 채권, 채무 분개시 베니스은행-보통예금, 이태로-대여금, 한필교-차입금 등과 같이 현행 부기의 과목에 해당되는 보통예금, 대여금, 차입금 등의 과목은 기입하지 않고 인명만 기입한다. 줄 돈인지 받을 돈인지는 적요란 기록으로 파악한다. 또한 상품출자 분개의 경우, 비단, 무명, 후추, 설탕 등과 같이 상품 명칭을 계정으로 분개해야 한다. 상품계정도 인명계정이므로 숨마부기는 송도부기처럼 인명계정으로 분개 기록하는 부기이다. 오히려 송도부기보다 더 인명계정 원칙을 준수하는 부기이다.

　- 송도부기에서는 인명을 주계정으로 하고, 과목을 부계정으로 하므로 분개기록시 "인명 과목"으로 계정을 기입하는 것이 원칙이지만, 숨마부기에서는 인명만을 계정으로 기입하여 분개하기 때문이다.

분개 원칙과 분개의 예시

분개 원칙

- 대차 양방 동액으로 분개해야 한다.
- 대차기호 다음에는 인명을 계정으로 기록해야 한다.
  - 분개기호는 Per, A 이 두 가지이다.
  - 분개시 언제나 좌측이 Per, 우측이 A이므로 이 두 기호는 생략해도 무방한 쓸모없는 기호이다.

■ 분개 예시

거래의 종류	숨마부기	송도부기(현병주 방식)
현금출자	Per 현금 // A 출자자 명칭	입 출자자 명칭_자본금 上
현물출자	Per 비단 // A 출자자 명칭	거 비단질 // 입 출자자 명칭_자본금
현금차입	Per 현금 // A 차입처 명칭	입 차입처 명칭_급차 上
현금상환	Per 차입처 명칭 // A 현금	거 차입처 명칭_급차 下
현금대여	Per 대여처 명칭 // A 현금	거 대여처 명칭_봉차 下
현금회수	Per 현금 // A 대여처 명칭	입 대여처 명칭_봉차 上
채무자 변경	Per 신채무자 명칭 // A 구채무자 명칭	거 신채무자 명칭 // 입 구채무자 명칭
현금예치	Per 은행 명칭 // A 현금	거 은행 명칭_당좌예금 下
사업비 지급	Per 인건비 // A 현금	거 공용질_인건비 下
현금매입	Per 비단 // A 현금	거 비단질 下
운반비 지급	Per 비단 // A 현금	거 비단질_운임 下
외상매입	Per 비단 // A 외상매입처 명칭	거 비단질 // 입 외상매입처 명칭_급차
현금외상 혼합매입	Per 비단 // A 외상매입처 명칭 Per 비단 // A 현금(현금지급분)	거 비단질 // 입 외상매입처 명칭_급차 거 비단질 下(현금지급분)
외상대 지급	Per 외상매입처 명칭 // A 현금	거 외상매입처 명칭_급차 下
현금판매	Per 현금 // A 비단	입 비단질 上
외상판매	Per 외상매출처 명칭 // A 비단	거 외상매출처 명칭_봉차 // 대 비단질
현금외상 혼합판매	Per 외상매출처 명칭 // A 비단 Per 현금 // A 외상매출처 명칭	거 외상매출처 명칭 // 입 비단질 입 외상매출처 명칭_봉차 上

상기의 예시분개에서 송도부기는 송도사개치부법 상의 분개방법이고, 이는 송도부기 제1파에 해당된다. 송도부기 제2파는 대한천일은행의 분개방법이다. 여기서는 송도부기 제1파를 송도부기라고 칭하고자 한다.

송도부기의 입/거는 숨마부기의 A/Per와 일치한다. 상기의 분개예시에서 상은 현금입금, 하는 현금출금을 의미한다. 그리고 봉차는 받을 돈, 급차는 줄 돈을 의미한다. 이체 분개의 경우 숨마부기와 송도부기는 기호만 다를 뿐 상기와 같이 일치한다. 그리고 현금거래의 경우 송도부기는 "입 차입처 명칭_급차 상"과 같이 1변으로 분개가 완료되는 듯 하지만, 이 역시 숨마부기와 원칙적으로 같은 양방 분개이다. 입/거 분개에 부가되는 상 또는 하가 또 다른 1변이므로, 송도부기의 현금 분개 역시 양방 분개가 되기 때문이다. 요약하면, 숨마부기와 송도부기는 같은 내용이다. 이에 대한 세부적인 설명은 다음 책에서 하고자 한다.

그리고 상기의 송도분개에서 '//'는 행 분리 기호이다. 송도부기는 입변과 거변을 행을 달리하여 기록하는 것이 원칙이지만, 여기서는 편의상 숨마방식으로 분개하였다.

장부의 마감과 결산

장부의 마감

마감 전 절차
- 분개장 기록의 원장전기의 정확성 여부를 확인해야 한다.
- 한 사람은 분개장, 한 사람은 원장을 갖는다.
- 분개 내역을 하나씩 외치면, 또 한 사람은 그 분개에 대응되는 원장 기록을 찾는다.
    - 원장 기록을 찾아 그것이 분개와 일치하면 소인(전기필 표시)을 한다.
    - 이런 식으로 모든 분개와 원장 전기를 확인하고 소인을 한다.

분개장의 마감
- 분개장의 마감에 대하여 특별한 언급은 없다.
- 다만, 새해가 되면 분개장 페이지가 남아 있더라도 새 분개장을 만들어 쓰기를 권고하는 정도다.

원장의 마감
- 원장은 차변과 대변으로 나누어 기록되어 있다.
- 차변 금액의 합계와 대변 금액의 합계를 산출한다.
- 양자를 비교하여 적은 쪽에 차액을 기록하여 양자의 금액을 일치시킨다.
- 이것이 마감이다.
- 이렇게 마감 후, 상품계정의 잔액은 손익계정으로 전기한다.
    - 상품계정이 다수인 경우, 각 계정별로, 즉 상품별로 손익계정에 전기한다.
    - 상품계정에서 차변 잔액이면, 손익계정에도 차변으로 전기된다.
- 또한 소사업비, 가계비 등의 잔액도 손익계정으로 전기된다.
- 손익계정 원장에서도 차변과 대변의 금액을 합계한다.
- 손익계정의 차액을 자본금계정 원장에 전기한다.

- 자본금계정 원장에서도 차변과 대변의 금액을 합계하고, 차액을 적은 쪽에 기입한다.
  - 이렇게 하면 자본금계정 원장도 대차 양변이 일치하게 된다.
- 따라서 모든 계정 원장의 차대가 일치하게 된다.
- 현행 부기와 달리 결산분개를 하지 않는다.
  - 즉, 원장 전기를 통하여 손익을 산출하고, 자본금계정의 잔액, 즉 순재산을 확정하는 수준에서 회계작업이 완료된다.

균형표의 작성

- 원장을 마감한 후에는 균형표를 작성해야 한다.
- 균형표는 잔액시산표가 아니라, 원장 전기의 정확성을 검증하는 표이다.
- 균형표를 작성하려면 먼저 커다란 종이를 준비한다.
- 이 종이의 좌측에는 원장의 모든 (계정의) 차변총액을 기록한다.
  우측에는 원장의 모든 (계정의) 대변총액을 기록한다.
- 기록한 후에는 차변과 대변 각각의 금액을 합계한다.
- 차변과 대변 합계가 같으면 오류가 없는 원장으로 간주하나, 다르면 그 원인을 찾아 교정해주어야 한다.
- 숨마에서 파치올리는 순이익과 순재산(자본금 잔액) 산출까지만 언급하였으므로 숨마부기가 일견 매우 소략한 것으로 보일 수도 있으나, 사실은 경제주체에 필요한 모든 정보를 해설한 것이라고 할 수 있다. 손익계정에서 순이익이 산출되고, 자본금 원장에서 출자 자본금 잔액이 산출되고, 나머지 대차 정보는 각 원장에서 확인할 수 있기 때문이다.

번역 후기

原文·眞文을 보는 것,
그리고 그 原文을 제대로 번역하는 것이
학문의 시작이다

　　1990년 대학동창과 함께 회계 소프트웨어 회사(현 더존디지탈웨어)를 창업하였으나, 경영에 대한 의견이 맞지 않아 그 2년 후 관계를 청산하였다. 그리고 아무 욕심 없이 시골에서 조용히 살고 싶어 1993년에 농촌진흥청에 농업경영연구사로 들어갔다. 그러나 전직이 회계 프로그램 제작업자라는 이유로 필자에게 대차변 없는 아주 쉬운 농업회계 프로그램을 개발하라는 과제가 맡겨졌다.

　　원래 프로그래머가 아니라 경영학도였던 관계로 그때부터 컴퓨터 프로그래밍, 데이터베이스, 회계 등에 대한 만리장정이 시작되었다. 일본, 미국 등 주요국가의 농업회계 그리고 복식부기 책자를 입수하여 꽤 보았지만, 그들 역시 회계에 대한 본질적인 논리 없이 그저 이럴 땐 이렇게 분개하고, 저럴 땐 저렇게 분개해야 한다는 복사기 부기, 앵무새 부기에 지나지 않았다. 대차변 없는 프로그램을 만드는 데에는 전혀 도움이 되지 않았다. 단지 복식부기 그리고 현행 회계에 대하여 필자가 그전부터 갖고 있던 환멸―학문이 아닌 중언부언의 암기과목―이 강화될 뿐이었다.

　　하지만, 농업인을 위하여 보다 쉬운 프로그램을 개발하기는 해야 했다. 연구결과 일단 회면 상으로는 농가에서 발생하는 거래의 유형을 제시하고, 이 유형을 농가가 선택하여 수입과 지출을 입력하면, 프로그램 내부에서 복식으로 처리하는 편법적인 방식으로 프로그램을 개발 보급하였다. 물론 완전한 차대 방식으로도 입력할 수 있도록 하여 전문적인 경리를 둔 영농법인도 활용할 수 있도록 하였다. 그리고 이 프로그램을 갖고 전국의 농촌지도사, 영농법인, 독농가 등에 대한 회계지도 사업을 하면서 회계 만리장정을 하게 되었다. 사용하기가 쉬워 10년 이상 사용하는 농가도 있었으나, 완전히 대차변을 탈피한 프로그램은 아니었기에 만족할 수는 없었다.

농진청 퇴직 후에는 주로 불경, 주역, 논어, 맹자, 노자, 그리스 철학, 삼국사기, 삼국유사 등 고전 서적을 읽으며 지냈다. 특히 불경은 산스크리트어 원문이 아니라 한국어로 번역된 책이지만 부처님 시대의 역사적 상황을 파헤친 책을 위주로 하여 보았다. 그러던 어느 날 우연히 회계도 최초에 발생한 시점을 다룬 책을 보아야 하지 않겠는가, 라는 생각이 들었다. 즉, 회계에서도 고전 원문의 탐구가 필요함을 깨닫게 되었다. 바로 찾아 나섰다.

국립중앙도서관에서 루카 파치올리라는 이름으로 검색하여 평정태태랑의 파치올리 부기서 연구(1918년 출간)라는 일본어 번역본을 찾아, 한동안은 꽤 열심히 보았다. 현행 일본어가 아니라 1945년 패망 이전의 일본 고어체로 되어 있어 난해한 책이었지만, 다행히 거의 한자로 되어 있어 웬만큼은 해독이 되는 책이었다. 그러나 이 책만으로는 부족한 것이 많았다. 단지 원문을 번역했다는 데 의미가 있을 뿐 앞뒤 연결이 안 되는 문장으로 되어 있어 이 책에서 어떤 의미나 논리를 찾는다는 것은 그야말로 연목구어 격이었기 때문이다. 어찌됐든 참고는 꽤 되었지만, 역시 파치올리의 原文, 眞文이 아닌 暇文(가문)이었기 때문에 다시 파치올리의 원문을 찾아 나섰다.

이어 국립중앙도서관에서 Basil Yamey가 편집한 회계학사 전집(Historic Accounting Literature)을 찾았지만, 그 시리즈에는 무슨 이유에서인지 파치올리의 숨마만 없고, 파치올리 이후의 회계학 서적들만 있었다. 즉, 숨마의 최초 번역자인 네덜란드인 Ympyn의 프랑스어판 숨마 1543년본, 독일인 Mennher의 독어판 숨마 1565년본 등부터 Bossi Andrea의 1816년본까지 수십 종의 회계학 고전서적들이 각 저자의 책 그대로 복사 인쇄되어 있었다. 파치올리의 숨마가 아니라 아쉬움이 있었지만, 일단 임핀의 불어본 1543년판, Peele의 영역본 1569년판 등을 보며 숨마의 진면목을 추리하고자 애썼다.

그러다가 우연히 평정태태랑이 쓴 서문에서 이 일역본이 미국인 존 가이스빅의 영역본(1914년 출간)을 그대로 번역한 것이라는 구절에 눈길이 닿았다. 그리고 드디어 아마존닷컴에서 존 가이스빅의 영역본(복사본)을 구할 수 있었다. 가이스빅은 숨마원문과 영역문을 좌우대조 방식으로 편집하였으므로 이제 숨마도 찾고, 또 숨마의 1대 1 번역본도 찾은 것이다.

이미 일역본으로 존 가이스빅의 영문판 내역을 파악해 놓고 있었고, 그리고 숨마부기의 원본인 송도부기, 서울부기(대한천일은행 부기)도 그 해석을 마친 상태였기에 영문을 해석하는 데에는 큰 문제가 없었다. 그리고 가이스빅은 좌측에는 영문, 우측에는 이탈리아어 원문방식으로 책을 편집하였기에, Per(Deve Dare, 그가 나에게 주어야 한다, 차변, 봉차), A(Deve Avere, 그는 나에게 받아야 한다, 급차, 대변), Conto(Count, 계정) 등의 중요한 단어는 라틴어 또는 이탈리아 원어로 그 내역을 추적할 수 있었다. 이렇게 이탈리아 원어와 영어를 대조해 보고, 또 번역의 논리성을 추적해 본 결과, 가이스빅의 영역이 사실상 거의 완전하다는 확신을 갖게 되었다. 그는 파치올리 원문의 오류 및 오기도 그대로 번역할 정도로 원문에 충실하였다. 이러한 확신으로 비록 이탈리아어 원문은 아니지만, 영역문을 저본으로 숨마를 한국어로 번역해도 무방하다는 생각을 갖게 되어, 번역에 착수하게 되었다.

그러나 가이스빅의 영역이 거의 완전함에도 불구하고, 이 책을 그 어떤 미국인도 제대로 이해하기 어렵듯이, 필자의 한역 또한 한글로 쓰여 있어 한국인이라면 누구나 읽을 수는 있겠지만, 이해하기는 어려울 것이다. 회계에 문외한인 사람들은 당연히 이해가 어렵겠지만, 회계학으로 박사학위를 취득한 전문가들도 이해가 어려울 것이다. 여기서 이해란 복식부기의 핵심에 대한 이해를 의미한다. 1) 왜 차변을 좌측에, 대변을 우측에 놓아야 하는지, 2) 인건비 등을 지급하면 왜 현금을 대변에 기록해야 하는지, 3) 출자 분개 시 왜 현금은 좌측에, 자본금은 우측에 기록해야 하는지, 4) 자본금 잔액은 왜 대변에서 차변을 차감하고, 예금잔액은 왜 차변에서 대변을 차감하는지, 5) 그리고 차변과 대변은 어떤 의미인지 등이 그 주요한 의문이 될 것이다.

필자는 숨마의 번역 시 원칙적으로 원문의 단어 하나하나 모두 다 번역을 하되, 직역을 위주로 하고, 가급적 의역이나 뭉뚱그리거나 하는 번역은 배제하였다. 즉, 대충 얼버무리거나 의역 등은 배제하였다. 이것은 필자가 대충 얼렁뚱땅 얼버무려 번역하는 방법을 몰라서 그렇게 한 것은 아니다. 원문이 어색해도 논리적 오류가 있어도 가급적 그대로 번역하였고, 또 원문도 좌측 페이지에 제시하였으므로 필자가 행한 번역의 정확성 여부 등은 독자들이 직접 육안으로 확인할 수 있을 것이다. 따라서 사실상 원문에 충실하게 번역하였다고 할 수 있다. 그러나 번역은 되었어도 이 글을 읽는 그 누구도 회계의 본질을 알 수는 없고, 앞에서 언급한 의문만 더 쌓일 것이다. 즉, 가이스빅이든 평정태태랑이든 필자든 숨마 원문을 제대로 번역하였지만, 아무도 알 수 없는 책이 되었다. 이러한 현상은 쓰레기를 넣으면 쓰레기만 나온다는 어느 속담처럼 원문 자체가 부실하기 때문이라고 할 수도 있다.

그러나 숨마는 중세 유럽 최고의 수학자가 쓴 글이므로 부실한 글이 될 수가 없다. 비록 회계의 본질과 원리에 대한 해설은 부족하고, 약간의 오류와 오기, 오타가 있지만 숨마는 사실상 완벽한 책이다. 즉, 숨마는 해설은 부족하지만 현병주 선생처럼 회계의 진리는 제대로 전달한 책이다. 문제가 있다면, 숨마에서 비롯된 현행회계가 숨마의 바람 풍을 바담 풍, 바탐 풍으로 번역하여 사용하는 데 있는 것이다.

필자는 송도부기와 서울부기, 조선왕조 관청부기를 숨마부기와 대조 분석하면서 숨마에서 파치올리가 바담 풍이 아니라 바람 풍이라고 기록했음을 확인할 수 있었다. 따라서 필자는 숨마의 바람 풍을 그대로 살려, 필자 역시 바람 풍으로 번역할 수도 있었으나, 본서에서는 현행회계 방식대로 바담 풍 또는 바탐 풍으로 번역할 수밖에 없었다. 현행회계는 묵비사염(墨悲絲染)의 회계이므로 그 물을 빼려면 꽤 긴 설명이 필요하기 때문이다.

묵비사염(墨悲絲染)
어느 날 묵자는 흰 실이 검은 물에 들어가면 검게 물들고, 빨간 물에 들어가면 빨갛게 물드는 것을 보고, 사람들의 하얀 의식 또한 그렇게 검은 물, 빨간 물이 든다는 것을 깨닫고 탄식하였다.

즉, 현행회계는 송도부기와 달리 부지지(不知知)의 회계이므로 그 인식을 지부지(知不知) 상태로 바꾸려면 긴 설명이 필요하기 때문이기도 하다. 현행회계는 그 원본인 숨마부기를 거의 본 적도 없고, 이해하지도 못하면서 그들의 회계가 정법이라고 주장한다. 또한, 송도부기를 원문 그대로 살펴본 적도 거의 없고, 해석도 제대로 못 하면서 송도부기를 단식부기 또는 비복식 불완전 부기라고 한다.

知不知 上, 不知知 病 (노자)

지부지 상, 부지지 병

모른다는 것을 아는 것이 상이고, 모르면서 아는 체 하는 것이 병이다.

但知不知 是即見性 (조계종 어록)

단지부지 시즉견성

모른다는 것을 아는 것이 견성이다.

나는 내가 모른다는 것을 알 뿐이다. (소크라테스)

오직 모를 뿐 (숭산 선사)

    요약하면 숨마를 숨마답게, 원저자인 루카 파치올리가 1490년대의 어느 날 관찰한 어느 베니스 상인의 기록과 계산, 즉 회계 그 모습 그대로 볼 수 있도록 번역하려면, 숨마의 원본인 송도부기, 서울부기, 조선왕조 관청부기에 대한 이해가 필요하다. 그렇게 해야 반역이 아니라 정역이 되고, 동시에 회계가 중언부언의 암기과목이 아닌 순수한 학문으로 다시 태어난다.

    하지만, 숨마에 대한 정역은 본서가 아닌 회계 고전 시리즈 마지막 부분에서 제시하고자 한다. 이것은 번역 전체를 다시 한다는 뜻이 아니라 정역에 필요한 키워드 몇 개를 제공한다는 의미이다. 그러면 그 열쇠로 바담 풍을 바람 풍으로 바꿀 수 있으리라.

2011년 1월

이원로

부록 1494 베니스 회계 원문

Proceedings of the Conference

ACCOUNTING AND ECONOMICS

in honour of the 500th anniversary of the publication of

Luca Pacioli's
Summa de Arithmetica, Geometria, Proportioni et Proportionalita

Siena, 18th - 19th November 1992

Edited by Martin Shubik

APPENDIX

Frontispiece of the "Summa" dedicated to Guidobaldo of Montefeltro.

Tractatus particularis de computis et scripturis

De quelle cose che sono necessarie al vero mercatante: e de lordine a sape bē tenere vn q̄derno cō suo giornale i vinegia e anche p ognaltro luogo.   Capitolo primo.

J reuerenti subditi de. V. D. S. Magnanimo. D. acio a pieno de tutto lordine mercantesco habino el bisogno: deliberai. (Oltr' le cose dinanze i q̄sta nr̄a opa ditte) ancora particular tractato grandemēte necessario copillare. E in q̄sto solo lo iserto: p che a ogni loro occurrēca el p̄sente libro li possa seruire. Si del mō do a conti e scripture: cōmo de ragioni. E per esso intendo dar li norma sufficiente e bastante in tenere ordinatamente tutti lor conti e libri. Pero che. (cōmo si sa) tre cose maxime sono opor tune: a chi uole con debita diligētia mercantare. De le q̄li la potissima e la pecunia numerata cōgni altra faculta sustantiale. Juxta illud phȳ vnū aliquid necessarioru̅ e substantia. Sēca el cui suffragio mal si po el manegio traficante exercitare. Auega che molti gia nudi cō bona fede cōmencando: de grā facēde habio fatto. E mediante lo credito fedelmēte seruato i magne richecce sieno peruenuti. Che asai p ytalia discurrēdo nabiamo cognosciuti. E piu gia nele grā republiche non si poteua dire: che la fede del bon mercantē. E a quella si fermaua lor giuramento: dicēdo. A la fe de real mercatante. E cio nō deuel sere admiratione: cōciosia che i la fede catolicamēte ognuno si salui: e senca lei isia ipossibile piacere a dio. La secōda cosa che si recerca al debito trafico: sie che sia buon ragionere: e prompto cōputista. E p questo cōsequire. (disopra cōmo se ueduto) dal pricipio alafine: ha uemo iducto regole e canoni a ciascuna opatione requisiti. In modo che da se: ogni diligē te lectore: tutto potra ipre̅ndere. E chi di questa pte non fosse bene armato: la sequete in va no li serebbe. La. 3.e vltima cosa oportuna sie: che cō bello ordie tutte sue facēde debita mēte disponga: acio con breuita: possa de ciascūa hauer notitia: quanto a lor debito e anche credito: che circa altro non satēde el trafico. E q̄sta pte fra laltre e a loro utilissima: che i lor facēde altramēte regere: seria ipossibile: sēca debito ordine de scripture. E sēca alcū reposo la lor mēte sempre staria in gran trauagli. E po acio con laltre q̄sta possino hauere: el p̄sente tra ctato ordiai. Nel q̄le se da el mō a tutte sorti de scripture: a ca°. p ca°. prcedēdo. E bē che nō si possa cusi apōto tutto el bisogno scriuere. Nō dimeno p q̄l che se dira. El pegrino ige̅g̃a q̄l cū altro laplicara.   E seruaremo i esso el mō de vinegia: q̄le certamēte fra gli altri e moito da cōmēdare. E mediante q̄llo i ogni altro se porra guidare. E q̄sto diuideremo i.2. pti pri cipali. Luna chiamaremo inuētario. E laltra dispōne. E p de luna: e poi de laltra successiua mēte se dira scdo lordie i la p̄posta tauola contenuto. Per la q̄l facilmēte el lectore porra le occurrentie trouare secondo el numero de suoi capitoli e carti.

Hi cō lo debito ordie che sa spectia vol sap tenere vn q̄derno cō lo suo g'orna le a q̄l che qui se dira con diligētia stia a tēto. E acio bē sintēda el p̄cesso idurre mo i capo vno che mo di nuouo comēsa a traficare cōmo p ordie deba procedere ne tenere soi conti e scripture: acioche sucitamēte ogni cosa possi ritrouare posta al suo luogo p che nō asettando le cose debitamēte a li suoi luoghi ncrebbe i grandissimi tra nagli e cōfusiōi de tutte sue facēde. Juxta cōe dictū vbi nō e ordo ibi est cōfusio. E pero a p fecto documēto dogni mercatante de tutto nr̄o prcesso faremo cōmo di sopra e ditto. 2. pti pncipali. Leq̄li aptamēte q̄ sequēte chiariremo: acio fructo salutifero sabia iprēdere. E pria dimostrando ch cosa sia iuētario e cōmo sabia fare   De la pa pte pncipale de q̄sto tractato de tā iuētario. E che cosa sia iuētario: e cōme fra mercatanei sabia fare. ca°. 2   Cōmēse adōqua pmēte psupponere e imaginare che ogni opante e mosso dal fine. E p poter q̄llo debitamēte cōsequre fa o q̄ni suo sforzo nel suo prcesso. vnde el fine de q̄l che traficante e de cōsequire licito e cōpetēte guadagno p sua substētatiōe. E po sempre con lo nome de meser domenedio: debiano cōmēcare loro facende. E i nel pō. dogni lor scripture: el suo sancto

Distinctio nona, Tractatus xi°. De scripturis

nome hauera mēte ʒc. E po p°. cōuen che facia suo diligente iuētario: i q̄sto modo. che sempre p°. scriua in vn foglio o uero libro da pte. Cioche se ritroua hauer al mōdo: de mobile: e de stabile. Cōmençando sempre da le cose che sōno in piu pgio e piu labili al perdere. Cōmo sō li o͞. cōtanti. Gioe. Argenti ʒc. P°.r che li stabili cōmo sōno. Casi. Terreni. Lacune valle. Peschiere e simili nō si possano sinarire: cōmo le cose mobili. E successiuamēte poi de mano i mano. scriuase laltre. Ponendo sēpre p° el dì: e milesimo: el luogo. el nome suo nel dicto iuētario. e tutto dicto iuētario si deue tenere in vn medesimo giorno: p che altramēte uarebe trauaglio nel māegio futuro. E po a tuo crēplo: porre q̄ vn p.r n°. cōmo se debia fare. Per lo q̄l tu pte porrai i ogni luogo el apposito sequire ʒc. v3.

Forma crēplare cō tutte sue solennita in lo inuentario requisite. ca°. 3

Al nome de dio. 1493. a dì. 8. nouembre in vinegia.

Questo se qūeste sie lo iuētario de mi. N. da vine°. de la cōtrada de scō apostolo. El qūle ordenatamēte io de mia mano ho scripto: o vo fatto scriuere dal tale ʒc. de tutti li miei beni: Mobili: e Stabili: Debiti: e Crediti che al mōdo mi ritrouo: sin q̄sto psēte giorno sopra dicto. p°. prita. In p°. mi trouo de cōtāti. fra oro e moneta: duc̄. tanti ʒc. Di q̄li tāti sōno doro veniniani. E tāti doro ōgari. E tāti. fio. larghi fra papali: senesi: e fiorētini ʒc. Lauāço mōete dargeto e rame de piu sorti: cioe. Troi. Marcelli. Carlini de re. E de papa. E grossi fiorētini. Testoni milanesi ʒc. 2ª. Itē mi trouo i gioie ligate e desligate. Peçi n°. tāti ʒc. De li q̄li tāti sōno balassi i tauola ligati: i oro anelli pesano. 3. e caratti grani ʒc. luno o uero i sūma. Qui poi dire a tuo mō ʒc. E tanti sōno safili pur a tauola iformagli da dōna. Pesano ʒc. E tāti sōno rubi oculegni desligadi pesano ʒc. laltri sōno diamāti grecci a tauola: e pōtidi ʒc. Narrādo le sorti e pesi a tua uoglia. 3ª Itē mi trouo veste de piu sorte. tāte de la tale e tante de la tale ʒc. Narrādo suoi cōditōi. Colo ri: fodre e fogie ʒc. 4ª. Itē mi trouo argēti lauorati de. p. sorti. Cōmo tacce bacili. Raimi. Cosiler i. Pironi ʒc. q̄ narra tutto le sorti a vna p vna ʒc. E pesa ciascuna sorta dapse sotilmēte. E tiē cōto de peçi e de pesi ʒc. de le leghe. E veneriana. O ragusea ʒc. alche stapo. o uero segno che haueffero farne mentioe ʒc. 5ª. Itē mi trouo i maßaria o panni lini: cioe Lençoli. Touagli. Camise. Fazu. li ʒc. Lapi n° tāti ʒc. Lēçuoli de. 3. rdi. Odi. 2. ʒc. rele padouane o altre ʒc. nuoui o vsati lōghi tanti bi. ʒc. E camise tante ʒc. touagle de rēle ʒc. fa quoli grandi n°. tanti ʒc. E piccoli tanti ʒc. noui vsati ʒc. a tuo mō narra ° le sorti. 6ª. Itē mi trouo lecti o pūa. n°. tanti ʒc. cō soi caueçali de piu° noua o vo vsata ʒc. federa noua ʒc. Qli pesano i tutto. o vo vno p vno. 8. tante ʒc. Seg°te del mio seg°. o dalt°. cōmo si costuma ʒc. 7ª Itē mi trouo de mercantie i casa ouer i magaçeni. ʒc. de piu sorti. p°. Colli tanti de çēçari. michini pesano. 8. ran°. ʒc. Segnati del tal seg°. ʒc. E cosi andarai narran°. a fortap p° sor°. e dicte mercantie cō tutti cōtrasegni sia possibile. e cō q̄ta. piu chiareçça si possa. de pe so n°. e misura ʒc. 8ª Itē mi trouo colli tanti de çēçari bellidi ʒc. carchi tāti de pip ʒc. pip lōgo. o uer pip tōdo scōdo che sira ʒc. E fardi tanti di canelle ʒc. pesa°. ʒc. E colli tanti garo. ʒc. pesa°. ʒc. cō fusti poluere e cappelleti. o vo seça ʒc. E peçi tāti. de ʒēçini ʒc. pesa°. ʒc. e peçi tanti san. rossi o bianchi pesa°. ʒc. cosi andarai mettēdo p ordie v°. sotto laltro ʒc. 9ª. Itē mi tr°. pelami da fodre: cioe agneli°. bia°. e albertoi pugliesi o marchiani ʒc. n°. tanti de la tal sor°. ʒc. e volpe mar. n° tante còçe ʒc. n°. tante crude ʒc. E camoçe conçe e trude ʒc. n°. tante ʒc. 10ª Itē mi trouo pelle si. fo°. arme. uolssi. vari. gebelini ʒc. n°. tanti de la tal sorte. E n°. tanti de la tale ʒc. Cosi destigüedo a v°. a v°. diligētemēte con tutta verita: acio el vero te habia a gnidare ʒc. Auendo sēp auerteça a le cose che uāno a n°. E a q̄lle, che uāno a peso. E a q̄lle cō vāno a misura. po ch di q̄ste. 3. for°. si costūa fare el trafico p tutto. e alcune si mercatio a. M°. Altre a. c°. altre a. 8. Altre a. G. altre a n°. cioe a cōto cōmo pella mi ʒc. altre a peçi. cōmo gioie: e perle fine ʒc. Si che di tutte sa ben nota a cosa per cosa ʒc. E queste te bastino a tua guida. Laltre per te poi sequirai sempre ʒc. 11ª. Item mi trouo destabile priam. vna casa a tanti sulari ʒc. a tante camere. Corte. Poççe. Orto ʒc. posta in la contra de sancto apostolo: fora canale ʒc. apresso el tal c: e tale ʒc. Nominando li cōfini: e referēdon ali instr si vi sōno ātichi piu veri ʒc. cosi se piu nauesse de le case i diuersi luoghi: nofare a simili ʒc. 12ª. Itē mi trouo terreni lauoratiui cāpi. o uero staiore. o uero panora ʒc. Nominādoli scōdo luso del paese doue se troui. o uero doue sōno situate ʒc. n°. tāti ʒc. Intrēdēdo el cāpo o uero staiora de tauole tāte o cāne o priche o beuolche ʒc. posti in la tal villa de padouana o altr°de ʒc. Apresso li beni del tale ʒc. Chiamādo li cōfini ʒc. E instrumēti. o uero prita de catasti. p li q̄li paghile fationi: e cōmuno ʒc. Quali lauora el tale ʒc. rēdano lāno de fitto cōmūo: stara tāti e. o. tāti ʒc. E cosi pte ua narādo tuoi possessi o ʒc. Bestiami. soci°. 13ª Itē mi tro° ba° ala cam°. o ipsm. ouer alt°. mōte iv°.

Distinctio nona tractatus .xi°. De scripturis

ducati tanti de cauedale nel sextier de canareggio zc. Duero pte i uno sextieri e pte i unaltro. Narrando ancora i nome de chi sonno scripti. E chiamando el libro de quello officio. El numero de le carti doue e la tua partita. El nome del scriuano che tien ditto libro: acio cō piu tua facilita qñdo uai a scotere li possi trouar. Pero che i tali officij bisogna hauere molti scontri alcuolte per la gran multitudine che ci interuiene zc. E nota el muissimo che respōdano a tēpo p tēpo acio sappia quādo uengano li so pro. e quāto per cēto respōdino zc. 14

Item mi trouo debitori numero tanti zc. luno e l' tale del tale zc. che me deue dare duca ti tanti zc. Laltro e el tale del tale zc. E cosi narrali a uno a uno con boni contra segni: e cognomi: e luoghi: e quanto te debano dar: e p che. E cosi ui son scripti de mā o in strumēti de nodari fra noi fāne mētione zc. In suma debo scotere ducati tāti zc. De boni d̄. Se li rā persone da bene zc. altramēti dirai de tristi d̄. zc. 15. Item mi trouo essere debito i tutto ducati tanti zc. tanti a al tale. e tanti al tale zc. Nominādo li toi creditori a uno a uno. E se ui sō no chiarecçe fra uoi. o de scripti o de instrumenti nominarli. E chi. E commo. el di e luogo per molti casi poteriēno occorrere in iudicio e for de iudicio zc.

Utilissima exortatione: e salutiferi documēti al bō mercatāre pritnēti. ca°. 4

Cosi discorso cō diligēça tutte le cose che se ritroui imobile e stabile: cōme e detto a una per una: se fosser ben diecimilia di che condirioni e faculta si sia: e banchi e imprestiti zc. tutte al buono ordine couiense nominarle in ditto cuetario cō tutti cōtrasegni nomi: e cōgnomi qñto sia piu possibile. Per ch al mercatāte nō possa no mai le cose essere troppo chiare. Per linfiniti casi che nel trafico possano occorrere: commo ala giornata so chi in esso se exercita. E pero be dici el prouerbio che bisogna piu ponti a fare un bō mercatāte. che a fare un doctore de leggi. Chi e colui che possa nūerare li prīti: e casi che ale mani uengono ali mercatanti. Ora p mare. Ora p terra. Ora a tempi de paci e d'abondantia. Ora a tempi de guerre e carestie. Ora a tempi de sanita e morbi. Ne quali tēpi occurrēte li coniuene saper prendere soi partiri. Si p li mercati: cōmo p le fieri che ora i una patria e cita si fāno. E ora in laltra zc. E pero ben le figura e asimiglia el mercatante al gallo. Quale e fragliaitri el piu uigilante animale che sia: e diuerno e di state fa le sue nocturne uigistie. che mai per alcū tempo resta. Auenga che de filomena se dica: cioe del rosignuo lo che tutta la nocte canti: non dimeno questo si po de state al caldo tempo uerificare: ma non dinuerno: cōmo la experiença e impronto adimostrarlo. E ancho sia sumigliata la sua testa a una che habia cēto ochi. che anchora nō li sono bastāti: ne in dir ne i fare. Le qual cose solole dica chi le pua. Marinolo. Uenitiani. Fiorētini. Genouesi. Napolitani. Milanesi. Ancōitāi. Bressani. Bergamaschi. Adriani. Senesi. Lucbesi. Perusini. Urbiati. Foxolim proniani. Cagliesi. E Ugubini. Castellani. Borghesi. e Fulignati cō Pisāi. Bolognesi. e Feraresi. Pātouāi. Uerōesi. Uigesi. e Padouāi. Trani. Leccia. Bari. cō Betōta. Legli spu'. tra laltre i ytalia del trafico tengano el principato. Marie la excelsa cita de uenetia cō fiorēça. Norma e regola d'ogni partito. chal bisogno aprender sabia. Si be dicāo le leggi municipali v3. uigilantibus 7 non dormientibus Jura subueniunt: cioe a chi ueggia e nō a chi dorme le leggi souengāo. E cosi neli diuini officij si canta da la sancta chiesa. che idio ali uigilanti e promesso la corona. E pero questo fo el documēto di virgilio dato a Dante: cōmo a suo figliuolo. Quando nel cāto. 14°. de lo iserno li dici exortandolo a la fatiga: per laqle al monte de le uirtu se peruiene. B z mai conuien figliuolo che tu te spoltri. Disse el maestro mio che pur in piuma. In fama nō si uiene ne sotto coltre. Sotto la qual chi sua uita cōsuma. Cotal uestigio disse in terra lascia. Qual fume e aire e i aqua la schiuma zc. E unaltro uulgar poeta al medesimo ci cōforta dicēdo. Non te para strania la fatiga ch marte nō concesse mai bataglia A quelli che possano se nutrica zc. Lo exemplo anchora del sapiēte molto fo acio conueniēte. Dicēdo al pigro che si spechiasse nella formicha. E paulo apostolo dici che niū fira degno di corona saluo che chi bara legitimamēte combattuto zc. Questi record i li o uoluti adure per tua utilita: acio non te para graue la cotidiana solicitudine in tue facende. maxime in tenere la pēna in carta: e tutto scriuere a di per di: qnel che te occorre: cōmo se dira nel sequēte. Ma sēp sopra tutto p' idio el p'rio te sia auāri gliochi e mai nō manchi da ludire la messa la matia Recordādote ch p le mai si pde camio. Ne p la carita si scema riēçce cōmo p q'sto scō uerso se dici. Nec caritas opes: nec missa miuit iter zc. E a q'sto ci exorta el saluator i sā matheo q'ndo dici. Primū q'rite regnū dei: 7 hec oia adijciētur uobis. Cercate xpiani pmamēte el reame ō li cieli e poi laltre cose tēporali e spūali facil

Distinctio nona Tractatus .xi°. De scripturis

mente consequirete. Pero chel padre vostro celestiale sa molto bene vostro bisogno zc. E q̃ sto voglio te sia bastāte a tuo amaestramēto diuersario zc. e altri boni documēti albenfare zc

De la .2ª. parte p̃cipale del p̃sente tractato dicta: dispōne: cōme la sabia a intendere e in che cōsiste: circa al trafico: e de li .3. libri p̃cipali del corpo mecatesco.   c°. 5

Equita ora la secōda parte principale del p̃sente tractato laqual vicēmo essere la dispositione di laquale alquāto piu longo cōuiē ch'io sia: che i lascēdete a ben chiarirla. E pero di lei faremo doi p̃ti. L'una dicta corpo o uero monte de tutto el trafico. L'altra dicta corpo o vero monte de botega. E prima dirēmo del corpo generale de tutto el manegio le sue exigētie. Al quale dico prima imediate doppo suo inuentario bisognare .3. libri p̃ piu sua destreza e cōmodita. L'uno dicto memoriale. E l'altro decto Giornale. L'altro decto. Quaderno. Auēga che molti p̃ le poche lor facende facino solo cō li doi secōdi: cioe giornale e quaderno. E pero prima dirēmo di l'uno cioe memoriale. E poi susequētemēte de l'altri doi de lor modi: nersi e vie cōmo debiano essere tenuti. E prima daremo sua diffinitione.

Del primo libro dicto memoriale o vero squartafoglio o vachetta q̃l che senten da e commo in esso se habia a scriuere: e p̃ chi.   ca°. 6

Vade memoriale o vero se condo alcuni vachetta o sq̃rtafoglio e vn libro nel q̃le tutte le facēde sue el mercatāte piccole e grādi: che amā li vegano. a giorno p̃ gior no e ora p̃ ora iscriue. Nel q̃le difusamēte ogni cosa di vēdere e cōprare (e altri manegi) scriuēdo se dichiara nō lasando vn iota. El chi. El che. El quādo. El do ue: cō tutte sue chiareçe: e mētioni: cōmo a pieno di sopra in lo cuentario te dissi: senza piu oltra te le replichi. E i questo tal libro molti costumano ponere loro iuētario. Ma p̃ che el puene a molte mani e ochi nō laudo de li mobili e stabili soi a pieno porre. E questo libro sol si fa p̃ la furia de le facēde che si fesse. nel quale deue scriuere el patrone. li fattori. Gar çoni :le dōne (se sāno) in absēça l'u ne de l'altro. Pero chel grā mercatāte nō terra sempre fermi li garçoni ne factori. Ma ora li manda in qua: ora li manda in la: i modo che alcuolte lui cō loro sōno fora. Chi a fiere chi a mercati zc. E solo le dōne o altri garçoni restano a casa che forse a pena sāno scriuere. Epure loro p̃ non erutare li auentori conuengano vendere e scoi tere: pagare: e cōprare secōdo lo ordine che ual principale li sia iposto. E loro secōdo loro po tere ogni cosa debono scriuere o dicto memoriale nominādo simplicimēte le monete e pesi che fāno: e trar fore a tutte sorte de monete che vendano e cōprano o uero pagano e scota no po che in questo tale non fa caso a che moneta si caui fore. cōmo nel giornale e quader no: cō disotto se dira zc. el quadernieri asetta tutto poi lui quādo deli pone i giornale. Dich tornando poi lo principale vede tutte sue facende e rasertale se li pare altramēte zc. E pero e necessario dicto libro a chi fa asai facēde. Per che serebe fatiga belleggiare: e per ordine ogni cosa la prima uolta mettere e li libri auctentici e con diligença tenuti. E i questo e in tutti al tri prima ponere el segno disora i sula copta: acio nel successo de le facēde siādo pieno ō scri ptura ouero fornito certo tēpo p̃ la qual cosa tu vorrai vnaltro libro prēdere. o uero de ne cessita te couerra quādo questo fosse pieno. Ma a le uolte molti costumano o diuerse p̃ti: bē che nō sia pieno a noualmēte far saldi e anche li libri nuoui cōmo desotto itēderai. E i dicto secondo libro per debito ordine bisogna renouare segnale differente dal primo: acio de tempo in tēpo si possa cō prestezza trouare loro facēde. Per tal uie ancora milessimo. E pero be ne si costuma fra li ueri catolici segnare li primi loro libri: de quel glorioso segno dal q̃l fug gi ogni nostro spiritual nemico: e la caterua tutta infernal meritamente trema del segno: cioe de la sancta croci dal quale ancora neli teneri anni i iparar ne legere l'alfabeto cōmen çasti. E poi li seq̃nti libri segnaral per ordine valfabeto: cioe de .A. E poi li terçi del .B. zc. discorrendo per ordine d'alfabeto. E chiāmase poi libri croci cioe   Memorial croci. Gioanal croci: cioe   Quaderno croci: cioe   Alfabeto o uero extratto croci: cioe.   zc. E poi ali secōdi libri se dici Memorial. A. Gioanal. A. Quaderno. A. zc. E de tutti questi li bri el numero de lor carti si conuen segnare per molti respecti e cautele che al operante fan no de bisogno. Auēga che molti dichino nel giornale e memoriale non bisognare: p̃ che le cose se guidano isilcate a di p̃ di: vna sotto l'altra che sia bastante a lor ritrouare.   Que sti tali direbono el uero se le facende de vna giornata non passassero vna carta. Ma noi ve demo che molti grossi traficanti non che una carta ma doi e tre ne piano in vn giorno de le qual poi (chi uolesse far male) ne potrebbe tagliare e causare una. La qual fraude nō si po trebe poi per uia d'li giorni cognoscere ne discernere. Per che li di son quelli che seça dubio

Distinctio nona tractatus.xi°. De scripturis

possano successiuamente seguire: non dimanco el man camento sira fatto. Si che per q̃sto e altri asai respecti sempre e buono numerare e signare in tutti li libri mercanteschi. E di casa e di botega tutte le carti 7c. ca°.7

Del mo cōmo i molti luoghi se habio auctēticare tutti li libri mercāteschi e p che e dachi.

Questi tali libri conuēgōsi secōdo l'usançe bone de diuersi paesi: neli quali luoghi mi so retrouato portarli: e apresentarli a certo officio de mercarāti cōmo son no consoli nela cita de perosa e a loro narrare cōmo questi sōno li toi libri i quali tu intendi scriuere o uero far scriuere de mā del tale. 7c. ogni tua facēda ordinatamēte. E dire a che monete tu li uoli tenere: cioe a.$.de picioli:o uero a.$.de grossi: o uero a duc.e.$.7c. O uero a fio.e.f.d.o vo a.g.rari grani.d.7c. Le qli cose sēpre el real mercatāre nel pricipio d'ogni suo libro deue pōere nella p̃ carta. E q̃do mano se mutasse nella scriptura valeriche nel pricipio se dicesse: conuense p uia del ditto officio chiarirlo. El scriuā poi d tutto ciò fa mētiōe i registri de ditto officio cōmo i tal di tu presentasti tali e tali libri segnati del tal segno 7c. Chiamano lū cosi e l'altro cosi 7c. Di qli el tale a tante carti el tale tāte 7c. li quali disse douere essere tenuti p mā sua o del tale 7c. Ma i vno ditto memoriale. O uo uachetta. o secondo alcuni ditto (squartafacio). ciascuno di suoi familiari de casa a la giornata poteua scriuere per le ragioni sopra asegnate. E alora ditto scriuā de sua propria mano in nome de l'officio scriuara el medesimo nella prima carta e li tuoi libri: e fara fede de tutto 7c. E bolleralli del segno del ditto officio: i fede autentica per tutti li iudici che acadesse p durli. E questa tal usança merita sumamēte essere cōmēdata 7c. E cosi li luoghi che la obseruano. Pero che molti tēgano li loro libri dopii. Uno n'e mostrano al copratore e l'altro al venditore. e che peggio e secondo quello giurano e spgiurano 7c. che malissio fāno. E po p tal uia d'officio degno andando: nō possano cosi de facili dir buscia: ne fraudare el primo 7c.

Li quali poi con diligença segnati e ordinatamente disposti tu teneuai co lo nome d'dio a casa agomēçare a scriuere tue facēde. E prima nel giornale ponere per ordine tutte le ptite de lo inuentario nel modo che sequente intenderai. Ma prima intendi cōme nel memoriale se costuma a dire 7c.

Cōmo se debino dittare le partite i ditto memoriale co crēpli ca°.8

Ja e ditto se bene ai amente cōmo i ditto memoriale: o uero uachetta: o uero sqrtafacio secondo altri che ognuno di tuoi li po scriuere. E pero del dittar tal ptite i esso nō si po dare piena doctrina. Pero che chi intēdera: e chi non di toi di casa. Ma el cōmū costume e questo cioe. Metamo che tu habi cōprato alquante peçce de pāno(vtputa.20.biāchi bresani) o duc.12. luna basta che semplicimēte ponga la prita, cosi dicēdo cioe. In questo di habiamo o uero io o cōprato da M feltro de rufoi o da m̃ lapāni n°.20. biāchi bressati posti i su la uolta di s stefano taglia pietra 7c. O ga lūa o le pecce di couēto br̃ tāti 7c. Per duc. tanti luna 7c. segnate del tal n° 7c. nominādo se sōno atre licci o uero a la piana basso o alti fini o meçani bergamaschi o uigētrini o veroēsi padoani fiorētini o matoāi 7c. E similiter nominar se cifosse sensale e narrar sel mercato fo a cōtāti tutto:o uero p parte cōtāti e pte termine: e dir q̃ato tēpo. O uero noiar se fosse pte d'.cōtāti e parte robbe E specificare che robbe. o de numero peso e misura. e a che pregio el. M°.o etc°: o uero.$. o uero a rasō de conto 7c. O uero se fossero tutti a tēpo e narrare che termic. O de galie o baruto. o de galie de fiādra o de retorni de naui 7c. E specificare la muta de ditte galie. O de naui 7c. o se fosse termine de fiere: o altre solenita: comme per la sensa proxima futura 7c. o uero p la pasqua de nadal 7c. o uero de resurectio. o uero carleuale 7c. Più e māco secōdo che uoi cōcludeste el mercato. E finaliter i ditto memoriale nō si conuerria lassare pōto alcuno. E se possibile fosse dir quāte parolle vesinterposero p che (cōmo nel inuentario sopra so detto) al mercante le chiarecçe mai sōro troppo 7c.

De li.9.modi p li quali cōmunamēte si costuma fra li mercāti cōprare e de le mercātie quali al piu d'le uolte de necessita a tempo si cōprano. ca°.9

Poi che al cōprare siamo nota che quello che tu cōpri po acadere cōmunamente i.9.modi: cioe a denari. contanti. o uero a termine. o uero ditt'in contro dar robba. Qual acto cōmunamente editto baratto. o uero a pte d'. parte termine o vero a parte cōtāti e parte robbe. o uero a pte robbe. e pte termine. o vero p asignatione de ditta. o uero parte i ditta e pte termie a te. o uer o pte ditta e parte robba. In li qli. 9. modi el più de le uolte se costuma comprare. E se per altro verso facesse in uestita: i qli

Distinctio nona. Tractatus. xi°. D: scripturis

modo proprio fa che tu e gli altri per te nel memoriale la narri aponto con verita e farai bene 7c. E cosi quando tu facesse le tue compre a tempo. Commo se costuma ale volte farsi de guati. O vero biade.vini.sali E curami vabecari. E seghi.che si obliga el venditore.al compratore.de dar tutto el guaro che per quel tempo bara. E cosi el becaio te vende e promette tutti li cori.pelle.sego.che per qllo anno in sua becaria.fara 7c. La tal sorta.per tanto la y.7c. E la tale per tanto 7c. E cosi de li seghi de manço.castroni 7c. E le pelle motonine nere:p tanto el c°. acoto. E tanto le montonine bianche 7c. E cosi de liguati. O biade specificar tanto el D°. E tanto lo staro.o el moggio.o la corba.de le biade: commo in sul chiusi de peroscia si costuma. E de guati.al Borgo sa lepolcro nostro. Mercatello. Santagnilo. Lita o castello. Furli 7c. Sicche de ponto in ponto. far mentione di tutto a pieno in ditto memoriale. o per te:o per altri che si scriua. E narra la cosa semplicimente.commo le nasciuta 7c. E dipoi el bon quadernieri.i capo de. 4.0.5.0 vero.8.giorni. Piu e manco che stesse del ditto memoriale metarle in giornale.a di per di tutte comme le sonno nascute. Ma solo in questo differente:che non bisogna che in ditto giornale se distenda.con tante filastoche de parolle.commo se fatto in ditto memoriale. Pero che basta a lui vna volta hauere lacosa ben digesta in ditto memoriale. Al qual poi el giornale sempre sa a referire. Pero che quelli che costumano tenere.3 libri(a modo ditto) mai debano ponere cosa in giornale.che prima non labino in ditto memoriale 7c. E questo basti quanto al ordine de ditto memoriale. O per te o p altri toi sia tenuto 7c. E nota che per quanti modi tu va altri poi comprare, cosi tu per tanti poi vendere. E per consequente altri po comprare da te. Nel qual vendere non mi stedo altra mente. Pero che tu per te habiando questa forma de comparare,porai a se tar lo 7c.

Del so libro principale mercantesco.ditto giornale: quel che l sia: e comme se debia disponere ordinatamente.   Capitolo   10

E L so libro ordinario mercantesco.e ditto giornale. Nel quale.(comme e ditto) deue essere el medesimo segno che in lo memoriale: E carti segnate 7c. Comino disopra del memorial e ditto. Per le ditte cagioni. E sempre nel principio de caduna carta; se deue mettere el Milesimo. e di. E dipoi demano in mano ponere prima le partite tutte del tuo euentario. Nel qual giornale. (per essere tuo libro secreto) porai a pieno narrare e dire tutto quello che di mobile e stabile te ritroui. Referendote sepre al ditto foglio che per te.o per altri fosse scritto.el quale in q iche cassa.o scatola.o filça.o maço. o tasca : che cosi se usa el seruarui. Commo te diro de le lettere. E scripture menute. ma le partite del ditto giornale; si conuengono formare e dittare per altro modo piu ligiadro: non superfluo.ne anche tropo diminuto : commo qui sequente de alquante partite te daro exemplo. Ma prima e da notare el bisogno di doi termini.che in ditto giornale si costuma usare.nela cita marime excelsa de Vinegia.Di qualli immediate diremo.

De li.2.termini nel ditto giornale vsitati.marie i Venegia. L'uno ditto. Per. e laltro ditto. A. e quello che per loro se habia a denotare.   Capitolo.   11.

D I sonno(commo e ditto)li termini vsitati i ditto giornale. Luno e ditto. Per E laltro e ditto. A. Li qli hano loro significati.ciascuno separato. Per lo. Per, sempre se dinota el debitore. o vno o piu che se sieno. E per lo. A. se dinota lo creditore.o vno o piu che se sieno. E mai si mette prita ordinaria i giornale(che al libro grade sabia aporre)che no se dinoti p p liditti doi termini.Deli qli.sepre nel principio de ciascuna prita si mette el. Per. Pero ch p°.si deue specificare eldebitore.e di poi imediate el suo creditore.diuiso lu dalaltro p doi rgolette cosi.|| Como ne lo er° disotto te sira noto 7c.   Del modo a sap ponere e dittare le prite i lo giornale del dare e de lauere co molti exepli. E deli doi altri termini nel q derno vsitati luno detto Cassa.e laltro Cauedale. E quello che per essi se habia intendere.   Capitolo.   12.

A Doca co lo nome de dio começarai a p°cre nel tuo giornale. La p³.prita del tuo iuentario. cioe la q°.deli d.cotati:che te ritroui. E p sape ponere ditto iuentario al libro.e giornale.bisogna ch tu imagini doi altri termini.luno ditto. Cassa e laltro ditto Cauedale. Per la cassa.s'intede de la tua p°.ouero borscia. Per lo cauedale.s'intede tutto el tuo mote e corpo de faculta prite. E l q le cauedale.i tutti li principii de q derni:e giornali mercateschi:sepre deu essere posto creditore. E la ditta cassa sepre deu essr posta debitrici. e'mai p nullo tpo nel manegio mercatesco.la cassa po essere creditrici.ma solo debitrici ouero para. Pero ch q ii nel bilacio del libro si trouasse creditrici denotarebe errore nel lib° como di sotto a suo loco te daro sumaria recordança.Ora nel giornale ditta prita de contanti si deue mettere e dittare in questo modo. v3.

P

Distinctio nona. Tractatus xi° De scripturis

Forma ō metter i giornale. M.cccc°Lxxxxiiii.a dì.8.nouēbre i venegia. pri°.
Per cassa de cōtanti. A cauedal de mi tale 7c̄.p cōtanti mi trouo i qlla al pn̄te.fra oro e mo
nete.arzēto e ramo ō diuersi cogni.cōc ape i lo foglio delo inētario posto i cassa.7c̄.i tutto
duc̄.tāri d'oro.E monete duc̄.tantiual i tutto al modo nr̄o venitiano.a oro.cioe a grossi.24
per duc̄.e picioli.32.per grosso a 8.a oro.   2ª.   8   ḡ   p̄
Per gioie ligate e disligate de piu sorti: A cauedal ditto. per balassi tanti, ligati 7c̄. pesano
7c̄.E safili tanti 7c̄.e rubini e diamāti 7c̄.Lōc ape al sopraditto iuētario.Quali metto ua
lere a comū corso.libalassi tanto. 7c̄. E cosi dirai de ciascuna sorta.suo p̄gio cōmo. mon
tano in tutto ducati tanti 7c̄. vagliano.   8   ḡ   p̄
E hauēdo tu nominato vnauolta el dì.E ancora el debitore.e ancora el creditore.nō trarne
çandose altra ptīta poi dire. A di ditto.Per ditto.E al ditto 7c̄.per piu breuita.   3ª.
Per argenti lauorati: Al ditto che sintēde pur el caudal de p pīu sorte argēti cal pn̄te mi trouo
cioe Bacili tanti 7c̄.E rami tanti 7c̄.e tacçe tante 7c̄. piron tanti 7c̄. cōslier tāte 7c̄.
pesano in tutto tanto 7c̄. val   8   ḡ   p̄
Destinguēdo.bene di pōto p q̄ste prime prite ogni cosa cōe festi in lo inuētario. Ponēdoli
tu p te vn comun p̄gio. E fallo grasso piu presto che magro.cioe Se ti pare che vaglino
20.ē tu di.24.7c̄. Acio che meglio te habia reuscire el guadagno.E cosi de mano in mano
porrai tutte laltre cose.con suoi pesi in n°.e valute.7c̄.   4ª.
Per panni de lana de dosso: Al ditto.p veste tante di tal colore 7c̄.E a tal foggia 7c̄. Fode
rate 7c̄. vsate o vero noue 7c̄.a mio dosso.o vero de la mia dona.o vero de figlioli 7c̄.Met
to valere a comune stima.luna p laltra.in tutto duc̄ tanti 7c̄. p mantelli tāti de tal colore
7c̄.E ōc diceresti dle veste e cosi dirai de tutti ditti pāni p tutto.   5ª. 8   ḡ   p̄
Per pāni lini: Al ditto p lenzoli tanti 7c̄. E tutto narra comme sta in lo inuentario. monta
no E vagliano.7c̄.   6ª.
Per letti de piuma: Al ditto 7c̄.p piume tāte 7c̄. E qui narra commo sta in lo inuentario.
montano o vagliano.   7ª.   8   ḡ   p̄
Per sençer mechini: Al ditto.p colli tanti 7c̄.narra cōmo i inuētario.si contene.montano e
vagliano a comune stima 7c̄.duc̄.tanti 7c̄.
    E cosi poi tu p te stesso seqrai di porre tutte laltre prite de qlaltre robbe.declascuna facie
do sua prita.sepata.cōmo ō de sēçer se ditto. Ponēdoli pgio de comū corso.conuīo disopra
e ditto.E lor̄ro segnī.e pesi.commo de ponto stāno i ditto foglio diuētario.Chiamādo den
tro laprita.cb̄ moneta cb̄ tu voli.E nel trar fora.conuē poi cb̄ sieno a vna sorta. Perchō non
staria bene.a cauar fora.a diuerse sorte 7c̄. E tutte ditte prite d giornale serçerai a 1°.ar_e ti
rando la riga. De q̄to dura tua scriptura. narratiua. fin al termine che si tra fora. E mede
simo modo seruarai ale prite del memoriale.E de tu ti del memoriale mettarai i giorna
le.cosi a vna a vna.andarai depēnando i lo memoriale.con vna sola.riga.a trauerso cosi./.
cb̄ denotara qlla tale prita.eēr posta i lo giornale 7c̄.E se tu non volessi trauersare la pri̅.cō
vna linea.e tu lacīarai.la p̄ fra del principio dela prita.o vero lultīa.commo al capo di q̄sta.e
fatto. O vero farate tu de te ql.b̄ alt°.segno.cb̄ tu itēda.p qllo ditta prita eēr stara mes
sa igiornale 7c̄.E auēga cb̄ tu da te pos=husare molti varij diuersi termini e segni.nō dime
no te debi sēpre studiare de vsare li comuni.che p li altri traficāti i tal paese si costuma di fa
re. Acio non para tu sia discrepante da lusitato modo mercātesco 7c̄.
    Del 3°.evlti°.lib°.priciple mercātesco.detto el q̄derno cōmo deba eēr fatto e ōl suo alfa
beto commo se debia ordinare. vgnelo e dopio.   Cap° 13.   E poste che tu ha
rai ordinatamēte tutte le tuoi prite al giornale.poi bisogna che di qllo.le caui.E portle in lo
3°. libro ditto qderno grāde.E ql comunamēte.si costuma fare de doi tāte carti chel giorna
le. Jn loqle conuerra eēr vno Alfabeto ouoi dir Trouarello so alcuni. ala
fiorētina se dici lo stratto. Nel ql porrai tutti debitori e creditori. Per le lfe che començano
con lo n°.dele sue carti.cioe quelli che comēça p.a.i.a.7c̄. E del dopio alfabeto. E questo
similmēte commo sopra dicemo conuē cb̄ sia segnato del medemo segno chl giornale e me
moriale. Postoui el n°.dele sue carti. E disopra i margine.da luna bāda e laltra. el milesimo
E in la prima. sua carta.dentro porrai debitrici la cassa. si commo ella e la p̄. nel giornale.
cosi deue eēre p̄.nel qderno. E tutta qlla faciata.si costuma lasiarla stare per ditta cassa. E in
var ne i hauere non si pone altro. E qsto p che la cassa se manegia piu che prita cb̄ sia.a ora
p ora.i metter e cauar dinari. E po lfe lassa el capo largo. E qsto qderno couiē che sia riga
gato. de tāte righe. q̄te che sorte monete voli trar fore. Se trarai. 8 ḡ p̄. Farai. 4. righe.
e dināçe ale 8.farane vnaltra. p metarui el n°.dele carti de le prite che isciemi de var. E ha

Distincto nona. Tractatus. xi°. De scripturis

uere se icatenano. E dināze farai.2.righe.p̃ potere mettere.li di ð mano i mano. commo ne li altri q̃derni hai visto che piu non mistedo i q̃sto ɫc.p̃.poter trouar p̃sto le p̃tie ɫc. E pur fira segnato croci commo li altri.

Del modo a portar le p̃tie de giornale in quaderno.e pc̃he de una in giornale sene facia doi in quaderno:e del modo a depennare le p̃tie in giornale e de li doi numeri dele carti del quaderno che in le sue margine si pone e pc̃he. Cap̃º. 14.

Er laqual cosa. sappi che di tutte le p̃tie che tu harai poste in logiornale. al qua derno grāde. te ne cōuē sep̃e fare doi. cioe una in dare e laltra in hauere pc̃he lui chiama debitore p̃ lo. Per. E lo creditore p̃ lo. A. cómo disopra dicēmo ch ð luno e de laltro. si deue da p̃se fare 1ª. p̃tia: q̃lla del debitore. ponere ala man sini stra. E q̃lla del creditore. ala man dextra. E in q̃lla del debitore. chiamare la carta. doue sia q̃lla del suo creditore. E cosi in q̃lla del creditore. chiamare la carta di q̃lla doue sia. El suo debitore. E in q̃sto modo sēp̃e uēgano incatenare tutte le p̃tie del ditto q̃derno grāde. nel q̃l mai si deue mettere cosa in dare che q̃lla ancora non si ponga in hauere. E cosi mai si de ue mettere cosa in hauere che ancora. q̃lla medesima cō suo amōtare nō si metta in dare. E di qua nasci. po albilancio che del lib°. si fa. nel suo saldo tāto cōuiē che sia el dare. q̃to laue re. Cioe sūmate tutte le p̃tie che sirāno poste in dare se fossero bene. 10000. da p̃te in su vn foglio. E di poi sūmate similmēte tutte q̃lle che in hauere si trouano. tanto debbe fare luna summa q̃to laltra. altramēte demostrarebbe eēr errore nel ditto q̃derno. cōe nel modo del far suobilancio se dira apieno ɫc. E cosi cōe duna de giornale ne fai. 2. al q̃derno. cosi a q̃lla p̃tia che del giornale leui farai doi righe a trauerso so ch̃ vai leuando. cioe se p̃. tu la metti i dare. p̃ia farai 1ª. riga atrauerso. verso al prin°. dela p̃tia. che dinora eēr posta in dare al q̃ derno. E se la metti in hauere. o prima. o poi cōe acade ale uolte fare al q̃dernieri q̃do li aca de scriuere i luogo. ch̃ l'in q̃lla carta li nandera. 2. o. 3. p̃ nō ui hauere a tornare. sene spaça di metterle li alora. E po fo che mette cosi deue depennare p̃ hauerla messa in hauere. farai tal tra depēnatura. verso man dextra. dal canto doue finesci la p̃tia che ðnotara eēr messa i ha uere. le q̃l linee staranno cōe disopra in q̃sto uedi figurato a la p̃tia. p̃. dela cassa. luna dirta linea. de dare. e lalt.ª de hauere. E cosi dalato i margine dinanze al principio bisogna che po ghi. 2. nu¹. luno sotto laltro. q̃l di sopra che denoti la p̃tia. del debitore. a p̃te carti che la sia posta in lo q̃derno E q̃llo de sotto che denoti le carti de ditto q̃derno. doue sia posto el cre ditore. cōe vedi li ala p̃tia dela cassa disopra i q̃sto. che sta cosi. ⅓. seça trameço. E ancora al cuni costumano cosi cō trameço. ⅓. a guisa de rotti. che nō fa caso. Ma e piu bello sença tra meço. Acio achi vede nō parciseno speçati. D vero rotti ɫc. E vol dire q̃llo. 1°. di sopra che la cassa. E nella p̃. carta del q̃derno. El caudeale. E nella fa carta de ditto q̃derno. i hauere. e q̃lla in dare ɫc. E nota che sep̃e q̃to piu p̃sto tu porai mettere el creditore al suo debitore. sera piu li cādro. auēga che posto doue si uoglia tanto mōri. Ma p̃ rispetto del milesimo. che ale uolte se iterp̃oēse fra 1ª. p̃ti². e lalt.ª resp̃ode male. E cō fatiga. nō poca. se ritrouano lor tp̃i cōe sa chi. pua. ch̃ ogni cosa cosi apieno nō si po dire. Ma bilo°. ch̃ ācora tu alq̃to cō tuo ha turale ingegno ta iuti. E po sep̃e studia dasettar ditto creditore immediate a p̃sso el suo de bitore in la medema faciara. o vero ila imediate seq̃nte. nō interponēdoui fra luno e laltro. al tra p̃tia. Peroche nel. pp̃io giorno che nasci el debitore in q̃llo medemo nasci el creditore E p̃ q̃sto rispetto sēp̃e se deue acostar luno a lalt° ɫc.

Del modo a sape ditrare le p̃tie de lacassa e caudeale nel quaderno in dare e hauere: e dl milesimo che disopra nel principio dela carta a lanti co si mette in esso: e dela sua mutatione e del cōptir lispaci dele carti fo le p̃tie piccole e grādi so el bisogno del facēde. Cap̃º. 15.

Or q̃ste cose discorse. a tuo amaestrimēto. ormai ditamo la p̃. p̃tita de la cassa i dare e poi q̃lla del caudeal in hauere in lo libro grāde. Ma cōe ditto p̃. deso pra nel quaderno porrai el milesimo alabacco antico. cioe per alfabeto cosi. M cccc. Lxxxxiiii. ɫc. El di nō se costuma mettarlo disopra in loquaderno cōe in lo giornale. pc̃he 1ª. p̃tita in quaderno. hara diuersi di. E pō nō si porra scriuar ordine deli di. disopra cōe apieno nel seq̃nte cap°. se dira. Ma detro dela p̃tita che intēderai la p̃. nostra E poi cosi dalato in lo spacio che disopra dicēmo dinanze ala p̃tia. q̃do tal partita nascesse daltro milesimo che disopra nel principio dela carta fosse scritto che sole auenire achi de an no in anno nō riporta e salda suoi libri sic̃he tal milesimo si porra difuora. nudo in margine ripetto a p̃oto a q̃lla p̃tita linata cōe uedi posto qui disotto. q̃sto solo auene in lib°. grande che in li altri nō po auenire. Doca uiaai cosi. traēdola fore pure alabacco atico p̃ piu belleça

p ii

Distinctio nona.Tractatus.xi°.De scripturis

non dimeno aqual che tu te caui non fa caso 7c. Donca dirai cosi.
　　ybs　　　M.cccc.Lxxxxiii.
Cassa de cōtanti die dare a di.8.nouēbre.per caudal per contanti de piu sorte fra oro e mo
nete me trouo bauere in quella in questo presente di in tutto ca.2.　　ß.xᵐ.ſ ḡ p̄
E qui nō bisogna che troppo te stēda.p hauer bē gia steso in giornale. Ma sempre studia
dir breue. La prima nel comēcare se dici alquanto; ale sequēti la medema sol se dici.e a
di ditto 7c.per lo tale. car.　　　　　　　　　　　　　　　　　　　　ß　ſ ḡ p̄
Laqual cosi posta che lharai.depēnarai in giornale in dare comme sopra te dissi. E poi i ba
uer per lo caudal dirai cosi.v3.
　　ybs　　　M.cccc°.Lxxxxiii
Cauedal de mi tale 7c.die hauere a di.8.nouēbre.per cassa.per contanti me trouo in quel
la fin al di presente in ori monete de piu sorte in tutto. car.1.　　ß.xᵐ.ſ o g o p o
　　E cosi ancora.i q̄sta basta succiniamēte dire per lacagion sopra dicta.laltre poi che q sotto
ala medema ptita.se haueranno aponere fin che la sia piena bastara a dire. E a di tanti 7c.per
latal cosa 7c. Cōe uedi acēnato qui da canto. e anco in fin di q̄sto barat exemplo. cosi sequi
rai con breuita in tutte maxime in quelle partite che a te solo aspettano.cioe che non hai a
rendere conto adal cuno. Ma in q̄lle che tu hauerai a rendere cōto adaltri.alq̄to piu ti cō
uerra dire.auenga che sempre se recorre.per le chiarecce al giornale 7c. E poi darai laltra de
pēnatura.a q̄lla del giornale in hauere. cōe sopra ti dissi in.12°.cap̄. E in lamargine dauen
ti.ala ptita.porrai li doi numeri cōe dissi pur in ditto loco dele carti doue sōno. El debitore
el creditore.cioe q̄llo del debitore desopra. E q̄llo del creditore de sotto cōe facēmo di sopra.
ala ptita de lacassa. E poi subito porrai in lo tuo alfabeto.cioe repertorio. q̄sto debitore e credi
tore.ognuno ala sua lra̅ cōe sai che disopra dissi. Cioe la cassa.al la.lra̅. E dicēdo dētro in q̄
sto modo.cioe. Cassa de cōtanti.　K.1.　E ancora el cauedal porrai al.C.dicendo. Ca
uedal de mi pprio.　K. 2.　E cosi p tuo ingegno ādarai asettando. tutte le ptite. e li nō
de li debitori persōe e robbe 7c. E cosi de creditori.porrai nel ditto repertorio. a lesue lettere
acio poi con facilita possi subito retrouarli in ditto quaderno grande 7 cetera.

　　E nota che hauendo tu pduto el tuo q̄derno p alcun caso derobaria.o incēdio di foco.o
naufragii 7c. E hauēdo tu luno de li altri doi libri. Cioe memoriale.o vero giornale. cō esso
porrai sempre refare vnaltro q̄derno.cō le medesime ptite a di p di. E ponerle al numero de
le medesime che i q̄l pso si retrouauano. Martime hauēdo tu el giornale. doue q̄do ne leua
sti le ptite. E pōesti al lib°.tu imargie ponesti.li doi nuᵒ.Oli debitori e creditori.suo soura tal
tro che chiamauano le carti. del q̄derno douerano situati. e di pōto atante cartī li porrai fa
re ritornar cō tuo ingegno 7c. E q̄sto basti q̄to a vna ptita posta 7c.　Poi la fa ptita ch
so dele coie al q̄derno ponēdola a suo cōdecēte luogo dittarai cosi. pᵃ. sempre senca piu
te replichi.porrai disopra nel principio dela carta.el milesimo se nō vi fosse posto p altra pti
ta. pᵃ. poche ale uolte in vna medema facia el quadernieri asettara.2.o.3.ptite ho che cogno
scera lo spacio eer bastāte al manegio di q̄lla. pche forse uedara q̄lla tale ptita bauerli chia
re fiade adoperar. E p q̄sto li dara vn luoco piu angusto. che a quelle che spesso li acade a
dopare: ala giornata cōe di sopra.al cap.13°.de la cassa e cauedal fo detto q̄l sicostumaua
lasarli tutta lafaciata del lib°. pche spessissime fiade.p cēre gradi le facēde si conuēgano ma
negiare. E q̄sto sol si fa p nō hauer tāto spesso a far reporto ināce 7c.ora al pposito trouato
li el loco cōe se dici.dirai cosi in dare cioe verso'man sinistra.cosi sempre fa aponere el debito.
Bioe de piu sorte. dienno dare a di.8. nouēbre.p cauedale.p pecci nᵒ tanti 7c.pesano tanto
7c.dequali tanti sonno balassi legati 7c. E tanti safili 7c. E tāti rubini coculegni 7c. E tanti
diamanti creci 7c.lequali in tutto.o vero a sorta per sorta metto valere a comun pgio.de cō
tanti duc.tanti 7c.val car.2　　　　　　　　　　　　　　　　　　　　ß 40.ſ o.g o.p o.
E cosi depennerai.la ptita in giornale.nel dare tirando la linea comme di sopra al.12° cap̄
te dissi. E poi andarai al caudal. E porrai q̄sta medema con māco parolle per leragion gia
disopra adutte in questo capitolo e porrala in hauere sotto quella pᵃ.chʼgia libat posto dela
cassa. E dirai cosi.v3.
a di o detto.per coie de piu sorte commo li apare 7c. car.3.　　ß.40.ſ o.g o.p o.
E cosi posta farai laltra depēnatura.al giornale in hauer.cōe te mōstrai disopra al.12°.caᵃ.
E porrai i margine li numeri ōle carti. doue tal ptite al quaderno ponesti cōmo dicēmo
vno sopra'laltro.comme qui denance apare che metto babi posta la ptita in dara carti.3. E
q̄lla del cauedal sta pure alogo suo a carti.2.fin tanto chʼella non e piena.che dipoi innāte

Distinctio nona. Tractatus. xi°. De scripturis

a tutte laltre la portarai. cōme disotto ne reporti intēderai a pieno. E qsto p qsta. e a sue simili te sia bastāte zc. E posta che larai al ditto qderno. E asettata in giornale. e tu subito laporai al reptorio o vero alfabeto. cōe disopra i qsto cap° fo detto. Cioe ala sua lra. 8. o vero .3. fo. pr̄be lra la pserirai. cōe idiuersi paesi acade. che qui i uinegia molto si costuma ponere el .3. doue noi in toscana ponemo el .g. siche acordarala tu a tuo Judicio zc.

¶Cōe se debino dittare leptīte delemercantie che per inuētario o altro modo lhomo se ri trouа: nel quaderno in dare e in hauere.   Cap°. 16°.

LE altre .4. ptīte poi su sequēti del tuo mobile. cioe argēti. pāni. lini. letti de piuma E veste de dosso zc. Poi p te stesso facilmēte mettarai del iuētario in giornale de pōto cōe li le ponesti. de notate. pche cōe dicemo disopra cap°. 6° qsto tal inuētario nō si caua del memoriale. p la ragiō li asegnara. E po suo dittare in giornale E ancora nel grā lib° i dare e hauere. e di porre alalfabeto. lasciaro or mai seqre al tuo pegri no ingegno del ql molto me cōfido. E solo la .7ª. prita de cēçer mechini che ti troui asettare mo i giornale. E ancora al qderno laql te fia bastāte e sufficiēte amaestramēto a tutte le altre che dimercātia alcuna te ritrouasse. hauēdo sēpre tu da te i nāte gliochi lor n°. pesi. e misure e valute i tutti li modi che tal mercātie se costumasse vēdere. e cōprare fra mercāti i rialto o fora. fo li paesi. dele qli cose q apieno nō e possibile ponere exēpli. ma cō facilita. da qsti pochi q cōpēdiosamēte posti porrai di glücaltri i prēdere a tua sufficiēça. po che se noi volēmo dar te exēplo del modo verso e via. di mercare atrani. lecia. bari. E betōta. cioe a lor nomi d̄pesi loro. E misure loro zc. E cosi dela marca. E anche dela nr̄a toscana. troppo serebbe grāde el volume. cōe cō breuita itendo cōcludere E p qlla. 7ª. de cēçer nel giornale. dirē cosi. ₺. Per çençeri mechini i mōte a refuso. o i colli dirai cōe a te pare zc. Al ditto che sintēde caue dal. pche li disopra imediate larai p ordine de ditto iuētario. cōe dicēmo disopra cap°. 12°. In la pr̄ta fa de le çoie. p colli tanti pesano. zc. E p. 8. tante qndo fossero arefusso i mōte zc. qli me retrouo hauere in lemani al di pnte metto di comū corso valere el c°. o vero la .8. zc. duc. tanti zc. mōtano in tutto netti duc. tanti zc. val   ₺   ₷   ᵹ   d̄

E cosi posta che larai nel giornale. E tu al memoriale. o vero inuētario. la dipēna. e faça. al modo ditto sop°. al. 12°. cap°. zc. E cosi obfruarai p tutte lalt°. zc. Di qsta cōe so detto e de qllū che altra che i giornale si metta. sēpre al gran lib°. si fanno doppie. cioe .1ª. i dare. e laltra i hauere cōe disopra dicēmo cap. 14°. La qual poi nel quaderno in dare. ponēdola dittarala i qsto modo. Posto pª. sēpre el milesimo se nō vi fosse in capo de la carta. seça mettarui el giorno disopra po che cōe dicēmo disopra cap°. 15°. El di nō si costuma porre sopra nel prī° de lacarta del quaderno o rispetto che in qlla medesima facia porrebono cēre piu prīte ō diuersi debitori e creditori. lequali bēche lenaschino sottoyn milesimo. L'Ma siranno in diuersi mesi e çorni. cōe discorrēdo p tutto poi aprēdere. E qdo bene ancora in ditta facia del libro grande nō vi fosse altro che .1ª. sola prita di cassa. o daltro ancora el çorno posto disopra nel quaderno. nō si potrebbe seruare. pche in ditta prita. ocorira di mettere casi ocorsi in diuersi mesi di e p qsto e che li antichi disopra nel quaderno nō hano i libri mercātescbi vsitato mettere el giorno. pche non hano ueduto verso ne via ne modo che con uerita si possa asettarcilo zc. Laqual parrita in dare cosi porrai dicēdo zc.

Zençeri me chini. in monte. o vero colli zc. dien dare a di. 8. nonembre per cauedal. per colli tanti zc. pesano. 8. tante zc. quali mi trouo hauere in casa. o uero magaçen al presente qual de comun corso stimo valere el cento zc. duc. tanti zc. E per tutti monta duc.   ₷   ᵹ   d̄   val cart. l. 2.

E cosi depennarai la partita del giornale in dare. cioe a man senestra cōme piu uolte to ditto E poi in hauere asettarala in qsto modo al cauedal comme te monstrai ponere quella dele çoie sopra a cap°. 15° cosi vz.

a di o detto. per çençeri mechini in monte o vero colli zc. car. 3.   ₺   ₷   ᵹ   d̄

E cosi posta che lharai depennarai la partita del giornale in hauere. cioe verso mande stra. cōe dinançe vedi fatto. E poni li numeri dele carti dināçe alei in margine vno sopra laltro. Cioe el .3. disopra el .2. disotto pche tu hai messo el debitore a carti. 3 nel quaderno. el creditore a a. 2. Cioe el capital. e subito poi la metti in alfabeto. o vero reptorio ala sua lra. Cioe al. 3. se p .3. la cōpitt. o vero al. 8. p la rasō ditta in lo precedēte ca°. a qlla prita fa dele çoie zc.

Del modo a tenere conto con li offiti publici: e perche: e de lacamera delimprēsti in venetia che se gouerna per via de sestieri.   Cap°. 17°.

p̄ iij

Distinctio nona. Tractatus xi°. De scripturis.

Ora de laltre nõ te ne do altra norma. cioe di q̃lla de pellami. dafodre cõce e cru de. e fine ⁊c. dele quali a 1ª. p 1ª. formarai la p̃ta in giornale e quaderno p ordine depẽnando. e segnando in tutti li lochi che non tescordi perche al mercante bisogna altro ceruello. che de beccaria ⁊c. Quella dela camera dip̃stiti dal tro mõte cõe in firença. el mõte dele dote i genoa li lochi o uero altri officii che si fossero cõ liquali tu hauesse a fare. per alcuna cagione fa che sempre con loro tu habia buono scõtro. de dare e de hauere in tutti li modi con qualche chiarecça se possibile e de man deli scriuani di q̃lli luochi q̃l riẽ sotto bona custodia al modo che dele scritture e lettere te diro. pche a q̃sti tali officii spesso se sogliano mutare scriuani. liq̃li ognuno a sua fantasia uole guidare lili bri delo officio. biasimãdo sempre li scriuan passati. che non tenuan bon ordine ⁊c. E sempre ognuno p̃suade el suo ordine migliore deli altri. i modo che ale uolte incrociano le p̃ite. De tali officii. che non sene tien 1ª. cõ laltra. Egual chi cõtali a afare. E po fa che sia a cosa. E col capo abotega cõ q̃sti tali. E certamẽte forsi el fano a bon fine nõ dimenõ mostrão igno rança. E cosi tirrai cõto. cõ li gabellari. e dariari de robbe che tu uedie cõpri. caui e metti nele terre ⁊c. Cõ si costuma fare in uinegia. che si tiene p li piu dela terra. cõto lõgo cõ lo officio dela messetaria. chi a 2. p. cº. E chi a 1ª. p cº. E chi a 4. p cº. ⁊c. Chiamando el libro del senẽ saro. che visinterpone. e notare al tuo libro. E anche la mare. in su ch fa. cioe el lib° doue va in nota li mercati al ditto officio che cosi lo chiamano in venetia po che ciascuno sensaro a uno libro. o uero luogo in qualche libro al ditto officio doue lui va a dare in nota li mercati che fa. si cõterrieri. cõe forestieri altramẽte caçano i pena. saltramẽte facessaro. E sonno pri uati. E bene q̃lla excelsa. S. licastiga e loro. e scriuani ch mal si portasero cõe de molti me ri cordo. gia neli tp̃i passati eere puniti strauiamẽte. E po santamente fanno a constituire uno elq̃le a solo q̃sta cura. in reuedere tutti lifficii. cioe se liloro lib̃i sono bñ. oq̃o male tenuti ⁊c.

Comme se debia tener conto con lo officio dela messetaria in venetia e del ditrare le sue partite in memoriale. gornale. e quaderno. e ancora deli impresti. Cap°. 18.

Si che q̃do vorai cõ tali offitii tener conto. la camera deimpresttiti. farai debitrici de tutta lasorte de cauedali a tanto el cº. ⁊c. Noiando li sestieri doue son posti. E similmente se piu ala giornata. necõprasse che molti se ne vendano p̃ te o p̃ altri cõe sa chi realto usa. Nota bñ inchi sono scritti e luoghi. ⁊c. E cosi nel scotere li loro. p. sep̃re sarala creditrici. a di p di. E sestier p sestieri ⁊c. E cosi cõlosslutio dela messetaria El cõto tirrai i q̃sto modo. cioe q̃do tu comprarai alcuna mercantia p meço d̃ sesari. alora de tutto lo amõtare. o rasone de. 2. o de. 3. o de. 4. p cº. farane creditore el ditto officio dela messetaria. E debitrici q̃lla tale mercantia. pla q̃l cagione tu paghi ⁊c. E po conuene ch el cõ pratore sempre ritega al uẽditore nel pagamẽto. de contanti. o uero p altro modo che labia asatisfare non fa caso. pch el ditto officio. non vol andar cercando altro senon larata che li aspetta. auenga che lisensari reportino el mercato in nota. cõmo. e cb̃ cho le stato fatto. per chiarecçe euidẽte de contraẽti q̃do fra loro. nascesse differẽça alcuna cõe acade. El comun puerbio dici. chi non fa non falla. e chi non falla non impara ⁊c. de le q̃li uolendose le p̃i chiarire hano regresso almercato notato. plo sensaro. al quale fo li decreti publici li si p̃sta fede cõe a publico instrumento denotaro. E so la forma di q̃llo. el piu dele uolte. El degno offitio deconsoli demercanti. formano le loro iuridiche sentẽçe ⁊c. Dico adonca compran do tu alcuna robba. tu die sape. q̃llo che la paga de m̃. E p lamita reticni. al venditore. Cioe se la robba paga. 4. p cº. a q̃llo officio p decreto publico del dominio. E tu alui retieni 2. p cº. E tanto manco li cõta. E hara el suo douere. E tu poi del tutto resti obligato al ditto offi tio. E del tutto larai asar creditore al tuo libro contado colui. E q̃lla tal mercantia farai obi trici. cõe dicemo ⁊c. pche el ditto offitio non uol cercare. chi vende. ma chi compra. E po pot a tal compratori li e concesso. di cauare tanto di q̃lla mercantia. p q̃to a pagato la m̃. fora d̃ la terra. in loro bolette. ala tauola. De lusciua. o per mare o p terra che la voglino cauare ala giornata. E po conuegano li mercanti tenere ben conto con lo ditto officio. acio sempre sa pino q̃to possino cauare. pche non si lassano cauar. per piu che si comprino se el non mon paghino la m̃. de contanti ⁊c. de le quali compre q̃ sequente ti pongo exẽplo. e cosi del ditto officio. comme se habino a dirtare in giornale. E anche in libro grande. E diro cosi. Pri ma. in memoriale. semplicimente. Jo o uero noi in questo di posto disopra o comprato da p̃ quan antonio da mesina. cucari palermini cassi nº. tante. pani nº. tanti. pesano in tutti. netti. de panelle. cassi. corde. e paglie. ꝓ tante per duc. tãti. el cº. montano duc. tãti ⁊c. abatto per la sua parte dela m̃. a ragion de tanto per cº. duc. ꝗ. p. tanti ⁊c. sensaro ꝓ quan de gagliardi. vale netti ducati. ꝗ. p. tanti ⁊c. pagammo contanti.

Distinctio nona. Tractatus. xi°. De scripturis

La medesima in giornale dira cosi   acontanti.
Per zucari de palermo. A cassa contati a ſ quan de antonio damesina. per cassi n°. tante pani
n°. tanti. pesano netti. de cassi. panelle. corde. e paglie. g. tante. a duc. tanti el c°. motano duc.
tanti zc. abatto. p la sua parte dela m.a rason de tanti per c°. zc. duc. tanti zc. restanonetti.
duc. tanti zc. sensar ſ quan de gaiardi.   g   ſ   g   p

La medesima in quaderno dira cosi.
Zucari de palermo. die dare. adi tale. p cassa contati a ſ quan dantonio de mesina. per panni
numero tanti pesano netti. g. tante per duc. tanti el cento. montano netti in tutto a carti 1.a.

E farai creditrici la cassa di quel tanto zc.   g   ſ   g   p
E sempre farai loffitio dela m. creditore del doppio che tu retenesti aluʒditore. cioe p la
sua e platua pte. zc. E sepre subito notato la robba imediate i unaltra. ptita sotto farai creditore ditto officio per ditto zucaro come harai disotto. E dibitrici ditta robba. Per exemplo un
na pagata a contanti. Or prendine una pte a cotanti e parte. a tpo p°. imemoriale cosi dirai.
                    A contanti e tempo. a di tanti zc.
Io o comprato a di detto. Da ſ quan dantonio. damesina. zucari de palermo pani n°. tanti.
pesano netti. g. tante. per duc. tanti el c°. montano duc. tanti. abatto per sua parte de m. a raſo
de tanti per c°. duc. tanti zc. de quali al psente. li no contati duc. tanti p parte e del resto mi
fa tpo fin tutto agosto pti°. che vien zc. sensar ſ quan de gaiardi. val.   g   ſ   g   p

E sappi che de alle cose che se scriue mercato per losensaro. a loffitio non bisogna far scritto de man. perche el mercato basta. ma pure a cautela ale uolte si fa zc.
In giornale la medema dira cosi. prima quel tal de tutto creditore. E poi debitore de ql
la parte de d. che lui haue.
                    yhs. 1493. a di tanti del tal mese zc.
Per zucari palermini. A ſ quan dantonio de mesina per pani numero tanti pesano netti in
tutto g. tante. a duc. tanti el c° montano duc. tanti zc. abatto per la sua pte de messetaria a ra
son de tanti per c°. duc. tanti zc. resta netto duc. tanti zc. de quali alpsente li nedebo contar
tanti zc. E del resto. mi fa termine fin tutto agosto proximo che vien. sensaro ser quan de
gagliardi. val,   g   ſ   g   p

Fanne creditore subito lofficio dela m. dela sua rata.
Per li dittri lofficio dela m. per lamontar soura ditto. cioe de duc. tati zc. a raſo de tati p c°.
p la mia parte e qlla del debitore i tutto monta duc. g. p. tanti val. g   ſ   g   p

La parte de contanti. debitor lui. E creditore la cassa. cosi.
Per ſ quan datonio. de misina: A cassa cotati alui p pte deli soura ditti zucari so la forma dl
mercato. duc. tati zc. a pe del receuere scritto de sua mano val.   g   ſ   g   p

La medema in quaderno dira cosi.
Zucari de palermo. dien dare a di tal di nouembre. per ſ quan dantonio damesina. per pani
n°. tati pesano netti g. tante zc. p duc. tanti el c°. motano duc. tanti de m. k. 4. g ſ g p
Quando uolesse farne partita nuoua. Ma uolendo sequitare la preposta bastaua dire a di.
tanti zc. per ſ quan dant. damesina p pani n° tati pesano g. tate zc. mota. k. 4. g ſ   g   p
                    La medema in hauere dira cosi.
Ser quan datonio damesina. die hauere a di tanti de nouembre. per zucari de palermo. pani n°. tanti pesan netti g. tante per duc. tanti el c°. montano. netti de m. duc. tanti. de quali al
presente li ne debio dar contanti duc. tanti zc. delauanzo. mi fa tpo per tutto agosto prio fu
turo. sensar ſ quan de gagliardi. val   k. 4.   g   ſ   g   p

In dare la medema. Per la parte deli contanti. dira cosi.
Ser quan alincontro. die dare a di tale zc. p cassa. cotati alui p pte de zucari. hebi da lui fo
nsi patti duc. tanti zc. a pe suo scritto de man in libreto. val. k. 1.a.   g   ſ   g   p

La medema. ala m. e anche per la precedente i quaderno cosi.
D ffo. dela m. die hauer. a di tal p zucari de palermo dati p quan danto de mesina. p la
montare de duc. tati. a tati p c°. sensar ſ quan de gaiardi monta. k. zc.   g   ſ   g   p

Commo se debia ordinare el pagamento che hauesse a fare per ditta e banco o scritta ne
li tuoi libri principali: Cap°. 19.

Cosi p tal copre. qsta ti basta a guidarte. o sia a tutti cotanti. o a pte cotanti. E p
te tpo. o cotati e ditta. o tutti in banco. o cotanti e banco. o cotati. E robbe. o rob
ba. e ditta. o tutta ditta o robbe. e tpo. o robba e banco. o banco e tpo. o baco e dit
ta. o banco cotanti. ditta. e robbe. zc. poche i tutti qsti modi se costuma coprare.
le qli tu per te. al seso dela pcedete metterale imemoriale. E drizarale i giornale. e quaderno.

                                                                        v iiij

Diſtinctio nona.Tractatus.xi°.De ſcripturis.

Mà q̃do hat' á far pagamẽto a p̃te bãco e ditta. Fa ch̃ p̃° coſegni la ditta.e poi p re°.ſcriui i banco.p̃ piu ſigurtà.vnde ancora q̃ſta cautella ſuſa p̃ molti e bene.q̃do ben pagaſſero a contanti.de far per reſto in bancho. E p̃ cõpito pagamẽto 7c̃. E pagandolo p̃te.banco p̃te. robba .parte ditta. e parte cõtanti.de tutte q̃ſte faralo vebitore. E q̃lle tal coſe ſarale creditrici ognuna al ſuo luogo 7c̃. E ſe per altri modi te acadeſſe cõprare.per ſimili te gouerna. 7c̃

E hauẽdo inteſo eluerſo d̃l cõprare p̃ tanti uerſi p̃ederai el vedere tuo a daltri. facẽdoli debitori.e creditrici le tue robbe. E debitrici la caſſa.ſe te da contanti.e d̃bitrici le ditte.ſe te le cõſegna in pagamẽto. E creditore.el banco. ſe tel da. E coſi di tutto p̃ ordine cõe diſopra e ditto d̃l cõprare. E lui de tutto q̃llo ti da.in pagamẽto faralo creditore 7c̃. e q̃ſto ti baſti a q̃ ſta materia a tua inſtructiõe 7c̃.   Dele p̃rite famoſe e p̃ticulari nel maneggio traficãte cõe ſono baratti cõpagnie 7c̃.cõe le ſe habbino a ſettare e ordinare neli libri mercãteſchi. e p̃°.d̃ li baratti ſeplici cõpoſti e coltpo cõ apti exẽpli d̃ tutti i memoriale.gornale e q̃der°.   Ca.20.

E q̃ta. Douer var modo. cõe ſe habino a ſettar alcũe p̃rite famoſe p̃ticulari. ch̃ ne li maneggii traficãti ſi ſogliano el piu de le volte.ſolẽniçare. E metterle va p̃ſe.acio di q̃lle diſtintte valaltre.ſene poſſa cognoſcere.el .p̃ e vano che di q̃lle ſeiſſe.cõe ſono li baratti.e le cõpag°.viaggi recomãdati.viaggi i ſua mano.cõmiſſiõe haui te p̃ altri.banchi de ſcrita.o vero ditta. L'abi reali.ouncõto de botega 7c̃. De le q̃li d̃ ſequẽte ſuccitamẽte a tua baſtança.te varo notitia.cõe ſe debi guiuare. e reggere neli tuoi libri ordi natamẽte.acio nõ te abagli in tue facẽde. E p̃°.moſtraremo cõe ſe debia aſertare 1°. baratto. Sono li baratti cõmunamẽte de.3.ſorte cõe diſopra in leragiõ ſo detto.   Diſtictio.9ª.T.3°. carti.161.fin in.167.a pieno ſi che li recorri a itenderli.   Dico adõca che in tutti q̃ſti te a cadeſſe ſcriuere i lib°! el baratto.ſep̃e puramẽte.p̃°. in lo memoriale debi narrarlo ad lram vẽt°. vala p̃rita cõ tutti ſuo modi e conditiõi ch̃ el ſira ſtato fatto.e cõcluſo.o comẽcani.o fra voi ſoli. E q̃do larai coſi narrato. E tu poi alafine riduralo i ſu li cõtanti. E ſo che q̃lle tal robbe vederai valere.a cõtanti p̃ tãto tirarai fora la p̃rita. a che moneta ſi vogla i memoriale. che non fa caſo.poche poi el q̃dernieri la redura tutta a 1ª.ſorta alautẽtico.cioe q̃do lametara al giornale. E al q̃derno grãde 7c̃. E q̃ſto ſi fa pch̃e cauãdo tu fori le valute de le robbe a q̃l che ti ſtanno abazatto.nõ potreſti neli tuoi cõti.e ſcripture.cognoſcere ſença grãdiſſima difficulta.tuo vtile. o vero p̃ditta ſequita. Le q̃li ſep̃e couiẽſi redure a cõtanti. p̃ volerle ben cognoſcere. 7c̃.   E ſe di tali mercãrie hauute p̃ baratti: voleſſi vap̃te p̃ticularmẽte tenerne cõto.p̃ poder veder il ſuo retratto. ſep̃arametẽ da lalt°.robbe che viral ſorta haueſſe.p̃°. in ca ſa.o che vapoi cõpraſſe.p̃ cognoſcere qual ſia ſtata megliore icepta.lo poi fare. E ãcora acumulare tutte mercãtie inſiemi.cõe ſe haueſſe.p̃°. gençeri va te. E hora q̃ſti recceueſſi del baratto li quali voler metter cõ li altri.nel gornal virai coſi.cioe.

Per cençeri bellidi i mõte.o vero in colli: A cucari de laral ſorta 7c̃. p̃ collt tanti.peſano. 8 tã te haui val tal abaratto de cucari fatto i q̃ſta forma.cioe che mi li miſſi el c°.de cucari duc̃. 24.7c̃.cõ q̃ſto che mi deſſe e l.⅓.de contanti el c°.de contanti 7c̃. B li quali
gençeri.li cõti cucari.pani.n°.tanti peſan 8 tante che acontanti el c°. val duc̃.20. E p̃ li ditti
gençeri nebbe 8 tante 7c̃.pani n°.tanti 7c̃. vagliano ciaſcuno.   8   f   g   p̃

E pche ale volte nõ ſapzai.a põto lo n°. d̃li pani.che p̃ ditti çençeri intraſſe nõ fa caſo. po ch̃ poi nela p̃tita ſeqnte.ſi ſupleſci q̃l che li mancaſſe. q̃l che li foſſe piu i q̃lla de la caſſa.mãca ra nõ vimeno. alincõtro de cucari ſep̃e. harai e doucre aponto.pche tutte vua. vãno a cu cari i modo che la p̃tita de cucari non pde el n°.de pani. ne d̃l peſo.pche nõ e ſep̃e poſſibi le d'ogni fraſchetta. va p̃ſe tener cõto. 7c̃. Hora di q̃lla p̃te de cõtanti che vi ſono coſi. fara ne debitrici la caſſa. E pure del ſimile. creditori ditti çucari. vicendo coſi.cioe.

Per caſſa: A li vitti 7c̃.   Per contanti hebi nel ditto baratto. val ditto 7c̃. per pani n°. tan
ti 7c̃. peſano 8.tante val.   8   f   g   p̃

E ſimili p̃rite ſubito q̃lli mettano immediate nel giornale a piſſo q̃lla del baratto. nel q̃l haue
ſti li conti 7c̃. ſi che a q̃ſto modo ditta reſti.non volendone tener ſeparato conto. Ma ſe ſe parato louoi tener nel giornale virai coſi.cioe.

Per cençeri bellidi. per conto di bazatto ſebbero val tale 7c̃: A çucari 7c̃. narrando tutto. poi a ponto commo diſopra. E in lo quaderno. poi barano loro partita. diſtincta 7c̃. E queſto uo glio che ti baſti. per tutti li altri baratti che ſo per te ſença piu mi ſtenda. li ſapa rai guidare 7c̃.

De laltra partita famoſa ditta Compagnie: comme ſe debino ordinare. e ditare in tutti
li modi occurenti in ciaſcuno libro.   Cap°. 21.

Distinctio nona Tractatus xi°. De scripturis

Altra partita famosa e la cōp⁴. cb̄ cō alcūo facesse p ragiōe di qllũche cosa si facesse o di panni o de sete o de spetiarie o de gottōi e de tētoria o de cābi 7c. Queste tali simili sēpre uogliāo sua pr̃ita sepata i tutti li 3 libri detti. Nel p̄cioe memoriale posto che tu barai el di sopra narrarala seplicimēte tutta con modi e cōditiōi cb̄ lauete fatta alegan°scripto ouer altro istr̃o cb̄ fra noi fosse e noiando el t̃po q̃ to la sintēde: e di che faculta si fa eli fattori e garzoni cb̄ sauesse a tenere 7c. e quello che mette ciascū perse o de robba o de d. 7c. o debitori e creditori: e di tutto a vno a vno farane creditori li cōp¹. ognū di q̃l tanto che mette da pr̃se e debitrici la cassa d̄ la dc̄a cōp². se da per se la tiēi cb̄ me g°. se reggi el trafico tenēdola sepata va la cassa tua pr̃iculari q̃°in fosse q̃l cb̄ salcō². guidasse p la q̃l te cōuē fare libri. vap̄se cō qllordie mō evia cb̄ di sop̃ e dc̃o: d̄ tutto el tuo maneggio p mē briga: nō vinnēo potresti tutta tenerla nelli medēi toi libri. vericādo noue pr̃ite cōmo al pr̃ite dicemo cb̄ si chiamāo famose p cēr sepate va tutte laltr̃. d̄ le qli q̃ te do el mō succito cōmo labi adittare i tuo mēoriale e di poi i giornale e qderno 7c. Ma tenēdo di lei libri sepati nō ti vo altr°vocumito senō cb̄ liquidi si cōmo d̄ tutto el tuo trafico e dc̃o. Dirolla cosi ime.

In q̃sto di biamo sc̃o cōp². cō li tali e tali alarte d̄ la lana 7c. cō pacti e cōditiōni 7c. cōmo ape p scripto o istr̃o 7c. p ãni tãti 7c. onde el tal vette cōtãti tãti 7c. Laltr° balle tãte lana frãc. pesa netta 8. tãte 7c. messacōto duc. tãti el m°7c. elaltr° a seg°tãti veri debitori. cioe el tal de duc. tãti. el tal de tanti 7c. e cosi io sborsai d̄ pr̃ete duc. tãti 7c. e so i summā tutto el cor. duc. tãti 7c. Poi in tuo giornale dirai i q̃sto modo asettado tutte cose a suo luogo imagina v². cassa d̄ compagnia. cvn cauedal di cō². e cosi a tutte le pr̃ite cb̄ tu metterai dirai sēpre p cōto d̄ pp̃. acio labi a cognoscere dalle toi pr̃ite pr̃iculari 7c. e p². o mo sestri da la cassa comēzarai e poi succesiuamente asettarai laltre. Per cassa de compagnia. al tale de ragiōn de compagnia acio se hauesse altri conti non simpacino 7c. pe contanti misēi q̃sto vi p la sua rata. 2. e li nr̃i pacti cōmo apare p scripto ouer istr̃o 7c. val 8. s. g°. p. Poi similmēte dirai de le robbe che bano messe cosi. Per lana franc. de la cōp². al tale p balle tante pesano nette inutto 8. tante so cōta dacordo con tutti ducati tanti el m°secōdo la for². del cōtratto ouer scripto fra noi 7c. mōta iturto duc. 7c. val 8. s. g°. p. E cosi andarai ponēdo tutte. p li debitori cōsegniati dirai cosi. Per lo tale de ragio de cōp³. A tale q̃l secōdo nr̃i pacti ci cōsegno p vero debitore de duc. tanti val 8. s. g°. p. Dr̃mal che a lept°sci itrodutto nō mi curo stēderme piu si cōmo in lo princ°d°q̃sto trattato feci che troppo seria auolerte ogni cosa di nuouo replicare. E po del modo de metterle al qderuo grande nō ne dico perche se ti sia facile cognoscēdo gia tu in lo giornale el va debitore cō l creditore. siche asetrarale tu i dare e hauere in quel modo che di sopra i questo te segnai a ca°15°e depēnarale i giornale cōmo dissi di sopra al ca°12°ponēdo sēpre denanze i margine li nūeri del debitore e creditore: a q̃re carti li barai posti al libro. e cosi cōmo tu li metti al libro grande: cosi li asetta i alfabeto cōmo di sopra piu fiade hauemo mostro 7c.

De lordine de le pr̃ite de ciascuna spesa: cōmo de casa ordinarie: straordinarie: e di mercantie: salarij de garzoni e factori cōmo sabino a scriuere: e dittare nelli libri. ca° 22.

Oltra tutte le cose ditte te quiene hauere i tutti toi libri q̃ste pr̃ite. cioe spesi d̄ mercātia spesi de casa ordiarie spesi straordiarie vna de itrata e vscita e vna de pro e dāno o uoi dire auanzi e disauāzi o utile e dāno o guadagno e pdita che tāto va le q̃li pr̃ite sōno summamēte necessarie i ogni corpo mercātesco p potere sempre cognoscere suo capitale. e ala fine nel saldo cōmo getra el trafico 7c. le q̃li d̄ seq̃te abastanza chiariremo cōmo se debino guidare nelli libri. Onde q̃lla de spese mercātesche si tiene p rispecto che nō sēpre ogni peluzo si po mettere subito i la pr̃ita de la robba che tu uendi o cōpri cōmo acade che da poi piu di p q̃lla ti cōuerra pagare fachini e pesadori e ligadori e barca. e bastagi. e simili e chi vi soldo. achi. 2. 7c. de le qli volēdone fare pr̃icular pr̃ita sereb be lōgo e nō meriranno la spesa poche de mimimis nō curat pr̃or 7c. E ācora acade che tu adoprarai q̃lli medesimi bastagi. fachini. barca. e legatori i vn pōto p piu diuerse cose cōmo itruene. cb̄ i ū pōto scarcādo o carcādo diuerse sorte mercātie li a fattigarai e tu li pagbi p tutte a vn tratto che nō potresti a ogni mercātia carattare la sua spesa. E po nasci q̃sta pr̃ita chiamata spese de mercātia la q̃l sēpre sta acesa i dare cōmo tutte laltre spesi fāno. Salarij ancora de factori e garzoni de botega si mettano i q̃ste e alcuni ne fa pr̃ita a so posta p sapere i ditti che spēdano lāno 7c. e poi i q̃sta la saldano: che p niū mō nō possano essere creditrici: e qdo cosi le trouaisti seria errore nel libro. E però i memorali te dirai cosi.

In questo di habian pagato abastasi barcaroli ligadori, pesadori 7c. cb̄ carcaro e scarcaro 7c. le tali e tali cose. duc. tanti 7c.

p iiiij

Distinctio nona tractatus xi°. De scripturis

Poi in lo giornale couerra dir cosi. ¶ Per spese de mercatie: a cassa contati: per barche e bastagi corde e ligatori de le tal cose in tutto duc.tati 7c. val. 8. s. g. p. In lo q̃derno dirai cosi. ¶ Spesi d̃ mercātia die dare adi tāti p cassa 7c. val к. 8. s. g. p. Quella d̃ le spesi di casa ordinarie nõ si po far sença. E itēdanse spesi di casa ordinarie: cõmo formē ti: vini: legne: ogli: sale: carne: scarpe: copelli facture de veste: giupponi: calçe: e sartori 7c. be ueraggi: beuestite: mance: ouer bonemani 7c. barbieri: fornaro: aquaruoli: lauature de pan ni 7c. masarie de cocina vasi. bichieri. e uetri: tutti secchi. mastelli. botti 7c. bauega che mol ti de simili masarie vsino tener conto separato per poter presto trouar suo cõto e fāno prita noua. cõmo ācora tu poi fare nõ che q̃ste ma ni qualūche altra ti parra. ma io te amaestro di quelle chel trafico nõ po far sença 7c. e tal prita di spesi di casa dittarala si cõmo e ditto de quella de la mercātia. e secõdo che tu vai facēdo spese grosse adi p di metti in li libri cõ mo del formento e vini legne 7c. De quali ancora molti costumano fare prita daperse per poter poi alasine de lanno o a tēpo p tēpo facilmēte sapere quāto de tali cõlumano 7c. ma per le spesi piccole cõmo sono amenuto cõprar carne e pesci: barbieri e traghetti si uol torre o vno ouer doi duc. a vn tratto e tenersi da parte in vno sachetto e di quelli andar spēdēdo a menuto. perche nõ scria possibili a vna a vna di tali tener conto. E cosi dicano per li con tanti in giornale. ¶ Per spesi di casa. A cassa q̃li trassi per spendere amenuto in vno sachet to duc. tanti 7c. val. 8. s. g. p. E poi se ti pare ancora con queste spesi de casa meter ui le spesi straordinarie che non sa caso. cõmo quādo spendesse per andare asolaçço: o p tra cere alarco o balestro e altri giochi o perdite che ti cascassero o pdesse robbe o denari o ch te fossero tolte o perdesse in mare o per fuochi 7c. che tutti simili sintendano spese straordina rie. Le quali ancora se le voli tenere da parte similmente lo poi fare e molti lusano per sa per netto alasin delanno quanto hano speso de straordinario per le quali anco sintende do ni e presenti che tu facesse adalcuno per alcuna cagione 7c. d̃ le quali spese non mi curo piu oltra stenderme perche so certo che tu per te meglio ormai hauendo amente le cose dette dinance asettarai che prima non haresti facto siche vegni diremo del modo da settare le partite de vna botega si nel tuo q̃uaderno e libri ordinarij: cõmo se tu la volesse te ner tu da te cõmo laresti a tenere che sia bella cosa a sapere siche notale.

De lordine e mõ e sap tener vn cõto de botega i tua mão o adaltri recõmādata e cõmo se debino nelli libri autentici del patrone e anche in quelli de botega separatamente scriuere e dittare. capi. 23.

Ico adonca quādo hauesse vna botega la q̃l tenesse fornita ala giornata for de casa tua e fore del tuo corpo di casa. alora p bono ordine tirrai q̃sto mõ: cioe de tutte le robbe che tu ui metterai adi p di farala debitrici ali toi libri e crediptrici q̃lle tal robbe cho i metti vna p vna e sa tua imaginatiõe cõ q̃sta bote⁰. sia vna p sona. tua debitrici di q̃l tāto che li dai e p lei spēdi i tutti li modi. E cosi p lauerso de tutto ql lo che ne caui e receui farala creditrici cõmo se fosse vn d̃bitore che pagasse apre apre. E poi ogni volta che tu voli con lei cõtare tu porrai vedere cõmo ella te butta. o bene o male 7c. E cosi poi saprai q̃llo arai afare. e i cõ mõ larai a gouernare 7c. E molti sono ch ali soi libri fā no debitore el pricipale che li arede a ditta botega beche q̃sto nõ si possa debitamente sēça volūta di q̃l tale. poch mai si deue mettere ne ācora a ragiõ si puo porre vn debitore alib⁰ sēça sua saputa ne ach creditore cõ cõditiõi alcūe sēça sua uolūta e q̃l cose facēdo tu sere sti mãco che da bene. E li toi libri seriēno reputati falsi. e cosi d̃ le masarie ch i q̃lla metesse e ordegni necessarii al a ditta botega secõdo sua occurēça: cõmo se fosse speciaria ti conuerra fornirla d̃ vasi. caldieri. ramini. da lauorare 7c. di q̃li tutti farala debitrici o colui che li attē de cõmo ditto. e p bello iuētario li le asegna scripto d̃ sua mão odaltri d̃ sua uolūta 7c. acio de tutto sia chiaro. e q̃sto voglio sia bastate q̃do la botega hauesse consegnata a vnaltro ch p te la facesse o fosse tuo cõmesso 7c. Ma se la dc̃a botega vorrai tener a tuoi mãi q̃sto or die suarai e stara bene: e meriamo ch cõpri e trafichi tutto p la ditta botega e nõ haui alt⁰ maneggio alora formarai li libri cõmo e ditto. E di cio che vendi e cõpri farai credito⁰ ri chi te da le robbe per tanto tempo se cõpri a tempo e creditrici la cassa se cõpri a con tanti e debitrici la botega. E quando tu vendesse a menuto. cioe che non ariuasse a. 4. o. 6. du cati 7c. alora tutti ditti denari reporrai in vna cassetta. ouer salua denaro dõde i capo d̃. 8. o 10. giorni sine cauarai. e alora farae debitrici la cassa e creditrici la bo⁰. di q̃l tāto: e la prita dirai p piu robbe uēdute de le q̃li già hauerai tenuto el cõto e molte alt⁰. cose in le q̃li nõ mi

Distinctio nona Tractatus xi°. De scripturis

voglio troppo distendere, p che so cómo disopra diffusamételhabiáo dcó ormai saprai perte
itéderle cóciosia che cóti non sóno altro che vn debito ordine de la fantasia che si fa el mercatante per el qual uniforme seruato puene ala noticia de tutte sue facéde e cognosci facilméte p qllo se le sue cose uáno bene o male. p che el prouerbio dici chi fa mercatia e nó la cognosca li soi denari douétan mosca 7c. e secondo le occurrenze li fa remedio. E pero piu e má-
co li sipo sempre agiongere in numero e i multitudine de pute. E po de qsto tacóténta.

Cómo se habino aseltare nel giornale e quaderno le partite de li banchi de scritta: e li sei
tédino e doue ne sia; o de cábi: tu có loro siandomercatáte: e tu có altri q dio fosse bachieri:
e de le quie táge che p li cábi se fáno. e p che sene facia doi de medesimo tenore   ca .24

Ora per li banchi de scripta o quali se ne troua oggi in vinetia i bruggia iauer
sa e barçelóa e certi altriluoghi famosi e traficati ti cóuie sap có loro libri scótra-
re có gradissima diligétia. E pero da notar che có lo bancho te poi cómunamé-
te impaciare da te ponédoui denari per piu tua sigureçça: o uero p modo de di-
posito a la giornata poter con quelsi far tuoi pagamenti chiari apiero gioâni e martino per
che la ditta del bancho e comme publico istruméto de notaro p che son per li dominij alci
gurati. onde ponédoui tu da te. d. farai debitore ditto bancho nominaudo patroni o uero
cópagni del bacho e creditrici la tua cassa cosi dicédo i giornale   Per bancho de li pamani: A cassa per cótanti li misi có tali. io o altri che per me fosse in questo di. de mio conto fra
oro e moneta 7c. i tutto ducati 7c. U al. $. f. g. p. E farare fare dal banchieri doi uersi i suno
foglio p piu cautela. E cosi giongédogliune tu ala giornata farai el simile: cauandone tu lui
te fara scriuere a te el receuere: e cosi le cose si uengano sempre a máteneer chiare: Uero e che
aleuolte tal scritte nó si costumano p che cómo e ditto li libri del bancho sempre sóno publi
chi e autentichi; ma pur é buono la cautela p che cómo di sopra fo detto al mercante le cose
mai soró troppo chiare. Ma se tu uolesse tal prita tenerla con li patroni: o uero cópagni del
bancho ancora lo poi fare che tanto uale po che noiando tu el bácho a modo disopra sinté
de li patróni e cóp². de quello: per li patróni diresti cosi.   Per miser Girolimo lipamani dal
bancho e cópagni qdo fossero piu. A cassa ut supra sequita tutto. E sempre farai neli tuoi libri mentione de le chiareçe: patti: e códitioni che fra uoi nascessero cómo de scripti de má: e
del luogo doue li reponi isiga: scatola: tascha: a cassa acio possi facilméte retrouarle: po che
có bona diligéça simili scripture si debono seruare. ad ppetuam rei memoriá; p li picoli oc-
corrano 7c. E p che aleuolte có lo bachieri porresti hauerui piu facéde e maneggi i mercá
tia p te o per altri cómo cómesso 7c. po sempre cú lui i cóuie tener cóti diuersi p non itriga
re lance có ronchoni: la nascieria grá confusióne: e dire i le sue ptite p cóto che la tal cosa: o
p cóto del tal o p ragió de mercantia o p ragion de contanti depolita li tuo nome o daltri
cómo e ditto: le quali cose so p tuo igegno o; mai reggerai 7c. E simil mte te reggerai saltri te
aconciasse. d. a te pche cóto si uolesse: taralo debitore altrui libro p ql tal cóto: cioe o pagamé
to noiando p pte o p resto 7c. e ql tale creditore p lo medesimo cóto e stara bene. E q̈
do tu de dcó bancho cauasse. d. i cótáti o p paga méti che adaltri facesse p pte o resto o uero
p remetter a daltri i altri paesi 7c. alora farai el cótrario de ql che finora e dcó: cioe se caui
cótanti farai debitrici la tua cassa: e creditore el bancho o uer patrói di quel tanto che ne ca
uasti. E se tu li scriuesse adaltri farai debitore ql tale e creditore do patrói di ql tanto noiando
de pche dicédo i giornale p li cótanti cosi.   Per cassa albancho o uer mi-
ser girolimo li pamani p contanti i tal dio i qsto di ne trassi a mio bisogno 7c. i tutto. duc.
tati 7c. ual. $. f. g. p. E te adaltri li scriuesse vtputa a martio di fiti cosi.   Per marc° del ta
le. Al ditto ut supra per duc. tati 7c. li scrissi p pte o p presto o abó cóto o p ipsto 7c. i qsto
di. ual. $. f. g. p. E cosi leuádo ditte ptitte dl giornale sépre a suo luogo i qderno asettarale: e
l alfabeto comodi disopra dari e depenandole cómo to mostro in memoriale e giornale. p. e
mancho per te stesso giógnédoli parolle. po che non e possibile d̄ di tuutto a picno narrare
si che cóuiē dal tuo cáto sia uigilante 7c. El medesimo mó te couerra obseruare p remette
re li cábi altroue. cóme lon²: brugia: ro²: lió 7c. per ritrar daltro 7c. nominando le termini 7c. o ala uista o aladata o al suo piacere cómo se costuma facédo métióe de p². 2². e. 3². 7c.
acio non nasca crrrore fra te el tuo respondente e de le monete che tu trai e rimetti e le lor
ualute e, puistói e spesi uâni e interessi che có li protesti poderebono nascere 7c. si che di tutto
si uol far métióe el p e cóme. E cóme o messo che tu habi afare con bácho: cosi uersa uice
prédi se fosse tu el banchieri mutaris mutandis che quando paghi fa debitore quel tale e la
tua cassa creditrici e sel tuo creditore sença cauare. d. adaltri li scriuesse dirai nel tuo giorni

Distinctio nona tractatus.xi°.De scripturis

se per quel tale tuo creditore a quel tale achi lui li acócia.e cosi vieni a far cómutatione da vno creditore a unaltro e tu rimani pure debitore e vieni in qsto atto essere persona meççana e cómuna.cómo testimonio e factore de le parti a tuo inchiostro carta sitto satiga e tempo si che di qua si caua la honesta puisióe nel cambio essere sépre licita qdo mai nõ ui corisse picolo de uiaggio altre remesse in mano de terçe psone 7c.cómo nelli cambi real i in qsto a suo luogho estato apieno detto 7c.Ma siando bache ri ricordare nelli saldi coi creditori sarte tornare sogli polize o altri scripti che di tua mano hauesse de leqli quando ne sai sépre sanne nel tuo libro mentióe acio te recordia sartele tornare e straçarli:acio nõ ucnisse a tépo cõ qlli altri a domandarte e satte sare sépre bone quietançe cómo costumano sare chi attéde al cãbio:po che lusança e che se tu vieni.verbi gra da gineuera con vna di cãbio q in vi°.a mis giouãnisresco baldi da sio°.e cópa.cb alauista o data:o a tuo piacere te douesse pagare metia mo duc. 100.p altre tanti che dila hauesse nele man de chi li scriue cõ segnati:aloza il ditto mis, giouãni e cóp².acceptãdo la lsa:e sbozsciãdote ditti.õ.re sara scriuere õ tua mano doi de tançe de vn medesimo tenoze: se tu nõ sapesse scriuere le sara vn terço pzo õ notro: nõ sa cõ tentara duna p che luna cóuie che rimandi a ql banchieri a gineuera:che li scriue che a te p suo cõto paghi li ditti duc.100.i sarli sede cómo cozresemète a satto ql tanto che li scrisse i una sua li mãda laquietãça di tua mano:e laltra tene i silça apresso di se: acio qdo cótasse cõ lui non potesse negarlilo: di la ancora tu tornãdo nõ potesse.lamétarte di lui ne de mis giouãni po che se tu lo sesse el te mostraria ditta quietança di tua mano e remaresti consuso:si che tutte qste cose sonno cautele che ti conuengano de necessita sare p la poca sede si troua oggi di Del quale atto ne nascano voi ptite i lo qderno loro.vna in ql di mes giouãni sacédo õbitore ql che li scriue p vigoze de la dicãbio: laltra i qllo del respódéte a gineuera sacédo creditore mis giouãni di quelli duc.100.per virtu de ditta tua quietança receuuta.e questo e el debito modo e ordine de cambiatori p tutto el módo: acio le loz cose vadino cõ chiareççe;si che dal tuo lato alquãto affatigãdote pozrai ogni cosa con summa diligença asettare.7c.

De unaltra partita che ale uolte se costuma nel qderno tenere detta entrata e uscita e ale uolte senesa libro particulare: e per che.   ca.25.

Onno alcuni che ne loz libri usano tenere vna ptita detta entrata e vscita i la ql pógano cose straozdinarie o altre cómo ala. santasia pare. Altri ne tirra una õ spese straozdinarie e i simili mettano cómo i qlla dintrata isita psérí che li sosser satti.v.gra.e cosi scdo che riceuano e vãno e tégano cóto i dare e hauere e poi a la sine cõ laltre le saldãno i .p e dãno e cauedale cómo irenderai nel bilancio 7c.Ma i uero qlla detta di sopza spese di casa p tutte e bastãte se nõ chi uolesse per sua curiosita tener conto da p se sin a vn pótale de stréga che lo pozria sare ma ach sint:epo si dba a le cose cõ breuita asettarse. Altri luoghi costuma de litrata cuscita tenér vn libro a sua posta: e poi quello saldano a tépo del bilãcio nel vltimo autético isicini cõ le altre sacéde;laql cosa no e dabiasmare auéga sia de piu satiga.

Cómo se habino asettare neli libzi le ptite de li uiaggi i sua mano: e quelle de li viaggi recomandati: e cómmo di necessita de tali nascono doi quaderni   ca.26.

J uiaggi si costumano sare i doi modi:cioe i sua mano e recomandato. vnde nascano diuersi modi i tener lo: cóti po che sépre si prosupógano libri doppio sia i tua mano o sia recómandato. Perche luqderno resta i casa e laltro ti cóué sare i uiaggio.vnde sel ditto viaggio sia i tua mano p bó ordie de cioche tu pozti sorma tuo inétario qdernetto:giozrnaletto 7c.rutto cómo di sopra se detto: e uéddedo cópzãdo baratãdo 7c.de tutto sa debitori e creditori psone:robbe: cassa:cauedal:de uiaggio:e p e van no de uiaggio 7c.e qsto e lo piu schietto e dica ch si uoglia altri. Auéga ch pozresti tener cõto la casa dalaql tu togli la saculta de al ditto uiaggio pozti sacédola nel libretto del tuo uiaggio creditrici:e le robbe debitrici a una p v¹: cosi sormaresti tua cassa:tuo cauedale 7c. ordenataméte cómo nel tuo samoso.E tornãdo a saluaméto rédaresti alacasa altre robbe ali contro. o uero.õ.e cõ lei saldaresti cóto e lutile o dãno seqto asettaresti a suo luogho nel quaderno grãde.siche aqsto modo ancoza le sue sacéde uerebono chiare.Ma sel viaggio recómãdasse adaltri:aloza saresti cómo del rutto nel tuo libro debitore ql tale achi larecomãdi dicédo per uiaggio recómãdato al tale 7c. cõ lui terresti conto cómine se sosse vn tuo auétore de tutte robbe:e õ.a ptita per partita 7c.E lui dal cãto suo sormara suo qdernetto: e iqllo te conuerra sare creditore de tutto.E retornãdo saldara conteco.E sel tuo cómesso sosse i le bãde

Distinctio nona. Tractatus. xi°. De scripturis

De 1ª. p̄rita famosa ditta .p e dāno o vero auançi e desauançi. cō. 'asabia, a tenere nel q̄der/
no.e pche ella nō si metta nel cornale comme le altre p̄tie.   Cap°. 27

Eq̄ta doppo ogni alt³ p̄tiª. 1ª.chiamata de .p e dāno o voi dire vtile e dāno seq̄ro
o vero auançe desauāçi fo alcūo paese ilaq̄le tutte lalt°.del tuo q̄der° sēp se ha
no a saldare cōe nel bilācio se dira. E q̄sta nō bisogna si metta i giornale. ma ba
sta solo nel q̄der° pchē lanasci i q̄llo d̄le cose auāçate o vero mācate i dare e bēre
p laq̄le dirai .p e danno die dare. E .p e dāno die bēre. cioe q̄do valcūa robba hauesse p̄du
to.lacui p̄rtª.più nel tuo q̄derno restasse i dare cb̄ i bēre.alora aiutarai el suo bēre p pegiar
la al dare acio se saldi.de q̄l tanto che li mancasse.dicēdo. e die bēre p .p e dāno q̄l q̄ metto
p saldo de q̄sta.p danno seq̄to 7c̄.e segnarai le carti d̄l .p e danno nel trar fuora lap̄tiª. E al
.p e dāno andarai i dare.dicēdo .p e dāno die dare a di 7c̄.p latal robba.p danno seq̄to tan
to 7c̄.posto i q̄lla aldie bēre p suo saldo ap̄e a carti 7c̄. E se la fosse più i bēre ditta robba cb̄
i dare.alora faresti p lo aduerso.. E cosi andarai facēdo a 1ª.p 1ª. de tutte robbe finite. o ma
le o bn̄ cb̄ sieno andate acio sēp̄e.eltuo q̄derno se ritroui paro de p̄ti°.cioe cb̄ tante sene tro
ui i dare q̄nte i bēre.pchē cosi sedeue ritrouare a star bn̄ cōe se dira nel bilancio. E cosi succin
ta mēte vedarai se guadagni o x̄o p̄di e q̄to. E q̄sta p̄rita, poi ancora lei si cōuerra saldare
i q̄lla del cauedale.laq̄le e vl̄tia de tutti li q̄derni.e p cōseq̄nte receptaculo d̄ tutte le alt°. cōe
i tēderai 7c̄.   Comme se debino reportare innançe le p̄tite del quaderno.qn̄ fossero pie
ne e in che luogo sabi a portare el resto.a cio nō sia p̄sa malitia nel quaderno. Cap°. 28.

Ancora e da notar̄ q̄do 1ª. p̄rita e piena. o i dare o i bēre che nō uisinipo metter
più bisogna portarla innāçe i mediate a tutte lalt°. nō lasciādo spacio nel q̄derno
fra el ditto reporto.e lalt°. p̄ti°. cb̄ se reputaria fraude nel lib°. E deuese reportare
i q̄sto modo. cōe disop²a. dicemo d̄ saldarle i .p e dāno. cosi nelli reporti. il o² mede
sime cōuiēse obseruare i dare e i bēre sēça metterle in cornale pchē li reporti nō bisogna poner
li i cornale bēcb̄ si potrebbe a chi volesse e verria a respōdere ancor² bn̄. ma nō fa bisog°. pchē
se beria q̄lla fatica. più sēça frutto.siche bisogna aiutar la minor q̄ª.cioe sele.più in dare cb̄ i
bēre ditta p̄rti°. di q̄l tanto aiuta el suo bēre 7c̄. E per² chiaro tenemettaro d 1ª. e mettiamo
che Martino habia fatto cō teco cōto lōgo de più p̄ti°.i modo. che la sua posta sia .da repor
tare.e sia nel tuo q̄der°.a carti. 30. e lulti². p̄ti°. de tutto el q̄der°. sia a carti.60. i q̄tma .e la me
desima façata sia luogo da poterui ancora locare q̄lla de Mart°. E siote d̄bito el ditto §. 80
p̄ 15.ḡ. 15. p̄. 2 4. deliq̄li in tutto te nabia dato. §. 72. p̄ 9. ḡ. 3. p̄. 17. dico che batta el suo bēre d̄l
suo dare. cioe. 72. 9. 3. 17. resta. §. 8 p̄ 6 ḡ. 5 p̄ 7. E de tanto lo deui portar debitore auanti. E
de q̄llo medesimo deui aiutare la p̄rtia in bēre. e dirai cosi. adi. 7c̄.p lui medēo q̄l porto auan
ti in q̄sto aloia dare p resto q̄l pōgo q̄ p saldo. §. 8 p̄ 6 ḡ 5 p̄ 7. val a carti. 60. §. p̄ ḡ. p̄. E opēne
ral lap̄ti°. in dare e in bēre cō 1ª. linea diametraliter. E fatto q̄sto andarai a carti. 60. in dar
E porrai ditto resto pon̄edo sēp̄e disop²a.p².senō ci fosse el M°. cōe dinançe fo ditto. E di/
rai cosi. Martino die darca 7c̄. p lui medemo p resto tratto da drieto in q̄sto aloia
bēre p saldo d q̄lla. val a carti. 30. §. 8 p̄ 6 ḡ 5 p̄ 7. E q̄sto medesi° modo obseruai in tutte p̄ti°
che hauesse a reportare auanti incatenandole al modo ditto e sēça interuallo alcūo. po cb̄ se
p̄re le p̄ti°. si vogliano ponere cōe nascano d̄ luogo. sito. di. e milesi°. acio nisū te possi calu
niare. 7c̄.   Del modo a sapere mutare el milesimo nel quaderno fra le partite che ala cor
nata acascano. quando ogni anno non si saldasi li libri.   Capitolo. 29.

Orria eb̄ alcuolte che nele tue p̄rtite in quaderno. tu hauessi a mutar milesi°. E
nō hauesse saldato. alora ditto milesi°. deui ponere in margine a ripetto ditta p̄rti
ta cb̄ cosi e nata. cōe ho detto sopra in cap.15° E tutte lal tre che la seq̄teranno se
intēderanno al ditto mile°. Ma sēp̄e buono desaldare ogn̄anno. maxime chi
e in cōp²a. pchē el puerbio dici ragion spessa amista lōga. E cosi farai a tutte simili.

Comme se debia leuare vn conto al debitore che lo domandasse. e ancora al suo patrōe
siando fatore e commesso de tutta la aministratione de le robbe.   Capitolo. 30.

Bisogna oltra li dati documēti. sape leuare vn cōto al tuo debitore ch̄ te lo domā
dasse. E q̄sto nō si po de ragion negare. p̄rtim q̄do cō teco hauesse tenuto conto
lōgo. de più anni e mesi 7c̄. alora farate da prin°. ch̄ insiemi hauesse a fare. o da al
tro termine cb̄ lui el volesse q̄do tu fossero stari altri saldi da q̄l tp̄o cb̄ lo vo
le per vna volta volentieri li le leua. E de tutto farai vna partita in vn foglio che ui capa.
E q̄do in. 1ª. facia non capisse saldarai tutto quello che li hauerai posto. e porterai el resto
dalaltro lato del foglio in dare. overo hauere commo nel capitolo. 28° fo detto. E va con
tinuando. E a lultimo. redullo in resto netto duna sola partita in dare. o hauer secondo
che la nascera. E questi tali conti si vogliano leuare con grandissima diligentia.

Distinctio nona. Tractatus xi°. De scripturis.

E q̃sto modo obfuarai neli fatti tuoi ꝓprij. e tuoi auctori. Ma se tu amistrasse p altri. p usa de acomãde. o de cõmissiõi. aloza similmẽte cosi lo leuarai al patrõe cõe õ põto lbarai posto al libzo. facẽdote creditore de tpo e tpo dele tuoi. puisiõi ſo vri patti. E poi i finc p resto netto. del ritratto. farate suo debitore. o vero creditore q̃do del tuo libauesse messo. e lui poi lo re uedara. põtãdolo. cõ lisuoi. E trouãdolo star bene. te vorra meglio. E piu te fidara. p cbe bi sogna cbe de tutto q̃llo te a dato o mandato cbe del receuere a lre di tua mano li ne asegni aministrationi ordinatamẽte. E po nota bene. E p lauerso farai tu leuarlo a tuoi fattori. o vero cõmessi similiter. Ma p°. cbe foza se vieno li conti si uogliano ben pontare cõ tutte lo ro ptite i q̃derno i giornale e memoriale. E con tutti luogbi cbe lauesse scritte acio nõ nascef se errore fra le pti.   Del' modo e ordine a sape retrattare. o vero istornare 1ª. o piu ptite cbe p errore bauesse poste i alt? luogo cb douessero adare cõe auene p sinẽo agic. Cap°. 31.

Ancora necessario al bon quadernieri sapere retrattare. o voi dire storna re ala fiorentina vna partita. cbe per errore bauesse posta in altro luogo cbe el la douesse andare. comme se lauesse messa in vare. E douiala ponere in bauere Et econtra. E quando douia porla aconto de Martino E lui la misse a conto de Giani. et ecõtra. Pero cbe ale volte non si po tanto essere atento cbe non si falli comme el prouerbio sona. Cioe cbi non fa non falla. E cbi non falla non impara. E pero incetrat r tarla. tirrai q̃sto modo. Cioe q̃do bauesse messa lapita. poniamo in vare e douia andare in bauere p retrala. porraine 1ª. alt?. alicontro della i bauere dcl tanto de ponto. E dirai in q̃ sto modo a di. 7c̃. p altretanto posto vincontro al die vare. E douia metterla q̃ i bauereual a carti 7c̃. E tra foza q̃lle mdesime. §. f. g. p. cbe ponesti p erro. E denãce a ditta ptita farai 1ª. croci. o altro segno. acio leuando tu el cõto lauegbi alastare. E subito posta q̃sta p retrat to. cb e q̃to senulla bauesse scritto del deuere. E tu poi la reponi i ditto bauere cõe douia andare e stara bn̄.   Comme se debbia fare elbilancio del libro e del modo a reportare vn libro in laltro. cioe elq̃derno vecbio nel quaderno nuouo e del modo a pontarlo con lo suo giornale e memoriale e altri scontri detro e difuore del ditto quaderno.   Cap°. 32.

Veste cose finoza bẽ notate bisogna boza dar modo al reporto de vn libro in laltro. q̃do uolesse mutar libzo. p cagione cbe fosse pieno o vero p ordine annuale de milesimo cõe el cbi si costuma fare p luocbi famosi cbe ogni anno. marime amilesimi nuoui li gran mercatanti sẽpre lo obfuano. E q̃sto atto insiemi con li seq̃nti. E detto elbilancio del libro. L aq̃l cosa voler seq̃re. bisogna grandissima diligẽria. e p ordine tirrai q̃sto modo. cioe p°. farai de bauere vn cõpagno. cbe mal porresti p te solo farlo. E alui darai in mano el giornale p piu tua cautella. E tu tirrai el q̃derno grande e dirai alui gomẽçando vala p°. ptita del giornale cbe cbiami le carti del tuo q̃derno. doue q̃lla sta posta. p°. i dare e poi i bauere. E cosi tu lubbidirai. E trouerai sẽpre doue te manda. E q̃l te dira la ptita de cb o de cbi la sira. E q̃to sia el suo tratto foze. E cositu vedarai q̃l tal luo go doue te manda. se bauerai q̃l cb. o q̃l cbi. E q̃l ponto bauerai tratto foze. E trouãdola stare aponto cõe i giornale lançarala. cioe pontarala. overo farai q̃lcbe segno alibito e su le 8. o altroue cbe non te abagliasse. E q̃l tal segno o vero lançata cbe cosi in altri luocbi si co stuma vir. dirai cbe faça. el cõpagno nel giornale. ala medesima pti°. E guarda cbe mai tu se ça lui ne lui sença te põtasse. overo l̃çasse ptita alcũa pcbe potrebe nascere grãdi errozi. po cbe la pita põtata cbe sia vol dire star bn̄. col debito modo. E q̃sto ancora se obsua i leuar de conti a debitozi nançe cbe li le vagbi in mano bauerlo scõtrato e pontato cõ li luocbi dl q̃derno e del giornale o daltri luocbi cbe auesse notate ditte ptite cõe sopra al. 30. ca°. fo ditto. E fatto q̃sto p ordine a tutto el q̃derno e giornale. E trouando tu aponto cõe lui i dare e bauere le ptite siran giuste e ben poste. Nota cb lui nel giornale p bona memoria fara doi lançate o vero põti a 1ª. sola ptita. E tu nel q̃derno utẽi solo afarne 1ª. p pti°. si cõe ouna pti°. de giornale in q̃derno sene fa doi cosi si fa doi ponti. E po nel pontare del bilancio i giornale acb e buono far doi põti l̃ṣo sotto lalt°. ale 8. o uero doi lãçate 1ª. sotto lalt°. cb dinota dita pti°. star bn̄ i dare e bẽre al q̃der? Alcũi nel giornale p lodare põtano vauãti al. p. E p lo bauere drieto ale 8. cõe se sia luo e lalt°. sta bn̄. Nõ dimeno si porria far ãcora cõ 1ª. põtatura sola i giornale. cioe solo p lo vare. pcbe tu poi per te stesso porresti pontare lbauere a qual partita cbe bai in vare nel quaderno sempre te manda per cbe subito tu bai quiui el numero dele carti doue sia lbauere quando bene quel del giornale non te mandasse sicbe scontrandote tu con lui solo indare per te stesso porresti seq̃ire lo bauere ma piu commodo te sia cõ lo compagno a modo ditto. Ma se fornito el giornale de põtare a te auançase in quaderno ptita alcũa cbe non ueniesse põtata in vare o in bauere denoraria nel quaderno eser erroꝛ. cioe cbe q̃lla seraue posta supflua in q̃l vare o vero bauere. el qual errore tu subito retratta/

Distinctio nona. Tractatus. xi°. De scripturis

rai dando la medesima q̃ª. alincontro. cioe se la sira de più in dare. E tu altre tanto porrai in hauere. Et eccõtra. laqlcosa cõe sabia adittare disopra te so detto al cap°. pcedẽte. E cosi harai medicato tutto. El medesimo seria qñdo lui hauesse in giornale prita supflua. che a te nel quaderno mãcasse in dare o in hauere che pur fallo nel quaderno denotarebbe. El quale si deue reparę al modo contrario del supfluo. Cioe che tu aloza ditta prita subito laponghi i dare e in hauere in quaderno. facendo mẽtione dela varieta del giorno. pche lanascera molto più tarda in quaderno che nõ douia. Dele quali varieta. sẽpre elbõ quaderniero deue farne mẽtione pche lenaschino p leuar il suspetto del lib°. a modo el bon notaro neli suoi instrumẽti. nequali non po ne giongnere ne sminuire senza pricularę mẽtione de tal augumẽto. o vero decremento. cosi sẽpre tal respetto cõuẽ che sia nel bon quadernieri. acio la rialita mercantesca. debitamẽte se venga amantenere. Ma se la ditta prita. solo mãcasse val dare o da lhauere. aloza basta la ponghi ¹ª. sola volta. da ql tal lato doue lamancasse. con ditte mentioni. Cioe cõe p errore lai fatto ⁊c. E cosi harai tutte custate tue prite. lequali trouandole a sol scontri cõe a discorso denota eltuo quaderno cẽr giusto o ben tenuto. Unde nota che nel ditto quaderno siranno a lcuolte molte prite non pontate con lo scontro del giornale p chenon si hano aritrouare inesso. E qste siranno li resti posti al dic dare. o in hauere p saldi dele p tite nel portarle hauanti cõe dicemo in lo cap°. 28. aloza da te stesso di qlli tali resti trouerai i. ditto qderno suoi scontri. cioe in dare. E in hauere. recẽdote p lo n°. de le carti cõ ila ditta prita notate siranno. E trouãdo scontro a suoi luoghi giudica similmẽte elqderno star bñ ⁊c. E qllo che finora se detto del scõtro del quaderno con lo giornale. el simile intẽdi p°. douersi fare del memoriale o vero squartafoglio cõ logiornale a di p di. qñdo vsassi tener memoriale a modo che in principio di qsto trattato de lui te dirì. e cosi co tutti altri libri tenessi. Ma lultimo conuen essere elquadern°. cio penultimo el giornale. Ideo ⁊c.

Del modo e ordine ascriuere lefacende che occurrissero nel tempo che si fa elbilancio. cioe che si saldano li libri. e comme neli libri vechi non si debia scriuere ne innouare cosa alcuna in ditto tempo e lacagione perche. Cap°. 33.

Utte qste cose ordinatamente fatte e obseruate. guarda non innouasse più prª in alcũ libro antiano al quaderno. cioe immemoriale. E giornale. perche el saldo tutto de tutti li libri sẽpre si deue intendere fatto in 1°. medesimo corno Ma se facende te acadesse in ql meçço che fai el tuo saldo o vero bilancio. porrale in libri nuoui nequali intẽdi fare reporto. cioe in lomemoriale o vero giornale. ma nõ in quaderno p fin tanto che non li hai portati li resti del p°. quaderno. E se ancora non hauesse ordinati libri nuoui porrale facẽde con li suoi giorni daprte in 1°. sfoglio p fin siran fatti ditti libri. E aloza li leporrai. signati che siran tutti de nuouo segno. Cioe se qlli che saldi sirã segnati. croci qsti segna de. A. ⁊c. Cõme se debiano saldare tutte leprite del qderno vechio. e i che e pche: e de la summa sãmarũ del dare e delauere vltio scontro del bilãcio. Cap°. 34.

Atto ch harai qsto cõ diligẽtia. E tu dare saldarai tutto eltuo qderno aprita p prtª. i qsto modo. chₑ pª. comẽçarai dalacassa debitori. robbe e auentori. E quelle portarai in libro. A. cioe in quaderno nuouo che non bisogna cõe so detto diso pra li resti ponere ingiornale. summarai tutte lor prite in dare e hauere aiutãdo sẽpre lamenore cõe te dirì. sopra del portare auãti. che qsto atto de 1°. quaderno in laltro. E de põto simile aqllo e fra loro non e altra differentia senon che in qllo dretto si porta auanti nel medesimo quaderno. E in qsto de 1°. libro in laltro. E doue in qllo chiamaui le carti d ql libro pprio in qsto sichiama lecarti del libro sequẽte in modo che nel reporto de vn libro in laltro. solo 1ª. volta p ciascũo quaderno se mette laprita. E qsta progatiua a lultima prita sempre deli quaderni che nullaltra mai po hauere cõe nel. pcesso dato hai notato. E deuerle tal riporto cosi ditare. cioe mettiamo che tu habia. Martino debitore p resto nello tuo quaderno. croci. a carti. 60. de. § 12. ſ 15. g 10. p 26. E habilo a portare in quaderno. A. a carti. 8. in dare te conuen nel libro croci. aiutare lhauere. doue dirai cosi desotto a tutte laltre partite E a di ⁊c. ponędo sempre el medesimo di. che fai elbilancio. p lui medesimo porto in quaderno. A. aldic dare per resto qual q põgo per saldo de questa val a carti. 8. § 12. ſ 15. g 10. p 26 E depennarai la ditta partita in dare e hauere diametraliter cõe nel reporto te insegnai ponẽdo lasuma de tutta laprita sotto nel cãpo de ditta prita in dare e in hãre. cioe tãto da lun lato qñto da lalt°. acio p a lochio subito star bñ e iqlc cõe se recerca. al bõ saldo. ponẽdo nel trar fora. el numero dele carti del quaderno. A. doue tal resto porti. E poi in lo quaderno. A. in dare dirai cosi prima ponendo sopra incima de la carta. el suo milesimo. El giorno ne la partita per lacasone detta sopra in lo cap. 15°. cioe Martino deltale ⁊c. die dare a di. ⁊c. p

Distinctio nona. Tractatus.xi°. De scripturis

lui medemo p resto tratto del libro.croci.posto al die hauere per saldo de qlla.val a car. 60.
§ 12.f 15.g° 10.p 26.E cosi andarai saldado tutte le prite nel lib°.croci. tu intedi portare
i qderno. A. de cassa.caueda.robbe mobili. e stabili.debitori.creditori.officii.sensarie. pesa
dori de comun 7c. con liquali se usa ale uolte andare aconto longo 7c. Ma quelle partite
che non uolesse portare in ditto quaderno. A. che porrieno eere qlle che solo e se saptega
rio. E no se obligato a segnarne coro ad alcu: coe son spesi de mercatia.spesi de casa intrata
isita.e tutte spese straordinarie.fitti.pescioi. feudi. o liuelli 7c. qste simili conuegonse saldare
in lo medesimo libro.croci.nela prita del p e danno o uero anaci e desauanci o voi dire uti
le e vano.i qsto modo che loro dare portarai e dare cb raro si possano hauere i creditori qlle
de le spesi dicedo.nel saldo aiutando coe piu volte e ditto sempre la menore quantita in dare
o i hauere p p e vano i qsto a carti tate 7c. E cosi tutte le hauerai saldate i qsta del p e van
no doue subito poi sumando suo dare e hauere porrai cognoscere tuo guadag°.e pdita p cb
sira i tal bilancio fatto la parita.cioe cb le cose cb se douia diffalcare siran diffalcate qlle che
se douiano agiongnere sira pporcionatamete a suoi luochi agiote. E se de qsta ptita. sira p
el dare cb hauere tu hauera pdutto ql tanto i tuo trafico dache lo gomecasti. E se sia piu lo
hauere alora dirai che ql tanto habia i ditto tpo guadagnato 7c. E veduto cb harai p qsta
lutile.e vanno tuo seqto.alora qsta saldarai i la prita del cauedale.doue nel pricipio del tuo
manegio ponesti lo iuetario de tutta la tua faculta. E saldarala i qsto modo che sel vano se
qto sira piu che dio ne guardi ciascuno che realmete so buon cpiano se adopa alora aiuta
rai lo hauere o modo usato dicedo a di 7c.p caueda el qstop danno seqto a carti 7c. val 7c.
E depenerai la prita diametraliter i dare e hauere.ut su°.ponedo pure la suma nel capo i da
re e hauere che deue battere para. E poi ala prita del cauedale i dare dirai.cauedale die dar
a di 7c.p.p e vanno. p danno seqto posto in quella al die hauere p saldo suo val a cari 7c.
§. f.g° p 7c. E cosi senc fosse seqto utile. cb serebbe qdo qlla del p e vanno se retrouasse piu
i hauere che i dare alora sugiogiaresti al dare p saldo ql tanto chiamado el cauedale ale car
ti suoi 7c. e lui la porresti hauere isiemi co laltre robbe mobili e stabili.e di nuouo i qsto ca
uedal qle couie eere sepre l ulti°.ptita o tutti liqderni. porrai sepre cognoscere tutta tua facul
ta.giognedo li debiti e crediti che in lib°. A. portasti 7c. E qsta del cauedal del qderno. ero
ci saldarai ancora. E portarala coe laltre nel qderno. A. in resto e suma o voi a ptira p pti
ta che lo poi anche fare.ma si costuma farla in suma pche 1°.volta tutto tuo iuetario ape. E
recordate chiamas suc carti. 7c. E assetarai poi tutte leprite ol qderno. A. ne lalfabeto ogni
na al suo luogo coe disopra te dissi. cap°. 5°. E acio sepre possi co facilita trouare le tue facede
secondo loro occurrence e cosi fia saldo tutto el primo quaderno con suo giornale e memori
ale. E acio sia piu chiaro de ditto saldo. farai questo altro scontro. Cioe summarai in un so
glio tutto el dare del quaderno.croci. E ponlo a man sinistra. E summarai i tutto suo hauere
E polo a ma detra. E poi queste vltime summe resumarai. E farane de tutte quelle
del dar una suma che si chiamara suma sumaru. E cosi farai una suma o tutte qlle ualuae
che si chiamara ancora lei una sumasumaru. Ma lap°.sira suma sumaru. del dare e la fa
si chiama summasumaru o lo hauere. Or se qste doi sume summaru sira pare.cioe che tan
to sia luna qto laltra. vi qlla del dare e qlla delo hauere. arguirai el tuo qderno eere be gui
dato tenuto e saldato p la cagioe cb di sopra nel cap°. 14.fo detto. Ma se luna o dicte sum
me summaru auancasse laltra denotarebbe erro nel tuo quaderno.el qual poi con diligetia
ti couerra trouarlo co la industria olo itelletto che dio tcha dato.e co lartefitio de le ragio
ni che harai bene inparato. laqual pte coe nel pricipio del prite dicemo summamete neces
saria albon mercatante altramete non siando bon ragioneri nel soi fatti andara a rastoi
coe ciecho. E porasine seqre molto vano. adonca co ogni studio e cura sforcarati sopra tut
to eere buon ragioneri cbel modo a tua comodita in qsta sublima opa a pieno a tua bastan
ca. te lo dato con tutte suc regole a tutti suo luoghi debitamente poste. si coe tutto facilmete
per la tauola nel principio di qsta opera posta porrai trouare. E ancora p le cose dette q se
quente come disopra nel cap°. 12° te pinisi a piu tuo recordo faro 1°.epilogo.cioe sumaria
recolta centiale de tutto el prite trattato.che molto senca dubio te fia utile. E p me recorda
rati latisimo pgare che a suc laude e gloria. Jo possa de bene i meglio opado pcedere 7c.

Del modo e ordine a sap tener le scripture menute coe sono scritti de mano lettere fami
liari police. pcessi snic e altri istrumeti e del registro de le l're. iportati. Ca° 35

Equita el modo e ordine de saper tener le scripture e chiarecce menute comune
sonno scritti de mano de pagamenti facti quitance de cambi. de robbe dare. let
tere familiari.quali cose sonno fra mercanti de gradissima stima. e molta impor

Distinctio nona. Tractatus. xi°. De scripturis

tança.e de gran pericolo in perderle e smarrirle.E prima. dele lettere familiari quali spesso fra te e li toi auctori possano acadere. queste sepre stendi e serba in vn banchetto ala fin del mese.E finito el mese legale in vn maço.e ripolle dapte segnando ogniuna defore cioe che la receui el di che li rispondi.E cosi si fa a mese p mese.E poi ala fin de lanno de tutti qsti maçi farai vn maço grande e luoga e segna suo Mº. E qdo voi alcuna lra a ql ricori. Dauerai i tuo studio overo scritoio vna tasca.nela ql repozrai lre cb li amici te dessero.sj tu cò le tuoi mandasse aloza.sedici che lamandi a roma. mettila in tasca di roma.e se a firença in qlla defirença 7c.E poi nel spaciare del fante pigliale con le tuoi al tuo respondente in quel tal luogo le manda. pche el seruire sempre e buono e anche susa dar suo beueragio per cèr seruito 7c. atorno esso cinta coptira cioe si fa i piu taschette.cioe in tante qte sonno le terre e luoghi in le quali fai le toe facede cone diciamo. Roma. Firece: Napoli. Milano. Zenoa. Lion. Londra. Bruça 7c.E sopra dicte taschette p ordine scriuerai illuo nome.cioe a luna dira Roma.a laltra. Firença 7c.in le quali poi repozrai le lre che p qlli luoghi te fossero mandate da qualch aico che lamandasse.E fatta de li barati respota e mandata.pure in ditta lia de fora. cone festi del suo recevere.e p chi. Cosi similiter porrai mentione de la respo sta. E pchi la mandasti con lo suo giorno. El qual di mai in alcua.tua facenda fa che machi.o piccola o grade cb la sia maxime in lre in le qli sepre si deue pore ilmilesimo el dic luogo.el nome tuo el qual no me si costuma mettarlo da pede aman dextra de la lra in vn catone.el Lº°, co lo dic luogo fra mercantis e usa ponere disopra nel principio dela lra. Ma pº.a modo bon xpiano barai sepre amete de ponere el glorioso nome de nra salute.cioe el doci nome de yhu.overo in suo scabio la figura de la sca croci.nel cui nome sep tutte le nre opationi debano eer principiate. E farai cosi.croci. 1494. a di.17.aprile i vinegia. E poi seqta tuo dire. cioe carissimo 7c. ma listudianti e altre genti cone sonno religiosi 7c.che non traficano. vsano nel luogo do ue la lettera e fatta poner di sotto con lo dic Mº. E li mercati costumano disopra a modo ditto altamente non vi ponendo el di scrbe confusione. E di te seria fatto beffe pche te dici la lia che non ha el di notato che le fatta de notte. E qlla che non a notato el luogo se dici che le fatta i laltº. modo.e non in qsto.e oltra le besse che pegio e ne seque scandalo ve dixi. Expedita che barai sua respota pocia al deputato luogo la poni cone hai inteso. E qllo che ditto habiamo de 1ª.sola iredilo p tutte. Unde e ancora dauotare che qdo le lre che tu ma di fossero de ipoztança.qlle tale se vogliano pº regitrarle in vn libro da pte solo a qsto deputato.nel ql registro si deue ponere la lia de verbo ad verbu scila sia di grande iportança cone sonno lre de cambio.o de robe mandate o d. 7c.o vero re gistrare solo la subitança.in tal modo memoziale dicedo i qsto di 7c.habiamo scritto al tale 7c.cone p lo tale 7c.limandamo le tal cose 7c.fo p 1ª.sua o di tanti 7c.ci conmise e richiese 7c.la qual ponemo in tasca 7c. E di fore sigilata che barai la tua che madi e fatto la sopra scritta su sa. p molti ponerui el suo legno di fuore.acio si cognosca che sia de mercantia.i quali molto se deue hauere di reuerentia el simile li Rmi. Cardinali.pongano defore elloro distito nome.acio nisu se possi lausare de non sape de chi la fosse. E molto piu apreamete el sancto padre fa le suc patentemete apte cone sono bolle breuilegi 7c. Auega che alcune cose piu irrisoche.poga sotto el sigillo dl pescatore 7c. Le qli lre poi a mese p mese o vero anno p anno recozrai i maçi. overo filce va pte le poni ordinariamete i vno armaro.o sularetto.securo. E cone nascano ala gozrnata co silasetta.acio possi piu pisto a tue occurece retrouarle d laqlcosa.no curo piu dire pcb so aba stança mal inteso 7c. Scritti de mano no pagati de tuoi debitozi cone te acenai disopra nel capº.17.seruarai in vn altro luogo piu secreto cone son caffi e scatole priuate 7c. E legta ce similiter.serua in luogo securo p ogni respetto. Ma qdo tu pagasse tu ad altri ol riceuere farai lo scriuere i 1º libretto de pagameti cone in pricipio te dixi.acio no li possa cosi facilmete smarire e pderc. E cosi obscuruarai de le polige che importano. cone sono notole de sensaria d mercati.o de pesadori o bolette o robbe messe o tratte de dogane o amare o da terra e seteçe o cartuline de consoli o altri officij o altri istrumenti de notari i pgamena qli se debano reporre i vn luogo da pte. E cosi copie scritture e pressi delite de peurator. E auocati. E similimete e buono hauere vn librº separato pgli chiami recordaite nel ql ala gozrnata farai le tue memozie dele cose che dubitasse no recordarte.che te pori tornar dano.nel ql ogni o al manco la sera nançe vadi adormire darai ochio.se cosa fosse daspedire o dasare che non fusse expedita 7c.alaql spaçata barai de pena. E cosi q farai memoria de cose che al vicino e amico p vno o doi di pstasse cone sonno vasa de botegga caldare e altri ordegni 7c. E quest

Distinctio nona. Tractatus xi°. De scripturis

ſimili documẽti con gli altri vtiliſſimi ſopra dati reportrai 7c. piu e mãco gonçando eſminuẽdo ſo ſuoghi e tpi a te per tuo ingegno parera. pero cħ non e poſſibile a pieno de tutto a ponto per ponto i mercãtia dare norma. e notitia pocħ cõme altre volte ſe dittoui piu põti a fare 1° mercatãte cbe un dottore de leggi. Ideo 7c. Coſe cħ finora ſono dette. ſe bũ la prẽderai ſon certo i tutte tue facẽde brĩ te reggiarai. mediãte el tuo peregrino ingegno 7c.

Sũmario de regole E modi ſopra il tenere vno libro di mercanti.   Cap°. 36.

   Tutti li creditori ſi debono mettere al libro vala tua mano deſtra. E li debitori vala tua mano ſiniſtra. Tutte le ptite che ſe metteno alliboħano a eẽre doppie: cioe ſe tu fai vno creditore al ſi fare 1°. debitore. Ciaſcũa ptita coſi i dare cõe i bẽre obbe cõtenere iſe. 3. coſe cioe il giorno del pagamẽto. La ſõma del pagamẽto. E la cagiõe del pagamẽto.   Lultimo nome vela ptita vel debito debbe eẽre il pro della ptita del credito. In qllo medeſimo giorno che e ſcritta la ptira del debito. i qllo medeſimo giorno debbe eẽre qlla del credito.

   Lo bilancio del lib° ſintẽde 1°. foglio piegato p lo lõgo ſul qle vala mano deſtra ſi copião li creditori del lib°. e vala ſiniſtra li debitori. E vedeſe ſe la ſũma del dare e qto qlla de laure. E allora il lib°. ſta bene.   El bilancio del libro debbe eẽre pari. cioe che tanto debbe eẽr la ſuma non dico de creditori. ne debitori. Ma dico la ſuma del credito qto la ſuma del debito. E nõ ẽdo ſaria errore nel libro.   El conto ci caſſa conuiene che ſẽpre ſia debitrice. ouerarnẽte pari. E ſe altrimẽte fuſſe ſaria errore nel libro.   Non ſi debbe e non ſi puo fare 1°. debitore al libro ſenca licẽſa e volũta di qllo tale cba a eẽre debitore e ſe pure ſi faceſſe qlla ſcritura ſeria falſa. Ne ſimilmẽte non ſi puo porre neppati ne conditioni a. 1°. credito ſẽca licẽſa e volonta del creditore. E ſe pure ſi faceſſe qlla ſcritura ſaria falſa. El lib°. conuiene che ſia tutto tratro fuori a 1². medeſima moneta. Ma dietro poi bũ noiare qllo cħ a cadeſſe o duc°. ſ. o fiorini. o ſcudi doro. o qllo che fuſſi Ma nel trarre fuori conuiene che ſia tutto a 1². medeſima moneta cõe pricipiaſti illib°. coſi conuiene ſeguire.   La ptita del debito. o del credito cħe ſi fa i conto de caſſa ſi puo abreuiare cbi vuole. cioe ſenza dire la cagione ſo lamẽte dire va tale di tale. o a tale di tale. pebe la cagione ſi vicine a dichiarar nella ptita opoſita. Hauẽdo a fare 1°. cõto nuouo ſi debbe ſcriuere i carta noua ſenza tornare a dietro ãcora cħ a drietro vi trouaſſi ſpacio da metterla. Non ſi die ſcriuere i drietro. Ma ſẽpre auãti per ordine cõe vanno li giorni del tpo che mai non ritornano indrieto. E ſe pure ſi faceſſe ſaria da reputare qllo libro falſo.   Se 1². partita foſſe al libro meſſa per errore che non doueſſi eẽre cõe adniene ale volte per iſmemoragine e tu la voleſſi iſtornare farai coſi ſegna qlla tale partita in margine duna croci o duna. H. E dipoi ſcriui 1ª. ptita alincontro. cioe a lo oppoſito di qlla nel medeſimo conto. cioe ſela partita errata fuſſe creditrice. poniamo che § 50 ſ 10 δ 6. E tu la farai debitrice. E dirai. e de dare. § 50. ſ 10 δ 6. ſonno per la partita dietro ſegnata croci che ſi ſtorna perche era errata e non baueua a eẽre. E qſta partita ſegna la. croci cõe e laltra e δ fatta.   Quando lo ſpacio duno cõto fuſſe pieno. in modo cħ nõ vi poteſſe mettere piu ptite. E tu voleſſi tirare qllo conto innanzi. Fa coſi guarda qllo cħ e reſto del ditto conto. cioe ſe li reſta hauere o a dare Ora poniamo che qllo conto reſti hauere § 28 ſ 4 δ 2. Dico che tu debbi fare 1°. verſo ſoletto va la parte oppoſita ſenza mettere giorno. e dirai coſi. E de dare. § 28 ſ 4 δ 2. per reſto di qſto conto poſto hauere in qſto a car. e fatto. E lo detto verſo ſi debe ſegnare in margine danant coſi. cioe R°. che ſignifica reſto cioe cħel detto verſo non ne debitrice ancor che ſia da la banda del debitore. Ma viene a eẽre traſportato qllo credito per la via del debito. Ora ti conuiene volgere carta e andare tãto auanti che truoui 1ª. carta nuoua. E qui fare creditore il detto conto. E nominarlo e fare ptita nuoua ſẽca metteruí il giorno. E dirai coſi tale di tale δ tali de bẽre. § 28 ſ 4 δ 2. ſono per reſto duno ſuo conto leuato in qſto a ca. E qſta partita ſi debbi ſegnare in margine coſi. cioe R°. che ſignifica reſto e fatta. E coſi conuíene io to moſtro quando ſi conto reſta a hauere coſi ancora bai a fare quando reſtaſſi a dare. cioe quello cai meſſo da la banda del credito metter da la banda del debito.

   Quando el lib°. fuſſe tutto pieno o vechio e tu voleſſi ridullo a 1°. alt° li°. nuouo fa coſi prīti cõuiene vedere che ſe il tuo lib°. vechio e ſegnato i ſu la couerta poniamo p caſo. A. biſogna cħ i ſul lib°. nuouo doue lo voi ridurre ſia ſegnato in ſu la couerta. B. pche li lib°. de mercanti vãno p ordie luno doppo lalt°. fo le lřé velo. a b c 7c. E dipoi leuare il bilancio del lib°. vechio che ſia giuſto e pari cõe debba eſſere e va qllo bilancio copiare tutti li creditori e debitori i ſul lib°. nuouo tutti p ordine cõe elli ſtanno i ſul bilãcio. E fare tutti li debitori e creditori ciaſcũo da pſe. e laſcia a ciaſc° tãto ſpatio

Distinctio nona. Tractatus. xi°. De scripturis

q̄to tu arbitrii b̄ere a trauagliare cō seco. E i ciascūa ptita del debitore hai a dire p̄ tāti resta a dare al lib°. uechio segnato. A. a car. e i ciascūa ptita del creditore hai a dire p̄ tanti resta a hauere al lib° vechio segnato. A. a car. E cosi e riducto al libro nuouo. Hora p̄ cancellar il libro vechio ti cōuiene a ciascūo cōto acceso ispēgnerlo cō lo bilancio sopra dicto. cioe se vno cōto del libro vechio sara creditore che louedrai p̄ lo bilancio faralo debitore e dirai p̄ tanti resta hauere a q̄sto cōto posto debbi hauere al lib°. nouo segnato. B. a. car. E cosi harai ispēto tutto il lib°. vechio e acceso al lib°. nuouo. E cosi cōmo io to moltro d'uno creditore cosi hai a fare d'uno debitore. Saluo che doue al creditore si fa debitore posto debbi hauere E tu hai a fare creditore posto debbi dare z e fatto.

Casi che apriene amettere al libro de mercanti.

Tutti li d̄. cōtanti che tu ti trouassi che fussino tuoi pprii. cioe che hauessi guadagnati i diuersi tp̄i pel passato o che ti fussino stati lassati da tuoi parēti morti. o donati da q̄lche prīcipe farai creditore te medēmo. E debitore cassa. Tutte le gioie e mercantie che fussino tue pprie che tu hauessi guadagnate. o ch̄ ti fussino state lassate p̄ testamēto. o che ti fussino state donate. e q̄ste tale cose si vogliono istimare da p̄ se luna da l'alt'a. q̄llo che vagliono a d̄. cōtanti. E tante q̄te cose elle sono tante ptite fare al lib°. e fare ciascuna debitrice e dire p̄ tā te mi trouo stimare q̄sto di tanti d̄. 7c. Posto medesimo creditore i q̄sto a car. E sarai creditore il tuo cōto. cioe te medesimo di ciascūa ptita. Ma nota che q̄ste ptite sintēde ch̄ nō sieno māco di dieci duc. luna po che le cose minute di poco valore non sinmettano al libro.

Tutte le cose stabile che tu ti trouassi che fussino tue pprie cōe sono case possessiōi botteghe hai a fare debitore detta cosa e stimare q̄llo che la vale a tua dis. cretiōe a d̄. cōtanti. E fane creditore te medēmo'al tuo sopra detto cōto. E vipoi fare debitore la posssissiōe da p̄ se e stimarla cōe e dicto e fane creditore te medemo al tuo sopradetto cōto. e cōe nelle regole to dicto tutte le ptite vogliono b̄ere i loro tre cose. cioe il giorno e la q̄'. dela pecunia e lacagiōe.

Lōpre che tu facessi di mercantie. o di che cosa si fusse p̄ li d̄. cōtāti debbi fare debitore q̄lla tale mercantia o q̄lla tale cosa e creditore la cassa, E se tu dicessi. io lacōprai a d̄. cōtāti cōe e ditto. Ma vno banco gli pago p̄ me. o veramēte vno mio amico gli pago p̄ me. Rispōdoti che a ogni modo hai a fare debitore q̄lla tale mercantia cōe disopra o dicto. Ma doue io t i dissi farai creditore la cassa tu hai a fare creditore q̄l banco. o q̄llo tuo aico ch̄ p̄ te glia pagati.

Lōpre che tu facessi di mercantie. o diche cosa si sia a termine d'alcuno tp̄o debi fare debitore q̄lla tale mercancia e creditore colui da cui tu l'ai cōpata p̄ q̄llo tp̄o. Lōpre che tu facessi di mercantia. o diche cosa si sia a p̄te d̄. e p̄te tp̄o debbi fare debitore q̄lla tale mercancia E creditore colui da cui tu l'ai cōpata p̄ q̄llo tp̄o cō q̄sti patti che li habbi hauere dicātāno il terzo dī d̄. cōtāti E loresto fra sei mesi p̄rini futuri: E doppo q̄sto fare un'altra ptita. cioe debitore colui da cui tu l'ai cōpata di q̄lla q̄'. di d̄. cōtanti che mōta q̄lla terza parte che fu di patto di cōtanti E creditore la cassa o q̄llo bancho che gli pagasse pre. Tutte le uēdite ch̄ tu facessi di mercantie o daltre cose hai a fare tutto cōme di sopra saluo chai a mettere p̄lo opposito. cioe che doue disopra ti diui che sēpre facessi debitore la mercancia: q̄ nelle vēdite hai a fare sēpre creditore la mercancia E debitore cassa se e uēduta a d̄. cōtanti o debitore q̄l banco che te li hauesse pmessi E se e vēduta a termine. hai a fare debitore colui a cui tu l'hai vēduta p̄ q̄llo termine e se fusse vēduta a p̄te d̄. e p̄te tp̄o hai a fare cōe disopra ti mostrai nelle cōpre q̄lle due ptite.. Se tu vēdessi una mercācia abaratto diciamo. Io ho vēduto libbre mille dilana d'īghliterra abaratto di peuere. cioe libre duomilia di peuere domando comme sa a cōtare q̄sta scrittura al lib°. fa. cosi istima q̄llo che vale il pipe a tua discretiōe a d̄. cōtanti. Or poniamo che tu lo stimi duc. dodici il cēto. ad q̄z le duomilia libbre vagliono duc. 240. cōtāti. e po farai creditore la lana d̄ duc. 240. p̄ q̄to l'ai vēduta E q̄sto modo obsua sēpre ī leptite tutte. Gli baratti de q̄li sene hauto §. Duomilia di peuere stimato. 240. duc. Posto detto peuere debbi dare ī q̄sto a car. E fane debitore il peuere. Danari cōtanti che tu pitassi a q̄lche tuo amico hai a fare debitore l'amico a chi tu gli hai pīstati e creditore cassa. Se tu riceuessi d̄. cōtanti ī pitansa da q̄lche amico hai a fare debitore cassa e creditore l'amico.

E tu hauessi p̄so otto. o dieci. o vēti duc. p̄ assicurare naui o galee o altra cosa debbi fare creditore sicurta di nauilij e chiarire che z cōe e q̄do e doue e q̄to p̄ cēto. E debitore cōto di cassa. Mercantie che ti fussino mandate da altri cō cōmissione diuēderle o barattarle d̄ le quali tu hauessi hauer la tua puisiōe. Dico che tu debbi fare debitore al libro q̄lla tale mercantia attenēte al tale di tale p̄ lo porto. o p̄ gabella. o p̄ nolo o p̄ mettere i magazino E creditore cōto di cassa. Tutte le ispese di mercantie di d̄. cōtanti che tu farai, o p̄ nolo. o p̄ gabelle. o vetture o sēserie. o portature fa creditore la cassa. E debitore quella tale mercantia per laq̄le tu gli hai ispesi.

Distinctio nona. Tractatus xi°. De scripturis

Casi che acade mettere ale recordance del mercante.

Tutte lemasseritie di casa o di bottega che tu ti truoui. Ma vogliono essere per ordine.cioe tutte le cose di ferro da perse con spatio da potere agiognere se bisognasse. E cosi da segnare in margine quelle che fussino perdute o vendute o donate o guaste. Ma non si intende masseritie minute dipoco valore. E fare ricordo di tutte le cose dottone da perse comme e detto. E simile tutte le cose distagno. E simile tutte lecose distengno. E cosi tutte le cose dirame. E cosi tutte le cose dariento e doro tē. Sempre con spatio di qualche carta da potere arrogere se bisognasse. e cosi da dare notitia di quello che mancasse. Tutte lemalleuerie o obbrighi o promesse che promettessi per qlche amico. e chiarire bene che e comme. Tutte lemercantie o altre cose che ti fossero lassate i guardia o a serbo di pstaxia da qlche amico. e cosi tutte lecose ch tu pstassi a altri tuoi amici. Tutti limercati conditionati cioe copre o vedite come p creplouno cotrato cioe ch tu mi mandi con leprossime galee che torneranno dingbliterra tanti cantara di lane dilimistri a caso che le sieno buone e recipienti. Io ti daro tanto del cantaro o del cento o veramete d' mandaro alincontro tanti cantara di cottoni. Tutte le case o possessioni o botteghe o gioie che tu affittassi a tanti duc. o a tante lire lanno. E quando tu riscoterai il fitto aloza ql li dinari sanno a mettere al libro comme disopra ti dissi. Prestando qualche gioia o vasella mente dariento o doro a qualche tuo amico per otto o quidici giorni diqueste tale cose no si mettono al libro.ma sene fa ricordo ale ricordance.perche fra pochi giorni lai bariauere. E cosi per contra se a te fossi prestato simili cose non li debbi mettere al libro. Ma farne memoria alericordance perche presto lai a rendere.

Comme si scriuono lire e soldi e danari e picioli e altre abreuiature.
Lire soldi danari picioli libbre once danarpesi grani carati ducati fioini larghi.
§   F   đ   p   libbre ɞ   đp   g.   ĸ   duc.   fio.lar

Come si debbe dettare le ptite de debitori.			Come si debbe dittare leptite di creditori.		
Mccccº Lxxxxiiiº.			Mccccº Lxxxxiiiº.		
Lodouico dipiero forestai de dare a di.xiiii.nouembre. 1493.§.44.F.1: đ.8. porto contāti in pstaça.posto cassa auere.a car. 2	8	44 F1 đ8.	Lodouico dipiero forestai de hauere a di.22.nouēbre 1493.§.20.F.4.đ.2.sōno p parte di pagamento. E per lui celia promissi a nostro piacere frācescho dātonio. caualcātti posto dare a c. 2.	8	20 F 4 đ 2.
E a di.18.detto §.18.F.11.đ. 6.promettemo p lui a martino dipiero foraboschi a suo piacer posto here i qsto. a c.2.	8	18 F11 đ6.			
Cassa i mano di simone da lesso bōbeni de dar a di.14. nouēbre 1493. §. 62. F. 13. đ.2. da francesco dantonio caualcanti in qsto a c.2	8	62 F13 đ6.	Cassa in mano di simone dalesso bōbeni de hauere a di.14.nouēbre.1493.§.44. F.1. đ.8. alo douico di piero forestani in qsto. a car. 2.	8	44 F1 đ8.
			E a di.22.nouembre.1493 §.18.F.11.đ.6. a martino di picro foraboschi.a ca. 2.	8	18 F11 đ6.
Martino di piero fora boschi de dare a di.20.nouembre.1493.§.18.F.11.đ.6. porto lui medesimo cōtāti posto cassa a car. 2.	8	18 F11 đ6.	Martino di piero fora bo schi di hauere a di.18.nouē bre.1493.§.18.F.11.đ.6. gli pmettemo a suo piacere p lodouico di piero forestani posto obbi here i qsto a c.2.	8	18 F11 đ6
Francesco dantonio caual cāti de dare a di.12.di nouē bre.1493.§.20.F.4.đ.2.ci p misse a nostro piacer p lodo uico di piero forestai a c.2.	8	20 F 4 đ 2.	Francescho dātonio caual canti de hauere a di.14.nouēbre.1493.§.62.F.13.đ.6. reco lui medesimo ptāti po sto cassa dare a car.2.	8	62 F13 đ6.